The Piety
of John Witherspoon

The Piety
of John Witherspoon

Pew, Pulpit, and Public Forum

L. Gordon Tait

GENEVA

Geneva Press
Louisville, Kentucky

Book design by Sharon Adams
Cover design by Lisa Buckley
Front cover illustration: Portrait of John Witherspoon, by Charles Willson Peale, which hangs in the faculty room of Nassau Hall, Princeton University.
Back cover illustration: Line sketch of Nassau Hall, by George Olson.

First edition
Published by Geneva Press
Louisville, Kentucky

This book is printed on acid-free paper that meets the American National Standards Institute Z39.48 standard. ∞

PRINTED IN THE UNITED STATES OF AMERICA
01 02 03 04 05 06 07 08 09 10 — 10 9 8 7 6 5 4 3 2 1

Library of Congress Cataloging-in-Publication Data

Tait, L. Gordon.
    The piety of John Witherspoon : pew, pulpit, and public forum / L. Gordon Tait.—1st ed.
        p. cm.
    Includes bibliographical references and index.
    ISBN 0-664-50133-8 (alk. paper)
        1. Piety—History of doctrines—18th century. 2. Witherspoon, John, 1723–1794. I. Title.
BV4647.P5 T35 2000
285'.1' 092—dc21
[B]   00-039312

To my son, Paul

Contents

Preface

At the time of the American Revolution, English author Horace Walpole remarked, "Cousin America has eloped with a Presbyterian parson." Walpole did not mention the pastor by name, but he could have had the Reverend John Witherspoon (1723–1794) in mind. Witherspoon came from Scotland to America in 1768; by 1774 he had become an ardent American patriot and in 1776 he signed the Declaration of Independence, the only minister to do so.

Long before he became an American and a minister-in-politics, he had a life of his own in Scotland and a successful career as a parish minister of the Church of Scotland. It was during that ministry that Witherspoon first began to think about what made a person pious or holy, or for that matter, virtuous. About the same time he also gave some thought to what made a parson pious. He did not always use the word piety, and he never wrote a treatise on the subject. Yet, as the present study will make clear, he wrote his sermons and the occasional essay to explain to his two congregations and other Scottish ministers what it meant to be a true or pious Christian. He continued to develop this theme after he arrived in the New World.

Witherspoon did not set out to be a minister-in-politics. That would come much later. In Scotland his overriding concern was the health of the Kirk, although he certainly was not blind to the fact that a healthy national church translated into a virtuous people and a strong nation. Only indirectly was he a reformer. He did not call himself that, nor did the others. Yet he saw nation and church infected by impiety and false religion and in need of considerable reform. In his estimation what was badly needed was a return by both people and pastors to a vibrant piety, to belief and practice based on the Bible and the church's confessional standards, in short, a turning from what he deemed to be false religion and a return to real religion. In that sense, even though he rarely summoned the

sixteenth-century Protestant Reformers to his side, he was attempting to reform the church of his place and time. Nor did he ever lose
that purpose in his preaching. Irreligion could be found anywhere,
he assumed. The need for a genuine Christian piety, therefore, was
universal, needed just as much in Princeton, New Jersey, as in Paisley, Scotland, where he preached before moving to America.

The present volume should find its place within the category of
theology rather than history. A more informed reader will find missing several aspects of Witherspoon's life and work, such as an examination of his moral philosophy and views on education, that would
rightfully belong in a larger intellectual history. Some historical
background is indeed necessary to understand Witherspoon's ideas,
for of course he belongs to a certain time and to several places. But
the reader should be advised that only a minimum of historical,
intellectual, or social context will be presented. This is a focused
work rather than a comprehensive one. To discover Witherspoon's
piety is the aim, to offer more of *what* he said about piety rather than
why he said it or what the connections were between his piety and
later theological trends. It is fair to ask where he might have gotten
his beliefs and, if possible, to point to some connections between
them and other statements of Reformed theology. Let the reader be
immediately warned: he did not go back to Calvin for his theological inspiration. He was more likely to base his beliefs on seventeenth-
century Reformed sources such as the Westminster Confession of
Faith. Some doctrines (e.g., human sin, grace, justification, and sanctification) will require comprehensive treatment, others less so.
Dissertations and monographs have examined Witherspoon's political, philosophical, and educational contributions, and even to a limited extent those of an ecclesiastical nature, but no one has yet
submitted and attempted to answer two questions: How did John
Witherspoon define a good person? How did he think one became
a good person? These are critical questions, not only for Witherspoon's time when Christian thinkers found they had some new
problems on their hands, but for any period of human history when
thoughtful persons reflect on the requirements for a faithful church
and a virtuous society.

Piety has not always had a good name. A positive understanding
of the term might be as simple as the *sacred*, distinct from the profane. Or, if somewhat more carefully drawn, piety could signify reverence for God and a life of virtue. But, for whatever reasons, in

many circles today piety is often thought to be out-of-date and something to be shunned, like conspicuous religiosity or even spiritual hypocrisy. In our time, many of the faithful probably would just as soon not be called pious.

However, my present claim is that there is a healthy and genuine use of the term *piety*. Perhaps the word does not strike modern ears as being so ancient or sanctimonious, if it is understood to mean true or authentic religion, a genuine love of God and of neighbor, or of faith and conduct joined with unqualified integrity. Those are some of the ways that John Witherspoon understood and explained piety. His piety, thus, is not outdated. His ideas deserve to be heard, and this is the impulse for the present work. He surely would have started with Genevan Reformer John Calvin's definition of piety: "that reverence joined with love of God which the knowledge of his benefits induces." Calvin continued, revealing great insight as he explained that piety is quite basic: "until men recognize that they owe everything to God, that they are nourished by his fatherly care, that he is the Author of their every good, that they should seek nothing beyond him—they will never yield him willing service."[1]

However, Witherspoon went beyond Calvin in his understanding of piety. He did not see piety in any restricted sense, nor as a mystical quality or virtuous lifestyle. Reformed piety has often been wide-ranging, including the cultivation of faith, experiences of the divine, appropriation of and gratitude for God's mercy, theological declarations, public and private worship and, of course, correct Christian conduct. Witherspoon also thought of piety in quite broad terms.[2]

Previous studies of Witherspoon, in particular the biographies noted below, have shown great interest in his service to his adopted nation—Witherspoon the patriot—and to his accomplishments as president and professor at the College of New Jersey, that is, Witherspoon the educator. Some of the previous scholarship on the life of Witherspoon will be noted below.

The present study, however, represents a fresh approach to a famous early American Presbyterian leader, and eventually will include some suggestions of whether and how he might have some things to say to contemporary people, especially to twenty-first-century Christians of the Reformed tradition. My attempt will be to demonstrate how an eighteenth-century Scottish-American minister was able to state clearly and forcefully the shape that he thought lay and clerical piety should take, first in Scotland and later in America.

What he presents will be of special interest to modern ministers and lay people and, of course, to all students of eighteenth-century Reformed thought and life.

Witherspoon's piety is important on another account. He is one of the signers of the Declaration of Independence who can legitimately be identified as an orthodox Christian. What contemporary Americans must remember, and unfortunately many do not, is that a number of the founders of the American nation, while they may have believed in a Supreme Deity, were not Christians in the conventional sense.

It is safe to say that most of the leaders of the colonies in 1775 had a far broader knowledge of the Bible than do political leaders today.[3] In general, educated citizens of the eighteenth century in the North Atlantic community had intensive knowledge of the Bible, but that did not mean that all of them were conventional Christians. Indeed, Princeton historian John Murrin has stated that the Revolutionary generation never agreed on a single set of fundamental value systems: Calvinist orthodoxy, Anglican moralism, civic humanism, classical liberalism, Tom Paine radicalism, and Scottish common sense philosophy. These six systems do not even exhaust all the options, he asserts.[4]

Historian Mark Noll has noted that it is not easy to recapture accurately the religious spirit of America's important founders— Washington, Jefferson, Franklin, and their colleagues. The difficulty is that they were religious, even genuinely so, states Noll, but not specifically Christian, which means that contemporary Americans should word any statement about early American leaders being religious or Christian very carefully. Many of the first-line founders, including Washington, Adams, Jefferson, and Franklin, tended to be deists, believing in "the Supreme Judge of the world" and in "the protection of the Divine Providence," phrases found in the Declaration of Independence. Only a few were Christians in the traditional sense, believing in human sinfulness, Jesus' atoning death for that sin, special revelation found only in the Bible, and the miracles happening as recorded in the Bible.[5]

One has to go to lesser known political leaders during the struggle for independence to find professing Christians, among them Patrick Henry and John Jay, and signers of the Declaration of Independence such as Roger Sherman of Connecticut and John Witherspoon of New Jersey, who proclaimed both traditional Christianity and political liberty. There was never any question of Witherspoon's stance. Even when he sat as a member of the Continental Congress for six years, he wore his ministerial robe and bands (two narrow stripes of white cloth hanging at the front of the neck).[6] Witherspoon's friend and New York Presbyterian minister, the Reverend John Rodgers, who was the author of a memorial tribute to Witherspoon at the time of his death, asserted that during the years Witherspoon was serving his country in the political sphere, "He did NOT [Rodgers's capitals] lay aside his *ministry* [Rodgers's italics]."[7] Hence, it will be instructive to examine the piety of one who made no secret of the fact that he was as much an American patriot as he was a Presbyterian minister.[8]

What was the basis for Pastor Witherspoon's piety? The answer is quick and easy: the Bible. What method, then, did he choose to transmit his ideas to others? He chose a traditional and at least for his time an effective one: the sermon. Modern readers must be aware of how much more important the sermon was in the life of the church, and even the culture, of the eighteenth century than it is today. In his time Witherspoon was not considered a spellbinding "pulpiteer," but he was a very effective preacher in getting across his ideas. There is no reason to think that he was unsuccessful in instructing his congregations on the subject of holiness or true religion.

In order to comprehend fully Witherspoon's piety it is important first to gain some insight into who John Witherspoon was, from whence he came, where he went, and what he did. The introduction will include a brief biography, with some attention to Witherspoon the preacher, the beginning of our understanding of what he would have us know. Following a brief biography of Witherspoon, the remainder of the introduction will be devoted to a discussion of his sermons: their construction, their relation to the Bible, and their reception by those who listened to them.

Witherspoon approached the subject of piety warily, yet systematically. So will we. Thus, in the first chapter we discover that Witherspoon sets his piety within the context of what has come to be known as the covenant theology of the seventeenth century, best expressed in the Westminster Confession of Faith (hereafter the Confession). He does not slavishly copy the doctrinal pronouncements of that confession, but it is the confine within which his piety is structured.

The reader of Witherspoon's sermons is struck by the way he may present and elucidate a text, and even stray far afield as he develops it, but sooner or later comes around to what I call the "foundational principle" of his piety, which discloses what he really thinks religion is all about. It is the truth of the first and great commandment of the law found in Matthew 22:37: "Thou shalt love the Lord thy God with all thy heart, and with all thy soul and with all thy mind." To Witherspoon, this is but a variant of the teaching of the Westminster Shorter Catechism that our chief end in life is "to glorify God and enjoy him forever."

The core of Witherspoon's piety is to be found in what he called "truths of such unspeakable moment." Those four doctrines constitute the essence of his piety as well as the essence of Christianity itself. They were, of course, to be found in the Confession, but what was even more basic, they constituted the good news, the gospel, proclaimed in Holy Scripture. These truths were (1) the lost state of man by nature, (2) salvation by the free grace of God, (3) justification by the imputed righteousness of Christ, and (4) sanctification by the effectual operation of the Holy Spirit.

Chapter 2 examines the characteristics and behavior of a pious person. Witherspoon believed that holy dispositions, the personal experience of the four leading truths, led to pious and useful actions: Faith produced good works; Christianity made a difference in a person's life. True religion, he would assert, enlarges the heart and "strengthens the social tie." He knew what Christians ought to be and he said so. He wanted them to be nothing less than outstanding examples of such qualities as humility or self-denial, self-control (especially in matters of one's speech), seriousness of purpose, application to duty, truthfulness, love of one's neighbor, and a renunciation of the world. His comments on each of these are wise, and of course, intentionally practical.

Witherspoon's "examples" were then told how to express their piety, what their "religious duties" or "the exercise of piety" should be. This meant that they needed advice on such matters as the Sabbath, the role of the church, public worship and sacraments, and private worship, especially prayer.

Piety for those in the pulpit comes next. In chapters 3 and 4, I explore how Witherspoon goes beyond what he has prescribed by way of lay piety to set a higher standard for the clergy. Early in his ministry he began to give serious thought to what constituted a pious minister. Without appearing to be sanctimonious or sounding superior, he began his prescriptions by asserting the need for ministers to experience personally the everlasting truths of the gospel and ended by contrasting the true cleric with a false one. In between he speaks from firsthand experience as he advises on such matters as ministerial integrity, the minister as an example, and the minister's need to be courageous as well as hardworking and truly humble before a sovereign God.

When Witherspoon arrived in America, he was forced to expand and sharpen his ideas of clerical piety. He had a new responsibility—that of training ministers for the American Presbyterian Church. By this time he was not only laying down the requirement of piety for clerics, he was also demanding that ministers be broadly educated. Immersing themselves in the Westminster Confession and reading their Bibles diligently was not enough; ministers were to be proficient in languages—Latin, Greek, Hebrew, and even French—and in philosophy, history, and "eloquence" or belles-lettres (rhetoric as it pertained to public speaking, composition, literary criticism). With this counsel Witherspoon began his "Lectures on Divinity," which he used in his theological instruction. These lectures also included material that, according to Witherspoon, should be part of the equipment of every eighteenth-century pastor: a rational defense of the faith, especially against deists and atheists, and a thorough comprehension of the main part of the Westminister Confession of Faith.

Chapter 5 contains an exposition of Witherspoon's understanding of the doctrine of providence. I contend that Witherspoon's broadening concept of divine providence enabled him to take up the patriot cause in America and enter politics by participating in the Revolution. An analysis of at least two of Witherspoon's sermons that were surely written within the context of the American struggle will disclose this new theological emphasis.

A short conclusion called "Practical Improvement" will suggest ways that Witherspoon speaks to the modern church and its members. The reader will see that his piety possesses an enduring quality because it is historic, theological, and very practical. Witherspoon believed that no divorce was possible between what one believed and what one did, so he concentrated first on developing a person's inner disposition before turning to the practical parts of piety. His practical bent also led him to develop a concept of common sense realism in philosophy, and to affirm the greater importance of piety in undergirding and thus guaranteeing a virtuous society and government.

Numerous quotations from Witherspoon's writings have been included in this study—paragraphs, sentences, sometimes only a phrase or two. This, of course, multiplies the number of notes. There are two reasons for doing this: first, Witherspoon's *Works* are not readily accessible to the modern reader, and second, I have found, and I trust others will also, that there is an irresistible energy, even a freshness to Witherspoon's writing about piety. Indeed, on a few occasions I felt I simply had to include long sections from his sermons that, in my judgment, continue to speak today.

I need to say a word about inclusive language. As much as possible I will avoid using "Father" and male pronouns with reference to God, but because I intend to quote Witherspoon accurately, that will require presenting his own very male language of God. Although Witherspoon will be of no help whatsoever on the matter of gender sensitivity in language, he will be of immense help to both women and men if they want to discover the kind of piety that he thought should be the possession of every Christian person, male or female.

The translation of the Bible that Witherspoon used and often quoted was the King James Version. I have not attempted to correct any of his infrequent biblical misquotations, nor have I called attention to or corrected his spelling, punctuation, or capitalization (except in the case of the titles in his *Works*), though I have modernized the typography slightly. Actually, compared to some other eighteenth-century writers, Witherspoon's usage is closer to our own than one might expect. As an interesting aside, even though he judged writing prose to be a heavy responsibility, Witherspoon held a low view of punctuation, despite the fact that he (or his printer?) peppered his writing with unnecessary commas. "There are few gentlemen or scholars who use [punctuation] much," he opined, "either in letters or in their compositions." And if a piece needed to be published, punctuation could be left up to the printers! Putting a surprising amount of faith in their judgment, he remarked that they understand "that matter at least as well, if not better than any writer."[9]

Sources

The major sources for Witherspoon's piety are to be found in the four volumes of his published *Works*. There were two editions of these *Works*, 1800–1801 and 1802, both published by William Woodward, Philadelphia, and both edited by Witherspoon's former student, the Reverend Ashbel Green (1762–1848), who himself was president of the College of New Jersey (1812–1822).[10] The manuscripts behind these published *Works* have either been lost or destroyed. We know that during the Revolution when British soldiers occupied Nassau Hall, the main college building, Witherspoon's office was ravaged, and his papers, along with any notes and letters, disappeared. At the end of his life, Witherspoon's second wife, on her husband's orders, destroyed a quantity of his papers, no doubt because he felt they were not ready to go to a printer. Carelessness on the part of Green and Witherspoon's son-in-law, Samuel Stanhope Smith, who succeeded his father-in-law as president of the college, would account for the loss of still other manuscripts. In his biography of his former mentor, Green explained that of the four sets of lectures that Witherspoon delivered at the college—Divinity, Chronology (History), Moral Philosophy, and Eloquence—only the latter two were complete as printed. The divinity lectures, also included in the *Works*, end after the topic "The Covenant of Grace," and the Chronology lectures were so incomplete that Green decided they should not be published at all.[11]

While the *Works* do include the majority of Witherspoon's writings—sermons, theological treatises, essays of political and cultural interest, and the three sets of lectures—with one exception (the Moral Philosophy lectures), they have not been critically edited. In the *Works* one might discover a rare footnote by Witherspoon but none by the editor, a scholarly introduction is absent, and there is no index of any sort—general, names, scripture references. Green and the printer simply reproduced the text of the various pieces from Witherspoon's handwritten manuscripts. Of course, Witherspoon must share some of the blame too, although it is probably not fair to hold him strictly to modern standards of scholarship. He usually did not properly identify his sources and, even when he quoted from the Bible or the Confession, he sometimes did so incorrectly.

As noted above, one important section of his *Works*, the "Lectures on Moral Philosophy," was expertly edited by Jack Scott in 1982. Other parts of the *Works* would profit by the same level of scholarship.[12]

It is important to recognize and appreciate the difficulty of unearthing and explicating the several parts and emphases of Witherspoon's piety without the aid of a critical edition of the pertinent sections of his writings. Furthermore, the task would have been easier if we owned a Witherspoon diary, journal, or spiritual manual. If any of these items ever existed, they have been destroyed. This means that only on rare occasions in his *Works* do we get a glimpse of the inner Witherspoon.

The earliest biographies of Witherspoon appeared in the first third of the nineteenth century: Ashbel Green's biographical essay was included in John Sanderson's *Biography of the Signers of the Declaration of Independence*, published in 1824. A Scottish account of Witherspoon's life by Thomas Crichton appeared in 1829, in which the author, once a youthful member of Witherspoon's Paisley congregation, related numerous incidents in Witherspoon's Scottish period. A copy of the brief biography, which appeared as a periodical article, is readily available in Firestone Library, Princeton University.[13] The first full biography was written about 1840 by Ashbel Green, who used many items from Crichton's account. Green's story, which was originally intended to be an introduction to a third edition of Witherspoon's *Works*, borders on hagiography but furnishes important insights into Witherspoon's work and character from one who knew him personally. Green's manuscript of 268 pages, lost for many years, finally came to rest in the New Jersey Historical Society and was edited and published in 1973.[14] All subsequent Witherspoon biographers have had to rely heavily on this avowedly sympathetic account. Two twentieth-century biographies have remained in print. *President Witherspoon* by Varnum Lansing Collins, a two-volume work published in 1925, remains even today the most comprehensive account of the life and work of the Princeton professor, preacher, and politician.[15] Relying largely on Green and Collins, Martha Lou Lemmon Stohlman wrote a brief, very readable account, *John Witherspoon: Parson, Politician, Patriot*, in time for the American Bicentennial in 1976.[16] A number of dissertations have been written on various aspects of Witherspoon's life and thought. These will be cited as needed throughout the present work. None have examined Witherspoon's piety; very few have even examined his religion to any extent.[17]

The particular sources for an examination of Witherspoon's piety within the *Works* are to be found chiefly in the first two of the four volumes. In the first edition, those volumes contain sermons and the two essays on justification and regeneration. In volume 4, the "Lectures on Divinity" merit careful study as well. These were the lectures he gave to ministerial students who studied with him in Princeton after they graduated from the College of New Jersey. Early in his ministerial career Witherspoon's sermons had attracted enough attention that by 1768 he had selected thirteen and published them under the title, *Practical Discourses on the Leading Truths of the Gospel*[18] (see appendix A). In a limited way they show the main emphases in Witherspoon's sermons and demonstrate that even at this early date he intended his preaching to be practical. These were included, along with other sermons preached in Scotland and America, to make a total of forty-seven pulpit discourses in his *Works*. A large majority of them were preached to regular Sunday congregations, while four dealt with ministerial piety and were preached on special occasions, namely, at the ordinations of two men to the ministry, and at Witherspoon's departure from Paisley and his arrival in Princeton. Nine sermons, which will be identified later, can be called "Action" or Communion sermons. In the eighteenth-century Kirk, the celebration of Communion was often called "the Action," "the Great Work," or "the Occasion." The "Action" referred to the fourfold action in the institution of the Lord's Supper: "He took . . . , gave thanks . . . , brake . . . , and gave . . ."[19]

Acknowledgments

My interest in John Witherspoon began many years ago when I received a National Endowment for the Humanities Summer Seminar award at Princeton University. The seminar director was Professor John F. Wilson. Other awards that have provided support for my project include a Cunningham Lectureship at the University of Edinburgh and a substantial grant from the Henry Luce III Fund for Distinguished Scholarship at The College of Wooster. The College of Wooster's generous leave program provided essential time for research and writing.

The directors and staff of the following libraries deserve special mention. I am grateful to them for routine and, at times, special assistance: in Princeton, the University Firestone Library and the Seminary Speer Library; in Philadelphia, the Presbyterian Historical Society Library; in Edinburgh, the New College Library of the University; and most of all, the Andrews and Flo K. Gault Libraries of The College of Wooster.

While several individuals have given me encouragement in my efforts to bring to light Witherspoon's ideas on piety, two College of Wooster colleagues must be named and thanked: Art History Professor Emeritus D. Arnold Lewis and English Professor Deborah P. Hilty, both of whom read the entire manuscript and provided gentle but constructive criticism from the standpoint of intelligent laypersons. The special interest that Arn Lewis has taken in my writing and my efforts to get a publisher interested in the manuscript has been both impressive and touching! I am also indebted to Dr. Thomas Long, director of Geneva Press, for his sound advice and wise suggestions for improving the text. Ardis Gillund faithfully typed almost all of the manuscript, with able assistance from Charlotte Wahl and Kathie Clyde.

Finally, I wish to thank my wife, Lois (who I am glad to say was not my unpaid, overworked research assistant), for her help in the early part of the project and for her ever-loving patience over the years and at the end of this long literary journey.

Abbreviations

Confession   "The Westminster Confession of Faith." *The Book of Confessions*. Louisville, Ky.: Office of the General Assembly, Presbyterian Church (U.S.A.), 1996.

Institutes   John Calvin. *Institutes of the Christian Religion*. Edited by J. T. McNeill. Translated by Ford Lewis Battles. Library of Christian Classics, vols. 20, 21. Philadelphia: Westminster Press, 1960.

Pictet   Bénédict Pictet. *Christian Theology*. Translated by Frederick Reyroux. Philadelphia, 1845.

Works   Ashbel Green, ed. *The Works of the Rev. John Witherspoon*. 4 vols. Philadelphia, 1800–1801.

An Eighteenth-century Pilgrim

Church historian Martin Marty titled his book on American religious history *Pilgrims in Their Own Land*. He reminds us that all those who settled in America, with the exception of Native Americans, were, as the French immigrant Jacques Maritain explained, still pilgrims. Of course, there was a select group of immigrants, called the Pilgrims, who came to New England, but most arrivals to the New World can rightfully be called pilgrims from other lands. It was as if they were prodded by a dream, always on the move, available for new responsibilities, prepared for possible loss and disappointment.[1] That description of a pilgrim can appropriately be applied to John Witherspoon. He may not have brought with him a well-articulated dream, but as a new arrival in America, he surely was on the move and more than ready for new responsibilities. Nor did he ever lose the Scottish imprint even as he became an American patriot, and he once confessed, though not in so many words, that if we are true Christians, we are all pilgrims on earth. He told the students at Princeton that true Christians always must be "pilgrims and strangers in the earth." As such, "they comfort each other in distress, they assist each other in doubts and difficulties, they embolden each other by their example, and they assist each other by their prayers." And pilgrims should give very little thought to their journeys in this life. The "great removal" in our lives, he explained, is from this life "into an eternal state." In that light, he did not regard his move from Paisley to Princeton as such a momentous event, though to him it was part of a providential plan. "I make no merit at all, of having left country, and kindred, and connections of the dearest kind," he confessed, "in order to serve the interest of the church of Christ, in this part of the globe."[2] Those are the words of an authentic pilgrim.

Witherspoon's pilgrimage and the story of his piety has its origins in the eighteenth-century Presbyterian manse of the tiny village of

Gifford, Scotland, in the rolling terrain of East Lothian, some four-teen miles from Edinburgh. There John Witherspoon was born on February 5, 1723.[3] We have some information about his father, James; very little about his mother.

The Reverend James Witherspoon was the Church of Scotland minister of Yester parish, which included Gifford, from 1720 until his death in 1759. Although very little trustworthy information about him remains, we do know he preached before the General Assembly, was frequently a commissioner (delegate) to that body, and in 1744 was appointed a royal chaplain.[4] There is no reason to question the general assessment of James Witherspoon as a capable but not outstanding cleric, "eminent for his piety, learning and fidelity as a minister of the gospel."[5]

Anna or Anne Walker married James Witherspoon in 1720 and was the mother of six children born within ten years, John being the eldest. She was a minister's daughter, and along with her husband provided a Christian upbringing for her children. John credits his "pious mother" for his early religious instruction, observing that with her help he was able to begin reading the Bible at the age of four, later memorizing passages from the Bible and a large number of Isaac Watts's psalms and hymns.[6] Her death occurred sometime before 1744, at which time her husband refers to himself as a wid-ower.[7] That she was descended from the famous sixteenth-century Reformer John Knox has often been alleged, and if true would enhance the standing of John Witherspoon, but the lineage remains unproven.[8]

John Witherspoon's upbringing was probably not very different from that of hundreds of children in rural Scotland, at least in the Lowlands, except that as a parish minister's oldest son his future might have been more carefully attended to. From what we know of his boyhood, he was a normal young Scot: he fished in Gifford Water, climbed through the heather of the Lammermoors, mastered the sport of curling, and profited from interacting with and learning from his brothers and sisters.

The Haddington Grammar School, four miles from Gifford, was the place where Witherspoon's formal education began. Of a long history, it had educated many famous Scots, including John Knox. There Witherspoon was taught the traditional subjects of the Latin classics, English grammar, mathematics, composition, and singing.[9] The students were also given the customary instruction in the Bible and the Westminster Catechism. The long days of instruction under schoolmaster John Leslie were tempered with such extracurricular activities as the occasional soccer match and a restricted form of drama—pedagogic and morality plays performed in Latin.[10] During Witherspoon's youth it was common for grammar schools to sponsor the performance of Latin plays, such as the "Bellum Grammaticale," in which various parts of speech were personified and vied with each other to see which was most important.[11] These Latin dramatizations became so popular that often parents and the public were invited to attend, and more than one town council, including Haddington's, was even willing to designate funds to construct a stage for these productions.

The reason for noticing these school plays is that years later when Witherspoon publicly denounced the theater, it must have caused him to recall that he had acted in Latin plays in his school. He did, however, draw a distinction between school plays and those produced in the public theater, approving the former, though reluctantly, and condemning the latter, noting that the public theater could never be a "means for instruction" and was wholly unnecessary "for our spiritual improvement."[12]

When the youthful Witherspoon left home to enter the University of Edinburgh in 1736, he was just thirteen, not an unusual age for university entrance in the eighteenth century.[13] However, there is reason to think that he was mature for his years. In his old age, the Reverend Alexander Carlyle (1722–1805) claimed to remember that Witherspoon came to the university with a "disagreeable temper" and an "awkward manner," but nevertheless judged him to be "a good scholar, far advanced for his age, very sensible, and shrewd."[14] He had been nurtured in a Christian home, indoctrinated in the rudiments of the Christian faith, and had received a solid grounding in those subjects deemed essential for an educated person. Biographer Varnum Lansing Collins has noted that Witherspoon went to the university with a good command of Latin, Greek, and French.[15]

We have no direct report from him regarding his university education, so it is difficult to know exactly what subjects he studied, what he thought of his teachers, and what he found particularly interesting. Fortunately, Carlyle, Witherspoon's acquaintance, who started at Edinburgh University in 1735, described his own course of study and his professors in some detail. We have to assume that Witherspoon's university career paralleled Carlyle's. The curriculum, which normally took four years, was fixed and thus virtually the same for every student: Latin first, then Greek; later came logic, natural philosophy (science), mathematics, and moral philosophy. The first four were required, the latter two optional.[16] Of these subjects the one that influenced Witherspoon the most was John Stevenson's course in logic and metaphysics. Stevenson, about whose background or training little is known, taught at the university from 1730 until his death in 1775.[17] Neither brilliant nor original in thought, he nevertheless had the ability to see the importance of trying out new ideas and appreciating constructive change.

Carlyle, Witherspoon, and their classmates heard him on a number of topics. Setting aside the traditional logic of Aristotle, he lectured on two more recent works: the *Elementa Philosophiae* of Heineccius, and Bishop Wynne's abridgment of *An Essay Concerning Human Understanding* by John Locke.[18] He also made an important contribution with his popular course on rhetoric, literary criticism, and belles lettres. He called up a variety of sources. Each morning he read with his students Aristotle's *Poetics* and Longinus's *Essay on the Sublime*, making allusions to Cicero, Quintilian, Horace, and Homer. English authors such as Dryden, Addison, and Pope were discussed. French critics were introduced.[19]

His reputation as a professor was further enhanced by his teaching style. He was reputed to be clear, thorough, and forceful in his presentation, at the same time employing Socratic and discussion techniques. Although he delivered his philosophy lectures in Latin, he ordered his classes to speak and write in English, not in broad Scots, the spoken language of his students, as they came to grips with the best examples of rhetoric and elegant prose and poetry. A large number of students, several of whom became eminent members of the Edinburgh literati, later testified to Stevenson's impact. Carlyle, Hugh Blair, William Robertson, John Erskine, and Thomas Somerville, not to mention John Witherspoon, all were indebted to John Stevenson.[20]

Although Witherspoon never mentions Stevenson's influence on his life and thought,[21] it is nonetheless possible to discover traces of Stevenson in Witherspoon. When Witherspoon later became a professor at Princeton, he, like Stevenson, encouraged classroom recitation, discussion, and oral examinations. Stevenson's appreciation of classical and modern writers and his insights into language and literature turn up in Witherspoon's "Lectures on Eloquence."[22] Likewise, Witherspoon's efforts to express himself simply and forcefully in his sermons, along with his sensitivity to literary style and proper use of words, must surely stem from his time with Stevenson.[23]

At a time when boys attended Scottish universities but did not often graduate with a degree, Witherspoon, Hugh Blair, and three other students requested and were each granted permission to present publicly a graduation thesis in the university common hall. Thus, in February 1739, having just reached sixteen and only three years after entering the university, Witherspoon and his friends defended successfully their theses and were awarded the degree of master of arts. Witherspoon's thesis, his first publication, was *Disputatio Philosophica: De Mentis Immortalitae* (Philosophical Disputation: Concerning the Immortality of the Mind).[24] In his twelve-page essay, in which he hoped to prove that the mind was indeed immortal, he ranged from Cicero's argument for immortality, to an empirical study of human nature, and finally to the religious belief that God created humans to enjoy an afterlife in which the mind would reach its highest development.[25] Roger Fechner rightly points out that even at this early stage in his thinking, Witherspoon "was groping for the epistemological foundations" for what later came to be known as Scottish common sense realism.[26]

It is not possible to tell when Witherspoon decided to enter the Church of Scotland ministry. Certainly the example of his father and other clerical relatives (maternal grandfather and an uncle), the Christian upbringing he received, as well as the feeling that the eldest son ought to follow in his father's footsteps, all played a part in his decision. What is known is that he remained at the University of Edinburgh to study divinity from 1739 to 1743. Though the divinity faculty was preeminent in the university, requirements were minimal and the quality of instruction poor. The teaching staff consisted of only three professors (divinity or theology, church history, and Hebrew).[27] Witherspoon apparently studied all three subjects.

Divinity was the single required course for theological students. Witherspoon's professor was John Gowdie or Goldie (1682–1762), who taught theology until 1754, when he was made principal of the university. He lectured on the *Theologia Christiana* of Swiss theologian Bénédict Pictet (1655–1724),[28] but his expositions were so slow and tedious that it took him seven years to plow through only half of the work. No wonder Carlyle dismissed him with the scathing comment that he was "dull, Dutch, and prolix."[29] Theological student Witherspoon may not have treated Pictet so cavalierly, for even a casual inspection of Pictet's *Theologia* uncovers the similarities between the contents of that work and the covenant theology of the Confession, the foundation of Witherspoon's thought. Common themes include authority of scripture, God and the Trinity, decrees, creation, fall of man, the double covenant, Christ the Mediator, justification, sanctification, church, sacraments, and life after death.[30] Pictet's theology was attractive to many in the Reformed world and for good reason. He attempted to remain faithful to Calvinistic orthodoxy while incorporating new developments in philosophy and science based on reason. At the same time he presented his thought in such a way that the average layperson could understand it.[31]

After completing his divinity training, Witherspoon prepared himself for his "trials," the examinations in theological subjects by the Presbytery of Haddington that would permit him to be licensed to preach.[32] Full status in the ministry—ordination—would come later. He passed these trials successfully, and on September 6, 1743, John Witherspoon was duly licensed and became a "probationer." For the next year and a half he assisted his father at Gifford, and finally, after further "trials" administered by the Presbytery of Irvine, Witherspoon was ordained and installed as minister of Beith parish in the west of Scotland on April 11, 1745. The new minister was just twenty-two years of age.[33] Two years later he married Elizabeth Montgomery, who lived nearby. Infant mortality rates were high in eighteenth-century Scotland, and of the ten children who came from this union, only five survived to adulthood.

Witherspoon soon discovered that his days were filled with the several activities of a Church of Scotland minister in a semirural parish of the mid-eighteenth century. The primary demand was the lecture and the two sermons every Sunday. The lecture that preceded the sermon in the morning service, in order to acquaint people with Holy Scripture, was customarily a verse-by-verse exposition of a chapter from the Bible. To prepare a lecture was enough of a strain. The writing and preaching of sermons themselves constituted a burden unremitting and oppressive. Sermons were long, often an hour or more. They could be written out ahead of time but were never to be read on Sunday; lay opinion did not tolerate a manuscript in the pulpit.[34] It is reported that Beith's new minister spent long hours in sermon preparation; the number of candles burned and books purchased surprised the townspeople. They commented that they saw the light burning late in the manse.[35]

The minister was also expected to "catechize" the congregation, and if the parish was a large one this could be time-consuming. Even though members were supposed to have learned their catechisms in their youth, the minister had the obligation to examine his flock periodically to make sure their beliefs were sound. In those days, theology mattered!

The faithful pastor was attentive to the spiritual needs of individual members and traveled on foot or horseback to their homes routinely and in emergencies. Pastoral supervision of the flock included oversight of the kirk session in its responsibility for monitoring the morals of the people; wrongdoing encompassed theft, swearing, dishonoring the Lord's Day, drunkenness, and sexual sins.[36] The goal was to reclaim the wrongdoer and insure an amendment of life. Punishments ranged from private warning to full excommunication. There are numerous examples of overzealous sessions exercising discipline and administering injustice, but extant Beith session records demonstrate that the session and the pastor were taking their duties of congregational oversight seriously and administering justice thoroughly and fairly.[37]

Outside Beith, Witherspoon was active at all levels of church government, his reputation expanding due to his participation. Several times he was elected moderator, the presiding officer, of the Presbytery of Irvine; he attended meetings of the next larger body, the Synod of Glasgow and Ayr; four times he was a commissioner (representative) to the national forum of the Kirk, the General Assembly.[38] Of more significance, he was fast becoming a leader of one of the two factions in the established church, the Popular party. By the 1750s in the Church of Scotland, two divisions were apparent on the national level, the Popular and Moderate parties. The former took its name from the view that ministers ought to be elected to their positions by a popular vote of the people. The latter name came to designate those who denounced the religious zealots and extremist views in religion and advocated moderation, politeness, and tolerance.[39] Numerically the Popular party was probably the larger, but from approximately 1760 through the early 1780s, the Moderates dominated church affairs, especially in the General Assembly where they were able to hold key positions.[40]

Two basic issues divided the parties. The first was the law of lay patronage, established by a parliamentary act of 1712, whereby wealthy lay landowners appointed ministers to parishes. According to the Moderates, this was the law, and the law should be obeyed not resisted; moreover, they believed that the system guaranteed a higher caliber of minister than a popular vote by a congregation. According to the Popular party, lay patronage denied the right of the congregation to choose the minister who would serve them, a principle that John Knox and his associates had inserted in the *First Book of Discipline* (1560–1561). The law of patronage was the key issue dividing the two parties, and according to K. R. Ross, was for a large part of the eighteenth and nineteenth centuries "to be productive of more mischief in Scottish ecclesiastical life than any other single piece of legislation."[41]

The second issue separating the two parties is at once harder to define but perhaps more significant in our understanding of how they differed. At base, there were two contrasting models of piety, though to be fair one must admit that even within each party there was not a uniform piety, and even between the two the lines of separation were sometimes blurred. Some divergences, however, were apparent. The Popular party regarded adherence to the Confession as essential; Moderates never renounced the Confession but generally ignored it.[42] The Popular model of piety included sermons on sin and salvation, and Popular party clerics frequently preached and published experiential and evangelical sermons. The Moderate model emphasized moral teaching and preaching to the end that personal and social morality might be enhanced. They published more on secular subjects and less on religious and theological topics. Popular religion meant being openly upright and religious in public and private, and wary of worldly pursuits, notably certain amusements like the theater. Moderates cultivated "politeness" in all its ramifications: mingling with persons of manners and refinement; composing rational, elegant prose; approving dancing and supporting the theater; encouraging scientific investigations; tolerating if not actually approving erroneous ideas; and striving to make persons virtuous and happy.[43] Understandably, the Moderates reckoned Popular party piety to be narrow, constrained, and unenlightened, whereas those of that party thought the Moderates worldly, unfaithful, and even heretical.

Both groups were reacting in their own way to the Enlightenment, the major intellectual development that spread across Europe and eventually to America. It was a form of eighteenth-century thought that found expression in such ideas as natural law, universal order and harmony, and especially the reliability of human reason. A more secular outlook on the world was the result of a rational or scientific attitude toward social, political, and religious issues. There was a general belief in progress and perfectibility. Human nature was understood to be universally uniform and a "science of man" now seemed possible. A utilitarian ethic became current, whereby an action was deemed the best when it produced the greatest happiness for the greatest numbers of persons. The expectation was that nature could be mastered and new discoveries and greater knowledge would make life better for everyone. Attitudes encouraged by the Enlightenment led to greater tolerance in religion and less reliance on dogma. Natural religion was encouraged; revealed religion was suspect, though not always attacked.[44]

The claim can be made that in no other European nation was the Enlightenment more completely assimilated by an established national church than in Scotland, though not all the laity and clergy endorsed Enlightenment principles. It is true that some of the leading scholars of the time were Moderate ministers of the Church of Scotland, including William Robertson (1721–1793), principal of Edinburgh University and an illustrious historian, and Hugh Blair (1718–1800), professor of rhetoric and belles lettres at Edinburgh University and minister of Edinburgh's St. Giles' Cathedral.[45] These two and Moderates like them were influenced much more by the Enlightenment than were Witherspoon and other members of the Popular party, who resisted many of the liberalizing emphases of the Enlightenment. What is of unusual interest in the present study is the discovery that during his life, and especially as he moved to America, Witherspoon faced up to some of the issues that the Enlightenment had raised and in the end was even influenced by this intellectual movement, perhaps more than he intended.

Members of the Popular party were sometimes called, pejoratively, "Highflyers," because they were seen to espouse extreme ideas and attitudes. Witherspoon often called members of his own Popular party "the orthodox."[46] He rarely used the term "evangelical," although later scholars have applied that term to him and to members of the Popular party. Evangelicals have traditionally taught such ideas as human sinfulness, salvation from sin through the death (often substitutionary) of Christ, the conversion experience, the centrality of the cross, and the new life in Christ after conversion.[47] It has often been assumed that the Popular party was an evangelical one, but this was not true in every case. Sometimes a Popular party member, fervid in his opposition to patronage, was close to the Moderates in belief and outlook. No doubt it is safe to say that all evangelicals of the time upheld the claim of the people to choose their own ministers, but not all who made that claim were evangelicals. Three conclusions seem to emerge. First, the only absolutely sure way to identify a member of the Popular party was to ask if he was opposed to the law of patronage. Second, there was not a single set of beliefs that encompassed all who belonged to the Popular party.[48] Third, Witherspoon was to put his own stamp on the label "evangelical" as a way of describing his own kind of piety.

Often feelings between the two parties ran high as they opposed one another, notably in disputes that reached the floor of the General Assembly.[49] Carlyle, who became a leading Moderate, could describe Witherspoon as hypocritical, "close, and suspicious, and jealous, and always aspiring of a superiority that he was not able to maintain." An anonymous pamphlet, *A Just View of the Constitution of the Church of Scotland* (1753), reflecting the Moderate position on a General Assembly action, called Witherspoon a "dupe."[50] Witherspoon could give as well as he got: Moderates were soft on heresy, he charged ("I never knew a moderate man in my life, that did not love and honor a heretic."). They were only "nominal Christians" who disguised or altered the gospel in order to defend it. They pretended "a warm zeal for the great doctrines of morality" and urged "the necessity of holiness in general," a sad corruption of true piety that induces "a deluge of profaneness and immorality in practice."[51] What projected Witherspoon into the larger world of theological debate in the Kirk and guaranteed his reputation as a leader of the Popular party was the publication in 1753 of an acerbic attack on the Moderates: *Ecclesiastical Characteristics, or the Arcana of Church Polity*.

Initially, this sixty-page satire was published anonymously, but Witherspoon's authorship was soon recognized. Before long it became very well known, appearing in four editions within two years. Using a favorite principle of Lord Shaftesbury (1671–1713), "Ridicule is the test of truth,"[52] Witherspoon satirized Moderate ideas and conduct in the form of thirteen maxims. These were, he explained, tongue in cheek, designed to be "a plain and easy way of attaining to the Character of a Moderate Man." The Moderate presumes to be an intellectual, well-read superior to dull quoters of the

Bible; is pleased to be chosen as a minister by noble, wealthy patrons disregarding what the poor common folk might think; would call orthodox church members "knaves" and "fools"; and would "never speak of the Confession of Faith but with a sneer." Buried in maxim 6 was an "Athenian Creed" to which all Moderates would surely subscribe. It begins, "I believe in the beauty and comely proportions of Dame Nature, and in almighty Fate," and concludes with a denunciation of Francis Hutcheson (1694–1746), professor of moral philosophy at the University of Glasgow from 1730 to 1746, a precursor or mentor of the later Moderates: "In fine, I believe in the divinity of L. S.— [Lord Shaftesbury], the saintship of Marcus Antoninus, the perspicuity and sublimity of A—e [Aristotle], and the perpetual duration of Mr. H—n's [Francis Hutcheson's] works notwithstanding their present tendency to oblivion. Amen."[53] With that, Witherspoon decided that he had put the Moderates in their place!

The importance of the *Ecclesiastical Characteristics* for the present study lies not so much in Witherspoon's success in honing his debating skill in an ecclesiastical squabble as in his understanding of what piety should *not* be. His 1753 sarcastic diatribe against the Moderates is valuable material in building Witherspoon's own construct of ministerial piety and even in the process of adapting his piety for life in the public domain.

Witherspoon's quarrel with the Moderates continued. A new skirmish between them and the Popular party began on December 14, 1756. The occasion was the performance of the play, *The Tragedy of Douglas*, presented on the stage of Edinburgh's Canongate Theater. The issue was whether Christian piety countenanced attendance at the theater. At a time when the basic question of theater attendance had not been resolved in the Kirk, many of the faithful were scandalized by the fact that the author of the play, John Home (1722–1808), a classmate of Witherspoon's at the University of Edinburgh, was a Church of Scotland minister (at Athelstaneford) and that he and several other ministers attended the performance on opening night. A major pamphlet war broke out between the two parties over the production of what, by today's standards, is a rather tame, sentimental drama. The opposition to *Douglas* and the theater raged on. Home was forced to resign, Carlyle was censured by his presbytery for helping to produce and for attending the play, and the General Assembly finally was compelled to act upon the "*Douglas* Affair."[54] Witherspoon joined the angry opposition to the play by writing perhaps the best antitheater piece of the period, "A Serious Inquiry into the Nature and Effects of the Stage" (1757).[55] The subtitle stated Witherspoon's position succinctly: "that contributing to the support of a public theatre, is inconsistent with the character of a Christian." In his mind the support of and attendance at the theater was a sin. His essay was another stroke of the pen in his attempt to portray a model Christian.

Witherspoon's party did not prevail in this controversy and others, especially on the floor of the General Assembly, where the Moderates increasingly gained and held power and influence. Nevertheless, Witherspoon's reputation grew both in Scotland and elsewhere. In 1757, he accepted a call to be minister of the Laigh (Low) Kirk in Paisley, fourteen miles from Beith.[56] Though the salary and the membership were larger (1300 "sittings"), Witherspoon's duties remained much the same as they were in Beith. The difference was that his sermons and other writings were now being published and widely read, and he continued to be active outside his parish.

Witherspoon's reputation was growing. Several times he appeared at General Assembly in Edinburgh; in 1759 the Synod of Glasgow and Ayr elected him moderator. In January 1758, he preached in Edinburgh before the Society in Scotland for the Propagation of Christian Knowledge, a missionary society, a stern message entitled "The Absolute Necessity of Salvation through Christ" (text: Acts 4:12). In part it was directed toward the Moderates who in Witherspoon's eyes were compromising the gospel by not holding fast to the only means of salvation, belief in Jesus Christ. Another published sermon was a jeremiad preached on the occasion of the annual public fast, or national day of prayer, in 1758: "Prayer for National Prosperity and for the Revival of Religion Inseparably Connected" (Isaiah 51:9).[57]

Two other discourses that received wide notice were an ordination sermon preached in Paisley Abbey in 1758 and one preached before the Synod a year later.[58] In these and other sermons Witherspoon's theology was taking shape. Also, in two theological treatises (they were more like extended sermons) certain Reformed doctrines came to be expounded. While still in Beith he had written the first of these, an essay on justification. Now in Paisley he produced its counterpart, a treatise on regeneration based on John 3:3 ("Except a man be born again . . .").[59] By the late 1760s these treatises and his sermons were being collected and published.[60]

Reformed circles soon acknowledged his spreading fame. The University of St. Andrews bestowed on him an honorary doctorate in divinity in 1764. Churches in Dundee, Rotterdam, and Dublin invited him to become their minister. Though he declined these invitations, he did accept one from Princeton in far-off New Jersey.

In 1766, the Reverend Samuel Finley died. An American Presbyterian minister, he had been the fifth president of the small Presbyterian college in Princeton, the College of New Jersey, which would later become Princeton University.[61] The college had been established by the New Side faction in the American Presbyterian Church, but since 1758, when at least officially the schism between the Old Side and New Side had been healed, the trustees were attempting to make the college an institution agreeable to both parties. The choice of Witherspoon as the next president seemed ideal. He had had no part in the contest between Old and New Sides.[62] His orientation within the Popular party in Scotland, his loyalty to the Westminster standards, and his reputation as an author, preacher, and church leader accorded him great appeal to both parties.

The generous invitation to become president included an annual salary equal to 206 pounds sterling, use of the president's house, a garden, land for pasturage, and firewood. At first, Witherspoon refused. He was well established in Scotland; moreover, he would have to leave the parish ministry to become chiefly an educator—and in a new country. His wife at first resisted, stating that if her husband suffered the same fate as the first five presidents, all of whom died in office, he "might soon die and she [would] be left in a strange land." Witherspoon listened to his wife. Letters and a visit from an alumnus of the College of New Jersey, class of 1760, Benjamin Rush (1746–1813), who at the time was a medical student at the University of Edinburgh, finally persuaded Mrs. Witherspoon to relent and the Reverend Dr. Witherspoon to accept the renewed invitation in 1768.[63] By this time, he felt that providence clearly intended that he should continue his ministry in the New World.

On August 7, 1768, after crossing the Atlantic for nearly three months in a sailing ship, Witherspoon, his wife, and their five children landed in Philadelphia.[64] At the end of five days' respite in the city, they went on to Princeton, where they were greeted enthusiastically by the staff and the entire student body. That night every window in the multipurpose college building, Nassau Hall, was illuminated by a candle, the closest the college could come to *son et lumière*. Formally installed on August 17, 1768, Witherspoon held the position of president of the College of New Jersey until his death in 1794.[65]

Witherspoon's move to America and from parish to college is similar to twentieth-century theologian Paul Tillich's experience of living and working "on the boundary."[66] Tillich was forty-seven when he escaped from the Nazis and came to America in 1933, thereafter living, as he explained, on the boundary between Germany and America. Witherspoon was forty-five when he arrived in the New World and began living on the boundary (though he never used that actual phrase) between Scotland and America. After he had been in America for several years, he declared, with no qualification and some excess,

> I am certain I feel the attachment of [native] country as far as it is a virtuous or laudable principle. . . . I have never seen cause to be ashamed of the place of my birth; since the revival of arts and letters in Europe in the close of the fourteenth and beginning of the fifteenth century, the natives of Scotland have not been inferior to those of any other country, for genius, erudition, military prowess, or any of those accomplishments which improve or embellish human nature.[67]

Witherspoon spoke and wrote proper English, but his Scottish accent sometimes prompted Americans to think of him as an untransformed Scot. Once in America, Witherspoon lost no time in joining the St. Andrews Society of Philadelphia, and for years encouraged Scottish emigration, even going so far as entering upon a land scheme in Nova Scotia designed for settling Scottish families. When Professor Witherspoon greeted his classes with "How do ye do, lads?" they responded enthusiastically, using a familiar Scots word, "Brawly, sir, brawly!" ("Fine, sir, fine!"). Manasseh Cutler (1742–1823), American Congregational minister, lawyer, and some-time scientist, described Witherspoon in 1787 as "an intolerably homely old Scotchman [who] speaks the true dialect of his country." Here indeed was a pilgrim very much still on the boundary between Scotland and America.[68]

Another significant boundary for Witherspoon came to be the one between church and college. When he took up his new post in Princeton, he added to the ministry the new roles of college administrator, professor, and, later, politician. College finances cried out for swift attention; the trustees had been lax in handling the funds. Witherspoon tidied the accounts and promptly set about raising money for the college and furthering what we today would call "college relations," which, of course, required making new friends for the college and recruiting students. Only a month after his arrival he preached in New York, and the next month, accompanied by John Rodgers, he toured New England, returning to Princeton with one thousand pounds contributed by Bostonians. In 1769, he set out on his first trip to Virginia, again gaining new friends for the college and raising funds.

Within the college he undertook curricular reform, assigning certain required courses for each of the four years. Green reports that he was responsible for introducing the lecture method at Princeton (previously each student studied a course textbook and recited on it in class).[69] Advancing the study of mathematics and science, Witherspoon purchased from David Rittenhouse of Philadelphia an innovative teaching tool for that time—his invention called an orrery. It was a delicate clockwork mechanism for illustrating the motions and phases of the planets in the solar system relative to one another.[70] Witherspoon also established a professorship of mathematics and natural philosophy (science) at Princeton in 1771.

Like most eighteenth-century college presidents, Witherspoon was both administrator and teacher. His formal lectures, as noted above, included moral philosophy, eloquence or belles lettres (composition, taste, and literary criticism), chronology and history, and divinity (for those students studying for the ministry). On demand, he also taught French and Hebrew, the latter to preministerial students. Equally as important as the formal lectures, especially in the 1770s, was Witherspoon's encouragement of student orations, the subjects of which were often political and public affairs issues.

We have already noted that much of Witherspoon's fame is based upon his participation in the American Revolution.[71] While his involvement in the Revolution is easy to trace and document, what is more problematic is the metamorphosis of Witherspoon from a loyal subject of the British king to an energetic American patriot. There are no well-defined stages in this shift during the period 1768–1774, though several factors may help to explain Witherspoon's developing patriotism.[72]

Witherspoon was apparently so impressed by what America had to offer, that merely by living in the new world a person would somehow become an American, that he once wrote, "A man will become an American by residing in this country three months . . . more easily and certainly than by reading or hearing of it for three years."[73] His friend John Rodgers testified that indeed this was what happened to Witherspoon, who, Rodgers said, "became almost at once an American, on his landing among us."[74]

In 1771, Pilgrim Witherspoon disclosed his American sympathies by sending a letter to the editor of the *Scots Magazine* in which he condemned "the absurd and ignorant manner in which persons of no inconsiderable stations in Britain, have talked of things and places in America."[75] During his numerous travels in the colonies on behalf of the college, he no doubt heard many an argument for colonial rights and independence. Back in Princeton he showed remarkable patience with student orations and demonstrations supporting the patriot cause. No discipline was administered when students declaimed against the British, when they insisted one commencement day on wearing only clothes made in America, or when in January 1774, after the news of the Boston Tea Party reached the college, they burned the winter's supply of tea in a huge bonfire, along with an effigy of the governor of Massachusetts. Witherspoon's own teaching allowed for the possibility of resistance to an oppressor. In his "Lectures on Moral Philosophy" he espoused the right of "resistance to the supreme power."[76]

Finally, in 1774, his words and actions began to coalesce. That year he joined eight others in forming the Somerset County, New Jersey, Committee of Correspondence, while simultaneously writing an essay entitled "Thoughts on American Liberty."[77] At this time, while not yet arguing for independence and still professing loyalty to the king, Witherspoon nevertheless criticized current British policy and supported the upcoming First Continental Congress. Later, he was elected to the New Jersey Provincial Congress and there took a leading role in denouncing the loyalist governor of New Jersey, William Franklin, son of Benjamin, and removing him from office. In late June 1776, Witherspoon was chosen as one of New Jersey's representatives to the Continental Congress then meeting in Philadelphia to deliberate on independence from Britain. By now John Adams judged him to be "as high a Son of Liberty, as any Man in America."[78] By this time too, Witherspoon was fast becoming a genuine American Whig.[79]

On July 4, he signed the Declaration of Independence, the only cleric to do so. Tradition has it that in the debate on independence, when one member of the Congress questioned whether the country was ripe for independence, Witherspoon responded vehemently, in my "judgment it [is] not only ripe for the measure, but in danger of becoming rotten for the want of it."[80]

Witherspoon's work in national politics did not end on July 4. For the next six years with only a few interruptions he served in the Continental Congress at a time when that body *was* the government. Witherspoon, ever the cleric and wearing his clerical attire, was appointed to more than one hundred short- and long-term committees, three of which were of special significance: war, finance, and foreign affairs. His writings reflect the same devotion; one example is his "Memorial and Manifesto of the United States of North America," which has been called his "apologia for the American Revolution."[81] In fact, Witherspoon was regarded by the British to be such a leading protagonist for the American patriots that on July 30, 1776, British troops burned him in effigy along with Generals Washington, Lee, and Putnam.

During his time in Congress, Witherspoon remained president of the college, though the war seriously interrupted instruction, and at different times both American and British troops occupied and severely damaged Nassau Hall. In 1782, he left Congress to resume his college duties, most importantly to begin repairs on Nassau Hall, to acquire funds, and to build up the enrollment to prewar levels. In his later years, Witherspoon was nominally in charge, but in 1779, when Samuel Stanhope Smith had been summoned from Hampden-Sidney College in Virginia to be professor at Princeton (in 1786 he also became vice president), Witherspoon turned over the president's house to Smith and moved to Tusculum, his country home, which remains today just outside of Princeton.[82] Still, his interest in matters political did not abate as he grew older. In the 1780s, he signed the Articles of Confederation and was a representative to the New Jersey convention that ratified the national constitution. Twice he served a one-year term as a representative of Somerset County in the New Jersey Legislature.[83]

Both Ashbel Green and John Rodgers attest to the fact that Witherspoon's daily round as an educator and politician might seem to minimize his role as a minister but in fact did not do so. They point out that he preached whenever asked and discharged other functions as a gospel minister.[84] In truth, he was always known as a Presbyterian minister in America, and in time he became a leader of the young

American Presbyterian Church. The piety that he expounded in Scotland was transported to the New World, where under new conditions it was repeated, expanded, and finally modified.

As a preacher just "off the boat," he got right to work. Three days after arriving in America he supplied the pulpit of the Second Presbyterian Church in Philadelphia, and a week later he preached his first sermon in the Princeton Presbyterian Church, a congregation made up of both townspeople and students. His duties at the college included preaching on a regular basis to that congregation, an obligation he fulfilled until his death. When he traveled on behalf of the college, he frequently preached in colonial pulpits.[85]

He, of course, joined New Brunswick Presbytery but through the years missed more meetings than he attended, a fact that might comfort some modern Presbyterian pastors.[86] The next higher court in the Presbyterian system was the Synod of New York and Philadelphia, which, because no General Assembly was yet in existence, functioned as the national government of the church. Here Witherspoon was seen more often at meetings and was more active in deliberations. At the first meeting he attended, in 1769, he was asked to serve on eight different committees. Several years later, a month after Lexington and Concord, Witherspoon's leadership was recognized when at a synod meeting in New York City he was asked to chair a committee to compose a pastoral letter to be sent to all the churches under the synod's care. It marked the church's intrusion into the politics of the day. Moderate in tone, showing awareness that war was now inevitable, the letter was replete with sound advice, both practical and spiritual: repent of your sins, personal and national; maintain respect for the king, but give full support to the Continental Congress and "adhere firmly to their resolutions"; remember that "no soldier [is] so undaunted as the pious man" but such a one never fights "till it is necessary, and who ceases to fight as soon as the necessity is over."[87] Witherspoon's leadership in the church along with his pro-American stance must have enlisted support for the cause from many colonial Presbyterians.

Friday, May 17, 1776, was declared a day of public prayer for the Continental Congress; the Tories sarcastically called it "Congress Sunday." Throughout the colonies, ministers were preaching sermons on the ramifications of independence. Witherspoon was no exception. For an hour or more he held forth in the Princeton Presbyterian pulpit on the subject, "The Dominion of Providence over the Passions of Men." Running to twenty-nine pages in the first edition of his *Works*, it constitutes Witherspoon's most impressive statement to the faithful during the War of Independence,[88] and will receive fuller treatment in a later chapter as an expression of piety that leads to politics. "You are all my witnesses," declared the preacher, "that this is the first time of my introducing any political subject into the pulpit."

The sermon, widely read, was not a diatribe against the king and parliament, nor was it an emotional call to arms. Rather, Witherspoon sought to justify the American cause and simultaneously to explain why he chose to support the colonial rebellion. "There is not a single instance in history in which civil liberty was lost and religious liberty preserved entire," he declared.[89] The leading Presbyterian minister in the colonies had placed his standing and influence behind the struggle for independence. Within a few weeks he joined the Continental Congress.

If this sermon heralded Witherspoon's entrance into the political arena, another sermon he preached on April 19, 1783, at the public Thanksgiving Day celebration at the end of the war, served to mark the end of his service in Congress and in the Revolution. Choosing as his text Psalm 3:8 ("Salvation belongeth unto the Lord"), he confessed again that it was necessary, especially on this occasion, to mix politics and religion, a duty, he said, to make his hearers aware of events of a public nature. He called attention in some detail to the dispensation of providence shown to America during the war and how the measures taken by the British had been confounded. He hoped his hearers would give thanks to God and show their gratitude by their lives and service as the new nation was born.[90]

Witherspoon, the minister, was called upon for one more contribution to his church: helping to create a national denomination. Presbyterians had grown in numbers and were scattered geographically. There was but one synod for the whole country. A more elaborate organization was required, so beginning in 1785 Presbyterians took steps to study their church government and make recommendations for changes. Witherspoon was one of those appointed to help draw up a new plan of government. His participation in the deliberations is mixed, and there is reason to think that John Rodgers played a more important part than Witherspoon in the process. Green explains that Witherspoon did prepare the brief but significant eight-point preface to the new form of government, the first point of which states

> That "God alone is Lord of the conscience, and hath left it free from the doctrines and commandments of men; which are in anything contrary to his word, or beside it in matters of faith or worship." Therefore, the synod reassert [*sic*] the rights of private judgment in matters of religion, repudiate all ties to the civil government, and call for full freedom of religion for all.[91]

The first sentence is a direct quotation from the Confession and has been frequently quoted by Presbyterians in upholding the principle of freedom of conscience.

By 1788, everything was in place and the standards for the American Presbyterian Church were formulated: a revised version of the Westminster Confession of Faith, the Westminster Larger and Shorter Catechisms, the Form of Government and Discipline, and the Directory for Worship. The General Assembly became official in that year, but it was not until May 1789 that it held its first meeting, in Philadelphia. Witherspoon was the convening moderator, opening the meeting and preaching a sermon based on 1 Corinthians 3:7: "So then neither is he that planted any thing, neither is he that watereth; but God that giveth the increase."[92] He also presided over the election of John Rodgers as the first official moderator of the new denomination. The national church could now boast of a General Assembly, four new synods, and sixteen presbyteries.

Witherspoon's influence in the church went beyond this formal appearance. In 1789, there were 177 Presbyterian ministers in the new denomination, and by one count 97 were Princeton graduates, 52 of them Witherspoon's own students.[93]

That same year in October, Witherspoon's wife, Elizabeth, died at the age of 68. Two years later, however, he married a widow, Ann Dill, twenty-four years old. There was a great deal of talk about this May–December marriage, but the happy bridegroom shrugged off all comment and delighted the students by granting them a three-day holiday to celebrate the nuptials. Witherspoon and his new wife had two daughters, one of whom died in infancy.[94] For several years his eyesight had been failing, and by 1792 he had become completely blind. Still, every third Sunday he entered the Princeton pulpit and preached one of his old sermons from memory.[95] Though his health was failing, he presided at the commencement exercises and at a faculty meeting in September 1794. At last, after a brief illness, he died at Tusculum on November 15, 1794. Always a person of enormous energy and resolute action, Witherspoon, even at the end, refused to give up and "go quietly into the night." His last request was to have the latest newspaper read to him.

Sermon and Scripture

Modern readers of eighteenth-century sermons must make a strenuous effort of imagination to realize that in an age which lacked the forms of media and entertainment that we often take for granted, the Protestant sermon was a significant instrument of both religious edification and social intercourse. The sermon, hallowed by years of tradition since the Reformation, held a position of considerable power and influence in social and intellectual as well as religious affairs. At its best it was a work of literary art and conveyed a vital message of God; the preacher was esteemed as a divinely inspired prophet and a literary artisan. By character and education the minister was a leader in church and community, and his sermons were the main source of information and instruction on all matters of local and national, moral and spiritual concern for his congregation.[96] A mere glance at Puritan church life and the election day sermon tradition in New England makes this point.[97]

In Scotland the sermon occupied a prominent place in the churches of both the Moderate and Popular parties. Beginning in the seventeenth century, church records frequently contained the phrase "in time of sermon" in place of "during divine worship."[98] John Calvin, of course, had declared that the true church exists "wherever we see the Word of God purely preached and heard, and the sacraments administered according to Christ's institution."[99] The *Scots Confession of 1560* echoed Calvin in stating that the "notes" of the true church were "first, the trew preaching of the Word of God . . . secoundlie, the rycht administration of the sacramentis."[100]

This was Witherspoon's understanding of the vital function of the sermon and the exalted role of the preacher. He knew without any doubt that Christ had established a standing ministry in his church which makes possible the proclamation and hearing of his word. "In no other way," Witherspoon explained, "doth he now communicate his will, and vouchsafe his presence to his people."[101] The Sunday sermons were the means that Witherspoon chose to generate pious persons in the pews. His sermons were biblical expository discourses, each based on a text, customarily one verse of scripture, and each neatly organized into main and subdivisions, often called "heads" and "branches." He took seriously the advice offered in the *Westminster Directory for the Public Worship of God* (1645), which advocated a plain direct style of sermon construction and delivery. Texts and doctrines were to be explained clearly and simply, and due attention was to be given to their application. This so-called plain style, made famous by the Puritans, was intended to reach both the minds and hearts of listeners. Plainness did not mean a simplistic or prosaic message; it did mean that the message was forceful, direct, and explicit, easy to understand and remember, couched in language designed for the understanding of the congregation. To be avoided were exotic words, flowery phrases, confusing rhetoric, and quotations in ancient languages.[102]

In Scotland the late seventeenth-century preachers and the evangelical preachers of the eighteenth century, following the *Directory* and the Puritan tradition, divided their sermons into three sections: "doctrines," "reasons," and "uses." (In passing, we might note that the modern three-point sermon enjoys a long heritage.)[103] While some Scottish preachers ignored the *Directory* and developed their own format, Witherspoon and others like him exhibited the best features of the plain style. In any given sermon he opened with a brief introduction that occasioned the need for the sermon and explained briefly the text. As he turned to the body of the sermon, he would revert to a tried-and-true formula: "In discoursing further on this subject, what I propose, through divine assistance is . . ." Usually a three-point outline followed. The "doctrine" or theological truth derived from the text would occupy the first main section. Next came the "reasons," proofs that the doctrine was valid, although in the second main section Witherspoon frequently undertook to discuss another significant aspect of the doctrine previously presented. Here, as in the first and third sections of the sermon, several numbered subheadings were offered. Throughout the sermon, but especially in the first two sections, he would furnish numerous scriptural proofs and illustrations.[104] The third division in Witherspoon's sermons was the "practical application" or "practical improvement," which brought the discourse to its conclusion. This last section provided Witherspoon with the opportunity to "improve" the sermon's text and theme(s) by applying them to the lives of his hearers. "Improvement," used in this sense, belongs more to the eighteenth century than to ours. The *Oxford English Dictionary* renders the term as "the turning of anything to good account for spiritual or moral edification." "Practical application" really captures Witherspoon's intent, and he sometimes used "application" instead of "improvement."[105]

Nowhere in Witherspoon's *Works* can one find a systematic overview of his understanding of the Bible. For instance, he seems to assume what is stated about the Bible in the first chapter of the Confession, but he never mentions that important chapter. He makes some interesting comments about the Bible as he discusses the validity of the Christian faith, miracles, the Trinity, and other doctrines in his "Lectures on Divinity," but again we look in vain for a key or keys to his use and understanding of the Bible. Nevertheless, as one studies his sermons it is possible to ascertain something of his approach to the Bible.

We must recognize at the outset that Witherspoon based his sermons on the Bible, not on articles of faith or on specific doctrines laid down in Reformed creeds and confessions, or even the Westminster Confession. Further, he did not view his Bible as a collection of proof texts to be shaped to selfish ends, nor was he guilty of a slavish literalism.[106] While Witherspoon appears in history before the rise of higher criticism of the Bible, he came after the Reformation and after those centuries during which there was such an outpouring of allegorical interpretations of the Bible, especially of the Old Testament. Witherspoon had his interpretative feet so firmly planted in this world and in human history that it never occurred to him to dream up a spiritual meaning of the text. In the sermon, "The Security of Those Who Trust in God," he reveals where he stands: "[S]o great a part of the holy scriptures [are] historical; because they serve . . . to engrave the truths of religion on the memory and the heart."[107] For the most part, he took statements in the Bible at face value—for instance, a miracle was a miracle, Jesus said what he said, angels existed as "exalted beings," events in the Old Testament were historical happenings. In that regard, by modern standards, he can be called a literalist. His sermons demonstrate that a person trained in theology could, with the aid of reason, take a text and say what it meant, and the pious listener of that sermon could comprehend and trust the words of the minister. Witherspoon was not a literalist in the sense that his work was done once he grasped what the original writer meant to say in each sentence or passage and passed it on to his congregation. As he developed his sermon texts each Sunday his intent was to drive those texts into the hearts and minds of his hearers. He knew that the language of the Bible was meant to direct the believer to truth beyond the actual words on the printed page.

Admittedly, he joined, infrequently, other interpreters of passages in the Psalms and Isaiah (interpreters of his time and even some modern ones) in employing "typology" to extract the meaning from the text. That is, in the Old Testament, the coming of the Lord, the suffering servant, the sacrifices—all were Christ-types, which stood for or prefigured Jesus the Messiah and his ultimate sacrifice.[108]

In his treatment of the Bible, Witherspoon did not bother to utilize the language of the Confession, but there is no doubt that for him scripture supplied "that knowledge of God and of his will which is necessary unto salvation" and that scripture was, in truth, "the Word of God."[109] Indeed, salvation was the point. The Bible was not a body of literature whose task it was to record history or support doctrinal propositions, and it was emphatically not a manual from which moral lessons could be or should be extracted. In sermon after sermon Witherspoon wove biblical texts to create a marvelous tapestry of piety for the inspiration and edification of his auditors. They could be reassured as well. The preacher was transmitting divine truth. The joint assumption of the preacher and the person in the pew was that the scriptures were authoritative and self-authenticating. This being the case, Witherspoon declaimed with the utmost confidence. There are no "it seems to me" or "possibly" insertions in his pulpit discourses. He knew that he was speaking for God as he preached from the Bible, God's very own revelation. Thus, the preacher had no call to be tentative or hesitant as long as he remained faithful to the Word of God written.

"Doctrines" and "reasons"—"practical improvement" less so—were woven together with verses and allusions from the Bible to make a consistent whole. Witherspoon's own thoughts and words grew out of and were parallel to God's gracious revelation found in the passages of Holy Writ. Thus, a symbiotic relationship linked the three divisions with scripture. A verse or passage served both as an illustration or support for any statement about God and his mighty acts and simultaneously as raw material that along with other passages would provide the basis upon which a doctrinal declaration could be formulated.

As a crafter of sermons, Witherspoon was sparing with illustrations. Most of them were from the Bible; there were plenty of persons and situations that could highlight a truth or a point. When, now and then, he reached beyond the Bible to find an illustration, he might invoke such worthies as John Knox; or further from home and the eighteenth century, Augustine; Ignatius; French cleric François Fénelon, archbishop of Cambrai; Calvin; the Waldensians; and Pliny the Younger in his letter to the Emperor Trajan. The tree with its parts served well to describe justification (roots) and sanctification (branches), as did his one reference to a microscope to illustrate the exceptional handiwork of "the almighty operator."[110]

He was likewise sparing in naming any masters of the pulpit who had influenced him in his homiletic labors. One apparent influence was the Puritan divine, Richard Baxter (1615–1691). Author of the devotional classic, *The Saints Everlasting Rest* (1650), and the famous volume on the ministry, *Gildas Salvianus: The Reformed Pastor* (1656), he had become well-known in Scotland.[111] Calling him in one instance "a very judicious and pious writer," and in another place quoting him briefly and describing him as the "pious, diligent, and catholic Mr. Baxter," Witherspoon followed him in adopting the plain style of sermonizing.[112] Both of them viewed preaching as a high calling and the means of saving souls. Baxter rejected the "witty" preaching of his day, which was known for its literary flourishes, classical references, and show of erudition. "God commandeth us to be as plain as we can, that we may inform the ignorant; and as convincing and serious as we are able, that we may melt and change their hardened hearts," he declared. In addressing persons of lesser ability, Baxter advised that ministers should express themselves "thoroughly and plainly, and give a full explanation of the whole truth to them."[113] Witherspoon echoed Baxter in 1758 in his advice to a young ordinand: "Preach plainly, or in a way that may be level to the capacities of the hearers, both as to sentiment and expression." Witherspoon charged that when one addressed a congregation of common people, it was absurd "to discourse in such a stiff and abstract way, as it is plainly impossible for them to comprehend. Nor is it any less absurdity [*sic*] to dress up an harangue with excessive elegance, and a vain, ornamented foppery of style."[114] Both Witherspoon and Baxter deplored "painted obscure sermons" which like stained ("painted") glass, though beautiful in itself, "keeps out the light." Baxter concluded, "Truth loves the light, and is most beautiful when most naked."[115] Without any reference to Baxter, Witherspoon repeated his complaint: "Some discourses may very well be likened to painted windows, which, with fine colours upon themselves, keep out the light."[116]

Witherspoon's drive for plainness apparently carried over to his horticultural pursuits. Green reports the incident of a woman acquaintance visiting Witherspoon at Tusculum and viewing his garden, then exclaiming, "Why Doctor, I see no flowers in your garden." "No Madam," was the reply, "no flowers in my garden, nor in my discourses either."[117]

I have already noted that Witherspoon was never known as an outstanding pulpit orator or a popular persuasive evangelist. Most assessments of his preaching were carefully modulated, primarily positive but never exuberant. Witherspoon was no George Whitefield (1714–1770), the famous itinerant Methodist preacher, who preached so powerfully in Philadelphia in 1739 that thrifty rationalist Benjamin Franklin, greatly moved by his message, emptied his pockets of all his money into the collection plate! English actor David Garrick is reported to have said that Whitefield could move his audience, which could number into the thousands, to tears simply by the way he pronounced "Mesopotamia."[118]

Witherspoon was not in Whitefield's league. He won over very few auditors, at least American ones, by his appearance, Scottish brogue, or by the power of his voice or gestures. What appealed to his congregations on both sides of the Atlantic were the written style, organization of the material, and his ideas, in other words, the content of the discourses presented simply and directly. Many would have agreed with John Adams who, after visiting Princeton in 1774 and hearing one of Witherspoon's sermons, called him "a clear, sensible, Preacher."[119] Similar assessments came from Ashbel Green and Benjamin Rush. Green concluded: "Yet take his pulpit addresses altogether as a whole; there was in them, not only the recommendation of good sense and powerful reasoning, but a gracefulness, an earnestness, a warmth of affection, and a solemnity of manner."[120]

While a medical student at Edinburgh, Benjamin Rush exclaimed in 1768 of Witherspoon that "he exceeds any Preacher I have heard since I came to Scotland." What impressed Rush more than Witherspoon's delivery was the sermonic content: "[H]is Appearance in the Pulpit is Solemn and graceful. His Sermons are loadned [*sic*] wth [*sic*] good Sense, and adorned at ye same time with all the Elegance and Beauty that Language can give them."[121]

In a more sober vein, after hearing additional sermons, Rush commented that "there was nothing in Dr. Witherspoon's sermons to recommend them but their uncommon good sense and simplicity."[122] Finally, at Witherspoon's funeral, John Rodgers also admitted he was "not a fervent and animated orator" but claimed that "it was impossible to hear him without attention, or to attend to him without improvement." His sermons, Rodgers continued, "were distinguished for . . . mingling profound remarks on human life, along with the illustration of divine truth—and for the lucid order that reigned through the whole."[123] These evaluations of Witherspoon's preaching tell us without question that we must pay attention to the content of his message, not his delivery.

One more careful review of his Scottish sermons does disclose an important development in his thinking and preaching. In several of those sermons he gave notice that he was beginning to think in terms of his later common sense philosophy. These early suggestions of a philosophy are rare and tentative. It was noted earlier that Witherspoon rejected allegory and accepted statements in the Bible in a straightforward manner. What a close reading of his sermons reveals is an unformed interest in reason and experience in the process of interpreting the Bible. Direct appeals to scripture are the norm, but on several occasions he summons Bible and reason, or Bible and experience. Here are some examples of "Bible and reason":

- Justification is "agreeable to scripture and sound reason."
- "Reason, as well as scripture, teacheth us, that in all acts of worship, the sincerity of the heart makes the chief ingredient."
- Placing ourselves in God's hands is "the doctrine of scripture, but [also] agreeable to reason and good sense."
- "This is the dictate both of scripture and reason, to whomsoever much is given, of them much will be required."[124]

The appeal to experience in his sermons is more subdued. He was to widen the understanding of the term later in America when, as Douglas Sloan has pointed out, it became virtually synonymous with common sense.[125] Here, however, experience is understood as being very close to the history of a person or race, that is, the record of human behavior. In one sermon in which he reflected upon the suffering some Christians must endure, Witherspoon noted "that the sanctifying influence of afflictions is no less the language of experience than of scripture." In sermons on sin and sinners he consistently taught that both scripture and experience disclose the fallen state of humankind: "that all mankind are by nature in a state of sin and misery, appears from the express, and repeated testimony of the word of God. . . . The same appears from the visible state of the world, and our own experience."[126] Years later, as he faced his Princeton students, he made it even clearer that they could trust their senses and their reasoning powers to arrive at truth, and they could be assured that such truth would never be contrary to "Scripture doctrine and history."[127] The few appeals to reason and experience in his Scottish sermons are adequate to demonstrate that Witherspoon was no Bible-thumping literalist ready to shout that all truth was to be found exclusively in the "Good Book," such and such chapter and verse. Innocently—or perhaps somewhat consciously—he was beginning to feel the effects of the Scottish Enlightenment and the realism it engendered. "Is there anything more manifestly reasonable," he once asked rhetorically, "than we should love supremely, what is supremely excellent [Matt. 22:37]?" Christ's first and great commandment based on reason and not on revelation? Really? That may not be Witherspoon's final word, but he did say it.[128]

Nor has he spoken his final word on the Bible. He had more to say about scripture when he taught his Princeton divinity students. But now it is time to turn to those biblically based sermons to define piety for those in the pew and the pulpit.

Part 1

Piety for Those in the Pew

Chapter One

Holy Dispositions

True piety is the same in substance in all ages, and points at one thing as its centre and its rest, the knowledge and enjoyment of God.

Works, 2:71

Now, we glorify God by cultivating holy dispositions, and doing pious and useful actions.

Works, 3:39

By modern standards the eighteenth-century Scottish Sunday worship service was a long, tedious affair. Simple in plan, it could last up to three hours, with the sermon an hour or so in length.

At the ringing of the church bell the worshipers entered the church and began singing a psalm led by a precentor who lined out the verses sung to a slow, doleful tune. There was no choir and no musical instrument. At the ringing of the next bell the minister entered the pulpit, signaled the precentor to end the singing, and commenced his part in the service by a long extemporaneous prayer. The ideal prayer was delivered with great ease and fervor and was expected to demonstrate great spiritual wrestling. The "lecture" followed, occupying most of an hour, in which a passage of scripture was explained verse by verse. Then came another prayer, a short one, followed by the sermon preached without or with only the briefest of notes. The latter part of the service included another long prayer of thanksgiving and intercession, the singing of another psalm, and the benediction.[1]

It was in these long Sunday services that the Beith and Paisley, and later Princeton, parishioners learned about Presbyterian piety. Sunday upon Sunday the Reverend John Witherspoon preached on texts that constituted for him, and he hoped for his hearers, the basis of true piety or true religion.

Context

The context of Witherspoon's and much of Popular party piety was the covenant or federal theology of the seventeenth century, grounded, of course, in the Westminster Confession of Faith and the Westminster Larger and Shorter Catechisms.

The Westminster Assembly of Divines that met in Westminster Abbey, London, 1643–1648, convened for a threefold purpose: (1) to reform the polity and liturgy of the Church of England; (2) to help bring unity to the Reformed churches abroad; and (3) to clarify the theology of the Church of England.[2] The eventual outcome of the Westminster Assembly affected the life and work of numerous Reformed churches, especially the Church of Scotland and American Congregational and Presbyterian churches, much more than it did the Church of England. The Assembly produced several historic documents, but the central achievement was the Westminster Confession of Faith.[3] Theologian Thomas Torrance has called it "the great confession of Calvinist scholasticism which brought into quasi-creedal form the core of the systematized doctrine of the great Reformed dogmaticians in the early post-Calvin era."[4]

The term "scholasticism" was first used in the Middle Ages to refer to a type of theology taught in certain medieval schools (a scholastic was a teacher who taught theology in one of these institutions). The theology was very abstract, analytical, logical, and systematic. Although the sixteenth-century Reformers revolted against medieval scholastic theology, their successors in the seventeenth century were not able to resist the temptation to frame Protestant beliefs in overly logical, abstract, formal terms. Their theology is customarily called Protestant scholasticism. As an example of Calvinist scholasticism, the Confession itself, so influential for Witherspoon, must be placed in its own context.

The Confession, of course, owes a solid debt to John Calvin (1509–1564), the great Genevan reformer, in its treatment of, for example, the concepts of the authority of the Bible, God's sovereignty, predestination, justification, Christ as Mediator, and sanctification. The Confession, it should be noted, absorbed developments in Reformed thinking during the late sixteenth and first half of the seventeenth centuries that changed some of Calvin's ideas and added some new ones.[5] Whereas Calvin had begun his *Institutes* with a discussion of God and then followed with a section on the scriptures, which were given by the Triune God, the Confession begins with a chapter on the Bible and follows it by one titled "Of God, and of the Holy Trinity." Calvin had founded the authority of the Bible upon the inner persuasion of the Holy Spirit, but by the 1640s the Westminster Divines had invented all sorts of arguments that proved the scriptures were authoritative ("the efficacy of the doctrine, the majesty of the style, . . . many other incomparable excellencies") in addition to the inner testimony of the Holy Spirit.[6] As we shall see, Witherspoon did the same. William Placher has noted correctly that the writers of the Confession were much more certain than Calvin that their theological conclusions were to be expressly found in or deduced from scripture. Calvin tended to be more restrained in determining what could be deduced from the Bible.[7]

Another change came about in the way the Confession treated God's sovereignty and predestination. In the final edition of his *Institutes*, Calvin placed predestination in Book 3, long after he had written about God as Creator (Book 1) and as Redeemer (2). He made predestination part of the redemptive work of the Holy Spirit and concluded that predestination should not be considered in a discussion of the nature of God. On the other hand, the Confession turned a Calvinistic understanding of God's sovereignty into God's eternal decree early in the Confession (chapter 3), in which the doctrine of double predestination was presented with its aspects of election to everlasting life and the corresponding damnation of sinners to everlasting death. Because it served as the basis for the work of salvation, the doctrine of predestination became a key item in the Confession. Decrees thus became far more important than God's free grace in the framework of salvation.

Finally, a major difference between Calvin and the Confession is covenant theology, sometimes called federal theology.[8] In the Confession, God's saving work is presented in terms of a double covenant, of both works and grace. Calvin and other sixteenth-century Reformers had taught a single covenant of grace, not the later double covenant. David Weir has demonstrated how the idea of a covenant of works came into being in the part of Europe known as the Palatinate between 1560 and 1590.[9] After 1590 the double covenant concept, or federal theology, spread throughout the Reformed world. In 1690, the Church of Scotland replaced the Reformation era Scots Confession (1560) with the Westminster

Confession of Faith.[10] Witherspoon, of course, had been brought up and educated under this confessional standard. When he was a divinity student at the University of Edinburgh, he would have again absorbed covenant theology from his theology textbook, Bénédict Pictet's *Christian Theology*.[11] Although Witherspoon takes up the two covenants in an extended way in his "Lectures on Divinity," he placed his piety for those in the pew in the covenantal context without making it very obvious. He understood that the first covenant made with Adam was a covenant of works, which would have guaranteed salvation to humanity upon condition of perfect obedience. Because of the fall and human disobedience, the covenant was broken and salvation was no longer possible. However, God took pity upon sinful humanity and freely offered a second covenant, a covenant of grace. Although it reached its fulfillment in Christ, it had already been announced in the Old Testament in the person of Abraham, in the exodus, the giving of the law on Mount Sinai, and in other promises and events. Nevertheless, there are, in fact, not two covenants of grace, one for the Old Testament and one for the New, but the same one under different dispensations.

Witherspoon did not quote or refer to Calvin in his sermons, and he seldom referred to the covenant. Nevertheless, there is no doubt that he thought in covenantal terms; he just did not always announce the fact. Sometimes he equated the law with the covenant of works; more often he proclaimed the covenant of grace. Jesus, he says, is what the covenant of grace is all about. Jesus is the mediator or the administrator of this covenant. "All the covenant-mercies of God to man . . . are to be referred to the love of Christ, as their price, their source, and their sum."[12]

The covenant of grace has meaning for acquiring piety. Witherspoon observes, "To enliven our duties by the comforts of the gospel is to follow the order of the covenant of grace." The faithful Christian will dwell upon the wisdom and power of God, taking "hold of his covenant, and the sure and everlasting mercy that is contained in it." The same believer will receive the sacraments as "seals of the covenant of grace." Ultimately, the covenant of grace extends right up to heaven "where many [will be joined] to the Lord in a perpetual covenant never to be forgotten or recalled."[13]

While Witherspoon without any quarrel adopted the federal theology of the time and was loyal to much of the Confession, he did not consistently follow that confession in every respect, nor did he find it necessary to pound the Westminster beliefs into the ears of his parishioners in any systematic way each Sunday. It will be enlightening to note in this study of his piety when and how he adheres to the Westminster standards and at what points he feels free to cast a different light on how the faith is to be understood. On rare occasions we will find him quoting from the Confession or the Shorter Catechism, but it is the Bible to which he resorts when he seeks support for his homiletic points, not Calvin or Knox or the Confession. If the laity did not require such a heavy dose of the covenant, it was a rather different matter for ministers. In a later chapter we will find him more insistent that ministers understand the covenants and subscribe to the federal theology of the Westminster documents.[14]

Foundation Principle

Witherspoon once began a sermon on worship with these words: "True piety is the same in substance in all ages, and points at one thing as its centre and its rest, the knowledge and enjoyment of God."[15] Piety or holiness (of life) is what men and women should seek after, what fulfills them, what the heart secretly desires, what is true and lasting happiness. Turning toward and reaching toward God is where it all begins. In his "Essay on Justification," Witherspoon asked, "Is not the love of God, I mean, the supreme love of God, precisely what is meant by holiness?" He pushed the question further: "Can we love holiness then, and not aspire after it? Can we love it and not endeavor to practice it? Nay, can we love it, and not possess it?"[16] It is here that some people make a big mistake, observes Witherspoon. It is utter folly to seek ultimate happiness within oneself, or to base it on our connections with others, beneficence of action, or even upon reason and the nature of things. It is not that these are totally useless; they will supply proximate happiness or well-being and be very tempting all the while. But it is pointless to settle for half measures or partial happiness. Only piety *based on the love of God* furnishes the full meaning to life and ultimate purpose for living. "Those alone are happy," Witherspoon avows, "whose God is the Lord." Using different words, he was merely repeating the famous question and answer from the Shorter Catechism—Question: "What is man's chief end?" Answer: "To glorify

God and enjoy him forever." Later, when he came to a discussion of regeneration, Witherspoon had this to say about its transforming effect in the life of the believer: It enabled that person "to love [God] supremely, and serve him ultimately, as our highest end; and to delight in him superlatively as our chief good."[17] Love of God is piety's "centre and its rest," its very foundation.

We can now begin to appreciate why Witherspoon is so keen to quote, as he does in so many of his sermons, the first and great command of the law, even more than the second: "Thou shalt love the Lord thy God with all thy heart, and with all thy soul, and with all thy mind" (Matt. 22:37). Today most Christians would not express belief in God the way Witherspoon does, but there is no denying that he exemplifies a strong theistic belief. All too often his God is revealed as abstract, majestic, distant. He employed the term *sovereignty* sparingly, but it is present nonetheless. The majesty and power of the Almighty shine through his sermons as much as they do in the Confession. American poet Oliver Wendell Holmes lived long after Witherspoon, but the latter would have voiced approval of Holmes's lines, made memorable in the hymn: "Lord of all being, throned afar, Your glory flames from sun and star." This majestic powerful being is the God that Witherspoon loved supremely. That this God was real to him is palpable.

The attributes of God in his theological lexicon are similar to those found in the Westminster documents. As he writes his pulpit discourses, we can almost hear him whispering to himself the answer to question 4 in the Shorter Catechism—Question: "What is God?" Answer: "God is a Spirit, infinite, eternal, and unchangeable, in his being, wisdom, power, holiness, justice, goodness, and truth." The reader does not have to look far to find these same attributes in his sermons.[18]

God is "most great, and therefore to be feared." God is "pure and holy," "an omniscient being, everywhere present," and it behooves us to make "a clear discovery of the infinite majesty of God, the unspotted holiness of his nature" as well as "the omnipotence of Providence." "I beseech you," pleads Witherspoon, to "contemplate the glory of God in the cross of Christ. See him, infinite in power, infinite in wisdom, infinite in holiness." And if one's prayer petitions are not immediately answered, or in the way one desires, then one humbly "dwells upon the wisdom and power of God, who alone can bring light out of darkness."[19] In the sermon, "The Object of a

Christian's Desire in Religious Worship," Witherspoon imagines
what pious Christians, the saints, experience when they yearn "to see
the glory of an eternal independent God." In a long, memorable section of the sermon he describes what happens:

> They dwell with adoring wonder, on all his attributes, which
> are boundless and unsearchable: the immensity of his being,
> who fills heaven and earth with his presence . . . ; his irresistible
> power, "who spake and it was done, who commanded, and it
> stood fast . . ."; his infinite holiness and purity, "with whom evil
> cannot dwell, nor sinners stand in his presence . . ."; his infinite
> wisdom, "who worketh all things according to his will . . ."; his
> boundless goodness, which fills the earth, and flows in plen-
> teous streams to all the creatures of his power.[20]

Witherspoon does not pause to challenge these attributes in any
way, or to ask seriously whether or not such attributes were divinely
revealed, or whether they might be a very understandable human
attempt, using human categories, to say the best that can be said
about God. There is certainly no room for mystery in discussing the
divine attributes. The list is complete as defined. If it had ever
occurred to Witherspoon to question the attributes, he undoubtedly
would have denied any human invention and searched Holy Writ to
find the appropriate passages from which the divine attributes could
be ascertained.[21] This is the place where one might well ask if Witherspoon does not have something to say about the Trinity. The
Confession, of course, affirms the doctrine, and Witherspoon does
have a short section on the perfection of the triune God and the
"felicity" of the three persons in the Trinity in one of his sermons.
More often, however, he was content to preach about the Father
sending the Son for our salvation, and the Holy Spirit as the agent
of our regeneration.[22] On the other hand, the Trinity merits fuller
consideration in the "Lectures on Divinity."

If the doctrine of the Trinity was virtually ignored, the concept
of divine perfection(s) was not. Witherspoon was quite taken with
perfection as it related to the divine attributes, that is, God possesses each attribute to perfection. We humans, conscious of our
imperfect fractured existence, do have, he asserted, an idea or
thought of perfection and what that means. Without acknowledging it, he made the leap from the human idea of perfection to its
actual existence somewhere—and where else but with God? God,

then, in his very being and in all his attributes *is* perfection. Of course, Witherspoon was not alone in thinking this way. The Confession announces a God "who is infinite in being and perfection," and Pictet wrote with even more enthusiasm of the idea: "The first idea we form in our minds concerning God is, that he is a perfect Being, which the scriptures confirm, everywhere proclaiming the divine perfections."[23]

Witherspoon put his own cast on this aspect of divinity. God is "absolutely perfect, and therefore to be loved and served," Witherspoon said, without informing his hearers and readers how one might go about loving perfection. But he does try to insert perfection into piety. If we would but read chapter 40 in the book of Job, we should be able to identify with Job as he discovers "the divine glory and perfection." Again, the believer should always place her or his dependence on the power of the Savior, "drawn from the perfections of an unchangeable God." God's nature is opened up for believers "in all his glorious perfections . . . to save and deliver them that put their trust in him." Finally, it is not acceptable to have a lukewarm general intellectual belief in the being and perfections of God. Truly pious individuals will "have a deep and awful impression of him upon [their] hearts."[24]

Witherspoon seemed unaware of any previous discussions of the problem of what the perfections of God might entail. To take just one difficulty, not all perfections are mutually compatible. One perfection might cancel out or exclude another.[25] No doubt Witherspoon was merely following the wording of the Confession when he preached about God's perfections. We can assume without too much risk that these claims about God were forthcoming because of the need he felt, on the one hand, to dispel mystery and enclose religion in distinct understandable ideas, and on the other, to preserve the sovereignty of the Supreme Being against all foes.

Witherspoon's God-language displays one of his understandings of God. It is a conception of deity that was metaphysical and static, and despite statements to the contrary, seemingly unrelated to this world. God is the absolute—eternal, utterly independent, unchangeable, entirely spiritual, and ever so distant from the particularities of human existence. This concept was close to a Greek-like view of God as the immortal, changeless, incorruptible Eternal One. However, although Witherspoon began talking about God in this way and delivered many sentences along these lines, this was not the dominant definition of God in his theology.

He saw no problem in talking about God as perfection in one breath and in the very next singing God's praises because of the saving work God does in Jesus the Christ. Here is how he combined and summed up both perfection and redemption: "There [in the Bible] all his various perfections, excellent in them selves and suitable to us, are enumerated and explained. . . . Here we must not forget that he hath in his word clearly revealed himself, as infinitely gracious to sinners through Jesus Christ."[26]

Whatever and whoever else God is, and all the talk about attributes carried to perfection notwithstanding, the final word about God is *salvation*. This gracious God who redeems is no distant uncaring abstract being who remains aloof from needy creatures and lost creation. This God does care. This God has a plan. This God acts, by becoming incarnate in Jesus of Nazareth. And this God saves sinners. That, in the end, is the most significant thing that the pious believer can ever say about God—not speculations about the perfections of God, not the recitations of the usual attributes of divine immensity, power, wisdom, holiness, justice, and the like. One notices and is mildly surprised that Witherspoon hesitates to include divine love, mercy, or kindness among the accepted attributes, although he is capable of making the connection: "Christ Jesus is the fruit of the Father's everlasting love to sinners of mankind. How great the giver! How unspeakable the gift! How mean and worthless the objects of his love! God is love. Power, wisdom, holiness, and justice, shine, indeed, in the doctrine of the cross."[27]

We will see later how, according to Witherspoon, God's love and mercy are uniquely manifested in the work of salvation. The truth was, he was ultimately incapable of thinking about and loving God apart from God's redeeming activity. So the basis of his understanding of piety is our love of God, and the rationale for our loving God is that we have received the mercy of God and are reconciled through the Savior.[28]

It was the first great commandment that caught and held Witherspoon's attention, but finally he does introduce the second, love of the neighbor: "It is love, supreme love to God, and through him, and for him, to all his creatures." The two great commandments were tied together once more: "The love of God, and the love of our neighbor, jointly concur in laying the strongest obligation upon every Christian."[29]

Does this love of God ever translate into a mystical union with the divine? Not for Witherspoon, though it might for others. He does not reject out of hand this kind of union. It could happen. At the same time he was no "enthusiast," one whose religious experience was grounded in the immediate direct action of the Holy Spirit. He saw no heavenly bright lights, he was never carried up to the seventh heaven to gaze upon the ineffable glory of the deity and the heavenly host. Still, he could fathom what some Christians had experienced, even if he had not: a union with the divine by affection, not just cognition. He spoke of an "inward and spiritual illumination" that was preferable to mere knowledge about God. Even more preferred were hearts "inflamed with the love of God." He even pictured the soul pointing heavenward, moving "up to the summit of present enjoyments, that it may see the farther into what still remains." The impulse for this trajectory of the soul is communion with the divine, which, he envisioned, would bring down something from heaven to earth and propel the soul from earth to heaven.[30]

What Witherspoon deplored was a person who professed a love of God but fell short of genuine devotion. These were the people who wanted to be known as Christians and praised by others but who persisted in their sins. His criticism was especially directed at contemporaries who might think about and speak of the perfections of God, but who never have had a deep penetrating awareness of God in their hearts. An intellectual acquiescence of the omniscience and omnipresence of God is one thing, but the overwhelming sense of God's presence is far more to be desired. The ideal situation would be when even one word spoken of the Eternal would strike a person's heart so vividly that God would become more real than ever before. The Bible, he continued, is precise on the difference between mild speculations on the nature and perfections of God and the *real* knowledge of God and the divine glory. He put it another way in a sermon on the commands of God. "A constrained outward obedience" to those commands counts for nothing and is unacceptable to God without "the inclinations of the heart." The service of God, then, must be based on love, the supreme love of God, which arises from the depths of one's being, not from a casual nod of the head and run-of-the-mill obedience.[31]

Truths of Such Unspeakable Moment

If Witherspoon based his piety upon the foundational love of a believer for God, he wanted those who heard or read his sermons to know that this was only the beginning of piety, an important point of departure, but nothing more. The substance of his piety is composed of several key doctrines found in the Bible and defined in the Confession that answer the question, What makes a true believer, a holy person, an authentic pious Christian?

It is, to be as emphatic as Witherspoon was, to acquiesce in, understand, and absorb into the very fiber of one's being what he termed "the everlasting truths of the gospel." These few basic beliefs constituted the heart of the Christian faith, the essence of true religion. Their importance for Witherspoon was that they were not just beliefs that challenged the mind. They represented authentic Christian experience: sinning, receiving God's free grace, knowing that one's sins were forgiven through the death of Christ, and the living of a new life as a forgiven sinner. This experience, he said, provided "every real Christian, an inward and experimental proof of the truth of the gospel . . . stronger and more stable than any speculative reasoning."[32] Here is one more affirmation of his head-and-heart religion.

These core beliefs were not of his devising, he insisted; they were drawn from the Bible, and he frequently called them "Scripture doctrines" or "truths of the everlasting gospel," supplying Bible passages to substantiate his claim.[33] They are so vital to the faith that they are like precious stones imbedded in the rock-like word of God. Only once does he draw upon the Confession as authority for the beliefs, though as we shall see, he sometimes falls back on the theology of the Confession when attempting to explicate each doctrine.[34] He liberally sprinkled these "truths" throughout his writings. Usually four doctrines were enumerated: "the lost state of man by nature; salvation by the free grace of God; justification by the imputed righteousness of Christ; and sanctification by the effectual operation of the Holy Spirit."[35]

These doctrines signify one's own salvation, one's personal transformation, but practical-minded Witherspoon considers them so valuable that he asserts that they will help in the reform of society! Hear his boastful claim:

> These doctrines I am persuaded are not only true in themselves,
> but the great foundation of all practical religion. Wherever

they are maintained and inculcated, strictness and purity of life and manners will be their natural effect. On the contrary, where they are neglected, and a pretended theory of moral virtue substituted in their room, it will immediately and certainly introduce a deluge of profanity and immorality in practice.[36]

With these words Witherspoon foreshadowed a conviction that he would express more forcefully in his American period—that is, public virtue is dependent upon the virtue of private citizens. While he remained in Scotland, and admitting responsibility for the public weal, he felt compelled to condemn those unfaithful Moderates who were preaching and teaching a wayward "pretended theory of moral virtue" in place of the four essential claims of the gospel.

To demonstrate that these truths were not recent or idiosyncratic, Witherspoon moved in two directions. First, he reassured his readers and hearers that these were, in fact, Reformation doctrines, the glory of the Protestant churches, he boasted, of such standing and importance that in all churches they ought to be "clearly explained, strongly inculcated, and frequently repeated."[37] They are not theological fads, they stand above and beyond any current ecclesiastical struggle or debate. Second, as has been noted, for Witherspoon they were biblical doctrines. In some cases he devoted an entire sermon to just one of these essential truths (e.g., "All Mankind by Nature under Sin," "Christ's Death a Proper Atonement for Sin"); at other times they were incorporated into another kind of discourse, perhaps an "action sermon" preached at a Communion service.[38]

The minister of Beith and Paisley was not the only preacher of his day who viewed piety as doctrine understood by the mind and acclaimed by the heart. John Erskine (1721–1803), longtime minister of Old Greyfriars Church in Edinburgh (1767–1803), heralded the gospel scheme of salvation as outward piety, and then continued by positing the need for inward piety as a basis for "conversion, progressive sanctification, a life of faith, the struggles of the flesh and Spirit, and such like subjects." He, too, noted the connection between the influence of gospel truths and a Christian's "public ministrations." Much less concise but equally convinced that piety was rooted in the atonement, Glasgow minister John MacLaurin (1693–1754) taught that there were two sides to piety: the doctrine of salvation through Christ and its influence upon life. It is from that doctrine, "from that rich source the inspired writers draw the chief motives to every duty, and against every sin," he argued.[39]

Witherspoon, Erskine, MacLaurin, and others of like mind knew with certainty that the human condition was such that it required divine intervention and transformation. Energetic summons to moral improvement of the person and fervent appeals to the improvement of one's nature were insufficient and, ultimately, useless. Witherspoon's prescription for the corrupt human condition was a piety based on four historic biblical beliefs, received by the mind and made very real indeed in the life of each Christian.

The Lost State of Man by Nature

Human sinfulness is the starting point for thirteen sermons that Witherspoon published in 1768 under the title, "Practical Discourses on the Leading Truths of the Gospel."[40] He commenced by announcing that it was necessary to prove the validity of the doctrine by both scripture and experience. That meant that in the first two sermons of the thirteen, verses from the Bible abound—from the first chapters of Genesis to the Psalms to Romans and finally to James and Hebrews—to declare that all humanity is under the burden of sin. A lengthy examination of world history makes the same point.[41] If even further proof is needed for universal sinfulness, one can draw upon reason, said Witherspoon. Reason and observation are sufficiently substantial and trustworthy that they can be invoked as testimony for the depravity of the race. One does not even need to be a student of history; a person only needs to watch how humans behave. A mere glance at what he calls the "state of the moral world" will be quite convincing. Reason and observation "plainly point out the guilt and apostasy of man, and loudly call for the interposition of a Saviour."[42] Where does all this lead? To the well established fact that human sinfulness is always present and universally pervasive.

Witherspoon was much more absorbed in propounding the nature and character of sinning than he was in tracing its origin. He assumed the Fall as reported in Genesis, chapter 3, but scarcely mentioned it in his preaching. He once offered the trite observation that sin has remained constant in its operation and influence since the fall of Adam, and a slightly stronger statement on the significance of the Fall and on the fact of original sin can be located in his sermon, "All Mankind by Nature under Sin." He explained that "the deplorable wickedness in which the world in general is overwhelmed, hath flowed in a continued stream from the first sin of Adam; and the sinfulness of every person's practice has the corruption of his nature as its fruitful source."[43]

If the whys and wherefores of the Fall were of little interest, what did claim his attention was that, tragically, Adam's sin had infected all his posterity leading to "a universal corruption of human nature," a phrase similar to one in the Confession. He did speak of human depravity, even "excessive depravation," but he never described humans as being in a state of "total depravity" as some Calvinists have done, nor did he describe that state in the sometimes extreme colorful language found in Calvin's *Institutes*.[44] He saved his own colorful language to narrate the many kinds of reprehensible sinners. He noted that original sin has infected our judgments, thoughts, desires, passions, and carnal inclinations, even our consciences. The sin-dominated conscience can no longer be trusted to be a reliable moral guide. It may serve its purpose for a time, he admitted, but under the onslaught of continued sinning, it frequently shuts down and stops doing its job. "Though the great lines of the law of God are written upon the conscience in so strong and legible characters, that it is difficult to efface them, yet it is plain that men have often brought this about to a surprising degree."[45]

Simultaneously with his doctrine of original sin, Witherspoon preached forcefully the principle of responsible human behavior. Men and women had to own up to their actions. He knew human nature all too well, particularly when it came to making excuses for sinning, and he would tolerate none of the many that people offered. He rejected the one he called "the commonness of it" (the everyone-is-doing-it excuse), and two more that might be named, in modern idiom, "my sins aren't really big ones" and "my basic goodness far outweighs any sins I commit." There were two more that really got under his skin, both of which were, in his words, "profane perversion of divine truth": (1) I cannot help sinning and should not be blamed for it, because due to original sin it is just my nature; and (2) God's absolute determinism removes any guilt of what appear to be my voluntary sinful actions. These two excuses, especially the first, bring out the worst of the preacher's ire. After admitting that God's sovereign providence rules absolutely and often does overrule the creatures and their actions, he insists just as absolutely that each sinner is charged with her or his sins and on judgment day must answer for them. Under no circumstances will Witherspoon make God to be the author of sin.[46] On any number of occasions while addressing directly the sinners in his congregation, he took it for granted that they were entirely responsible for their sinful behavior.

Let us look ahead several decades to see how Witherspoon's student at the College of New Jersey, James Madison, absorbed his professor's ideas of human sinfulness. Historian James Smylie has compared Witherspoon's teaching on sin with some of Madison's ideas on human nature contained in *The Federalist*, and has concluded that Madison learned his lessons well. Like his teacher, he held to a view of human depravity while asserting that humans were responsible for their actions and possessed virtue sufficient for self-government.[47]

Now to the act of sinning. This is where the problem finally rests. The worst sin of all is withholding the service and glory that are rightfully God's. Indeed, all other sins are nothing more than derivatives of this first and greatest of sins. Witherspoon has already declared that piety is founded upon the love of God, above everyone and everything else. The exact opposite is the most heinous of sins, namely, "the alienation and estrangement of our heart and affections from God, to whom alone they are due." This is, in a word, *pride*. The message from the pulpit is that pride is "the master-passion of the human frame," because it is nothing more than the "dethroning of God, and setting up self to be loved, honored and served in his room." In naming pride the chief of sins, Witherspoon was repeating the time-honored definition of sin in the long history of the church. As early as the fourth century, Augustine (354–430) was saying "the beginning of all sin is pride," and John Chrysostom (ca. 347–407) took aim at the sin of pride and called it "a rock where wild beasts lurk that would tear you to pieces every day." Sin as pride, taught Witherspoon, is indeed the pulling down of God and setting up of self in God's place. Pride causes us to think we are strong, independent, and self-sufficient. Pride makes us think we have to answer no one and are in complete control of our own lives. Pride instills the feeling that we can do anything we desire. Twentieth-century theologian Reinhold Niebuhr (1892–1971) summed it up this way: "The real issue is the universality of the corruption which results from undue self regard."[48]

Gross sinners have more than pride to answer for. They come in for severe condemnation from Witherspoon's pulpit. In a livid outburst he identified all those who "lived in the open habitual practice of gross sin": "Swearers and profaners of Jehovah's name, despisers of his Sabbaths, scorners of sacred things, neglecters of prayer, sons of violence, midnight rioters, beastly drunkards, unclean fornicators, takers and holders of unjust gain, liars and slanderers, hard-hearted oppressors, and whosoever liveth under the dominion of known sin."[49] This list would seem to cover a huge amount of wrongdoing, but elsewhere he detailed still other sins that God forbade—murder, fraud, perjury, lust of uncleanness, and—lest we forget—attending the theater.[50]

It is interesting to observe in this directory of sins that what some might today call sins are missing. There is no mention of abortion; Witherspoon meant the violent killing of one person by another when he denounced murder. It is possible that he would have included homosexuality under the category of "lust of uncleanness," but we cannot be sure.[51] What is not debatable is that he gave scarcely any consideration to the environment. He merely repeated the conventional wisdom that it was lawful for humans to use the "lower irrational animals" for labor and for food, since in the order of creation God gave humans dominion over all the other creatures (Gen. 1:26).[52] Nor is there any mention of the sin of owning slaves. We know that many early American leaders owned slaves—Washington, Jefferson, Madison, Franklin, even Puritan minister Cotton Mather—so Witherspoon was no exception. Tax records show that for a number of years he owned one or two slaves to help him farm his 500-plus acres at Tusculum. The inventory of his possessions drawn up shortly after his death lists two slaves valued at one hundred dollars each.[53] Many of Witherspoon's rural neighbors also owned a small number of slaves. While there is no evidence that he belonged to any abolitionist cause, he did go on record in his moral philosophy lectures as being opposed to slavery, stating it was unlawful to take away people's "liberty by no better right than superior power." Thus, slavery turns out to be unlawful as a violation of one's liberty, but Witherspoon never called it a sin. His answer to the slavery question was gradualism: time would solve the problem. In 1790, he chaired a committee of the New Jersey legislature to study the possibility of abolishing slavery in the state. He honestly expected that in the near future slavery would somehow disappear, so he and his committee submitted no law for action. He was certain that "from the state of society in America, the privileges of the press, and the progress of the idea of universal liberty," slavery would be gone within thirty years. On this issue his optimism was obviously unjustified.[54] Finally, Witherspoon saw nothing wrong with moderate consumption of wine. He loudly denounced drunkenness, but a social glass of wine was quite acceptable, a fact that some later teetotaling Presbyterians would undoubtedly have liked to forget.

It was by no accident that in the above directory of sins, "swearers and profaners of Jehovah's name" head the list. Witherspoon took very seriously what people said. Their words amounted to something; talk was not cheap, and idle conversation was a waste. He firmly believed that the words that flowed from a person's mouth indicated what kind of an individual that person was and, in particular, what that person believed about God. Each word was to be weighed for its meaning and its disclosure of one's inner life. So if an individual swore or used any form of profanity, it meant that he or she had rebelled against or, worse yet, renounced God, the worst of all sins. He continually inveighed against this evil stating: "Swearing, and taking the name of God in vain, is . . . of so atrocious a nature, and so direct an assault upon the majesty of God, that it ought not to be treated lightly, as only a small decorum, or breach of good manners. It ought indeed, to be despised for its folly; but, at the same time it ought to be deeply abhorred for its guilt."[55]

The one sin that required an entire essay for its analysis and condemnation was attending the theater. Curiously, theatergoing was not one of the sins Witherspoon denounced in his preaching. Perhaps he thought that he had said all that needed to be said in his 1757 critique, "A Serious Inquiry into the Nature and Effects of the Stage," the extended argument making the point that supporting stage plays was inconsistent with the character of a Christian.[56] Although it was worse that ministers were attending the theater, the sixty-eight page essay declared that the theater was a bad place for both clergy and laity alike. His arguments against theatergoing, which reveal a considerable bias, deserve a short investigation.

Is the stage amusement? Yes, of course, the stern preacher was forced to admit, but, "the truth is, the need of amusement is much less than people commonly apprehend, and, where it is not necessary, it must be sinful." Not only should Christians put their money to a better use than supporting the theater, but also going to plays causes distress and fatigue because the theater "agitates the passions too violently," he alleged.

Are plays instruction? They are supposed to be, but instead of having a positive effect, most theatrical productions render a "pernicious tendency." The subjects of love, pride, ambition, and revenge are distorted for the sake of entertainment. Regrettably, the moral teaching is ambiguous; an actor is applauded as much when he represents a wicked character as a noble one.

Are there other reasons not to attend? Of course. Contributing to the theater supports actors and actresses in an unchristian occupation. Also, even if a person of high moral character goes to the theater and is somehow able to withstand the inherent temptations, he or she by example may lead others into harm and sin. A final telling argument against the theater was to debunk the notion that going to the theater is necessary for one to acquire a "fashionable education," one that is designed to overcome such deficiencies as rusticity of carriage, narrowness of mind, ignorance of worldly topics, and a too-rigid character. To Witherspoon, this is utter nonsense. He heatedly discharged this point by declaring that it is "the greatest madness to seek knowledge of the world by partaking with bad men in their sins."

Whatever the modern reader might think of Witherspoon's critique of the theater, it is important to recognize that he was raising a question which has a long history, notably, in modern terms, to what extent do dramatic and literary productions, especially those on television today, influence social behavior? The eighteenth-century minister lacked the measurement techniques of modern social scientists as they analyze human behavior, but Witherspoon did not need to poll Scottish citizens to tell him the theater represented sin. He knew that it did!

He was just as worried about how one became a hardened sinner as he was about the sins themselves. In "The Deceitfulness of Sin," the same sermon in which he dealt with excuses that sinners invent, he set forth a useful eight-step morphology or structure of how a person develops into a sinner. As a pastor he wanted those under his care to know and, of course, avoid the several stages leading to one's downfall.[57]

The neophyte begins with small sins, occasionally stealing small items, for example, or engaging in "little arts of equivocation." Next, the beginner moves to "sins of a deeper dye" and continues to sin, in the process weakening the resistance to it. Third, greater sins throw the sinner into the company of the impious, removing the person from the beneficial influence of the pious. The sinner, therefore, is "emboldened, by seeing vice practiced, and by hearing it justified." By this time he or she has entered the next stage and has become a habitual wrongdoer. Repeating sins brings on a habit. Witherspoon did not have access to modern studies of alcoholism, so he cited drunkenness as an illustration of a habitual sin. At the fifth stage, the sinner loses all sense of shame and sins boldly, not caring any longer what others might think. In the sixth stage all remorse of conscience has vanished: "The frequent repetition of atrocious crimes stupifies the conscience." Proceeding to the next stage, the seventh, sinners are so deep into sinning that they actually boast of their wickedness and think it to be honorable. Lastly, they are now so wicked that they use every art and all their influence to drag down others into sin. Witherspoon then summarizes, "So will zealots in vice compass sea and land to make a proselyte to the devil." Through stage seven it is still possible for God to step in and of his grace rescue the hardened sinner, though, as Witherspoon comments, such instances are few and far between. However, once sinners have entered upon the eighth stage they are hopelessly lost and doomed to destruction. They have hardened their hearts so completely that God can no longer reach them. His only option is to pronounce judgment: "They are incapable of mercy, and marked out as vessels of wrath, fitted to destruction."[58] What is instructive about this multistep process is that in the end, Witherspoon is forced to set a limit to God's love and mercy if he is going to supply a rationale for the presence of incorrigible wrongdoers in society. They have put themselves beyond any possibility of restoration.

Now that we have discovered what Witherspoon understands about sin, sins, and sinning—the first of the "everlasting truths"—we can begin to grasp what he means by piety. Specifically, if we reverse much of what he subsumes under the heading of the lost and fallen state of humanity, the shape of the pious person begins to take on a recognizable form. Simply stated, the pious person shuns those lesser and greater sins and practices their opposites. It is gratifying to discover that Witherspoon himself saw what he had done. In the conclusion to the sermon on the deceitfulness of sin, he introduced a short morphology of piety. The progress of the person striving for piety is contrasted step-by-step with the progress of the individual becoming a gross sinner, which had been presented earlier in the sermon. The person of piety begins as a new convert, unsure about leaving those former enjoyable lusts, but seven steps later, while his feet are still planted firmly on earth, he is spiritually "raised above the world, his heart is in heaven, and he longs to be carried there."[59] The growth toward piety will be examined in a more detailed way in the next chapter.

Salvation by the Free Grace of God

Witherspoon reverted briefly to the double covenant as he preached about the free grace of God. As has been explained, the second covenant is called the covenant of grace, in which God freely offers to sinners life and salvation by Jesus Christ. Witherspoon taught that the penitent sinner seeking help would take hold of God's covenant and the sure and everlasting mercy contained in it, and then would pray earnestly to be able to submit to the divine will.[60] This free covenant grace represented the action of a merciful deity. The person who has experienced the grace of God as pure gift, with no strings attached, knows better than anyone else that God is indeed merciful—and that God bestows mercy exclusively in the wonderful way he treats sinners. Faith, it must be said, never comes first. Grace does, and then faith follows, although that turns out to be a gift too. Grace is so basic that Witherspoon declares that God's mercy is "the *only* [italics mine] foundation of our hope and peace."[61]

Earlier it was stated that beyond all the customary attributes Witherspoon attached to the Deity, mercy stood by itself, because the most outstanding activity of God is the redemption offered to unfaithful and undeserving creatures by the gift of his son. Strictly and justly speaking, sinners deserve only punishment for their wrongdoing; they do not deserve even one iota of free grace. That might seem to be the bad news. The good news is that God holds on despite human unfaithfulness and pours out his grace. The overwhelming sense of gratitude that sinners then feel, once they know they are forgiven, is directly due to "the astonishing means" employed by God in not sparing his own son. "Well might the apostle John say," Witherspoon noted, "'God SO [Witherspoon's capitals] loved the world, that he gave his only begotten Son, that whosoever believeth in him should not perish, but have everlasting life.'"[62]

When Witherspoon took up the classic Reformed doctrines of predestination and election in his sermons, he did not spend much time arguing the fine points of either. He concurred with the Confession that God works all things—including grace, of course—"according to the counsel of his own immutable and most righteous will," and he interpreted such a statement to mean that God wills to save sinners. The constant refrain that he dinned into the consciousness of his hearers was that God will save all who call upon him and repent of their sins. Sinners can in no wise save themselves, but there is, as a sermon title states, "Hope of Forgiveness with God" (Psalm 130:4).[63]

Clarifying the psychology of conversion for his hearers in this sermon, Witherspoon pointed out that once a full sense of sin takes hold of a person, it is so intolerable something has to happen at once. Borrowing nautical imagery, he declared dramatically that when the sinner feels he is drowning under the "waves and billows of divine wrath," "he must either fasten upon some ground of hope, or suffer shipwreck upon the rocks of despair." The ground of hope, of course, is God's mercy. When the awakened soul becomes aware of this unmerited mercy, he or she will stand astonished, and wonder why God did not assign immediate and deserved destruction but instead bestowed the "glad tidings of peace." The sinner manifests true penitence, but that too comes from God, not human effort. God's grace "opens the springs of penitential sorrow, and makes them flow . . . more copiously than before." There are no excuses for sins that were committed and no suggestion that the guilt was any less than it was. Thus commences a life of "serious, voluntary, deliberate humiliation" that affords peace with God and with oneself. The humble forgiven sinner is now ready for "the growth of true piety."[64]

It bears repeating that the source of this forgiveness is God and none other. Witherspoon cautions, "Forgiveness is always declared to be an act of sovereign grace." God's will is sovereign; Witherspoon does not want to hedge on that. He wants to say, and does say for now, that it is God who saves when, how, and whom he will. Later he will clarify if not modify that point. If it is the sovereign God who saves, then humans can claim no merit or part in the act of forgiveness. Nor are we humans to try to determine how or on whom God's grace works. That is God's business, not ours. Witherspoon explains, "God in many passages asserts his own sovereign and perfect liberty in the distribution of his grace: Rom. 9:15, 16." We Christians are forbidden to penetrate the depth of the divine counsels or in our own case speculate on why God's grace came our way. Our proper response is only to accept what has been offered and to be deeply humbled.[65]

Therefore, in predictable fashion Witherspoon took up the doctrines of predestination and election by pronouncing that God, according to his secret counsel and sovereign will, has predestined to life some, who are called the elect; others he passed by and ordained to his everlasting wrath for their sin. Such a belief is customarily called double predestination. While "election" and "the elect" are words found occasionally in Witherspoon's sermons, "predestination" rarely is. He did not find it easy to articulate the idea of double predestination and state outright that God damns all those who are not of the elect. When he had to, he did, but did not belabor the point, and he tried his best to show that the unregenerate were only getting what they justly deserved as sinners. "Every individual of the human race," he explained, "is not in fact partaker of the blessing of [Christ's] purchase; but many die in their sins, and perish forever. . . . Many have died in unbelief and impenitence, serving divers lusts and passions; and if the scripture is true, [God] will at last render unto them according to their works."[66]

It was more palatable for him and more in keeping with his interpretation of God's mercy to posit single predestination, that is, to praise God for saving some and not leaving all of humanity in a state of sin and misery, even though pure justice would decree that since all humans are sinners all deserve God's wrath. But he did not make too much of single predestination either.[67] When he did present election, it was often accompanied by warnings: We are not to speculate on who is saved and who is not; we must trust the goodness and sovereignty of God. Additionally, we must not let the doctrine of election produce either the extreme of an absolute guarantee that we are saved or the despair that accompanies doubt that we might not be saved. Just remember, he advised, the doctrine does double duty: it gives us hope but destroys our arrogance and pride, at once exalting and abasing us.[68]

A prominent feature of many of Witherspoon's pulpit discourses was his intense obligation to preach salvation through Christ to everyone in the pews. He longed to see lives changed. A radical life change was vital to Christian piety, so he attempted to make religion practical and life-transforming. This is the impulse behind the lengthy sermon-like essay, "A Practical Treatise on Regeneration"

(1764), with its text, John 3:3: "Verily, verily, I say unto thee, Except a man be born again, he cannot see the kingdom of God."[69] The reason for writing an essay on this subject was Witherspoon's lament that the church of mid-eighteenth-century Scotland was no longer stressing the inner renewal of individuals. Conversion, along with spiritual renewal, was not heard often enough from the pulpit, and he believed that it needed to be proclaimed. His intention was to write broadly on the topic, combining the doctrines of human sinfulness, election, and sanctification. He called regeneration a process, a change, from a sinful life to a life of a forgiven sinner. As such, both justification and sanctification belonged to regeneration.[70]

What is regeneration? Witherspoon answers that it is, at bottom, a unique spiritual rebirth, a startling renewal. It is a sinner moving from a state of nature to a state of grace, from one covenant to another, in a manner of speaking. It is becoming a new creature. It is a veritable change from death to life. It is a reviving inner experience leading to action, the recovery of the moral image of God upon the heart, leading to a supreme love of God and a desire to serve God as one's highest end. Here is his fullest and most eloquent statement on the subject:

> Regeneration consists in having the image of God again drawn upon the heart; that is, its being carried out to the supreme love of God, and delight in him or, in other words, brought to the supreme love of, and delight in, perfect goodness and immaculate holiness. When this is the case, the sinner is renewed, he again bears the image of God, which he had lost, he is again fitted for the presence of God, from which he had been expelled.[71]

The most important thing to see in the process of regeneration is that it is *God's* work, "a supernatural change," Witherspoon called it. Apart from the regeneration essay and Lecture 11 in his "Lectures on Divinity," he had little to say about the role of the Holy Spirit in the formation of piety. Nevertheless, the agency of the Holy Spirit in regeneration is crucial. Ordinarily one goes to the New Testament to read about the work of the Spirit, but Witherspoon assures his readers that the story begins in the Old Testament, where one finds predictions of the "plentiful effusion of the Holy Spirit" (see, for example, Isa. 44:3, 4; and Ezek. 36:25–27). But wherever one opens the Bible to read about regeneration, one thing is sure: "regeneration is the work of the Holy Ghost."[72] He appears to take the position that any human effort in effecting an inner change is worthless. With finality he declares, "We are of ourselves utterly unable to produce a change in our hearts." That would seem to be the last word and would seem to be consistent with his previous statements on predestination and election. Now comes a surprise. Human participation is a factor after all.

Immediately declaring that we can do nothing, he qualifies his statement by informing us that our sinful state is not so severe that our obligation to duty and the guilt arising from our sin can be easily dismissed. He never introduces the word "cooperation" in holding together divine intervention with human participation, but he does assert a measure of human responsibility. Is there a contradiction here? He does not acknowledge one, and perhaps in his own mind he saw none. His dilemma was that he strove to preserve the integrity of divine grace, but he also wanted to make room within human sinfulness for the possibility of an active responsibility. In sum, we are not totally depraved or completely corrupted. In a revealing sentence, he has nothing to say about divine intervention but much about human capability: "The moral inability, under which sinners now lie, as a consequence of the fall, is not of such a nature, as to take away the guilt of sin, the propriety of exhortations to duty, or the necessity of endeavors after recovery."[73]

To think about regeneration is to think about conversion, a term possibly more familiar to us today than regeneration, thanks to contemporary revivalists and televangelism. Witherspoon, of course, preceded the age of revivals that began in the nineteenth century, so he had nothing to say about mass revival meetings.[74] Nevertheless, he did know about conversion, and he deemed it important to inform his people about the change wrought by the Holy Spirit. Offering no standard by which all conversions could be measured, he observed that some persons can, others cannot, pinpoint the time and manner of their conversion. Conversion can be instantaneous or rapid, otherwise slow and gradual. Regenerate or pious persons will, in any case, be able to recall a sinful past, or at the very least be aware of the corruption in their hearts, and the resultant change of life brought about by the Holy Spirit. The fundamental change may be common to everyone, but the moment and the circumstances will not be the same for all believers.[75]

This truth is being repeated in our time by at least some mainline Christian leaders, proving that the Billy Grahams of the world do not have an exclusive claim on conversion itself or a particular method of achieving it. Henri Nouwen has attested both to the necessity of conversion if a person is to live a spiritual life and to the fact that conversion can be quite different—a sudden traumatic event or a long quiet process. Conversion means that the detail of our lives will no longer worry us as things we can hardly cope with, but will now be experienced as "affirmations and revelations of the new life of the Spirit within us." At Harvard, Peter Gomes, Preacher to the University, warns that being born again is not what some would like to claim for it—a badge of spiritual superiority announcing that they have already arrived—but instead, a "second chance," the opportunity to "enter afresh into the process of spiritual growth. It is to wipe the slate clean. It is to cancel your old mortgage and start again. . . . 'You must be born again' is an offer you cannot afford to refuse."[76]

Witherspoon gives us something else to consider. There is no telling what God in his freedom and sovereignty is up to. Sometimes it pleases God to snatch some of the most "abandoned profligates" from eternal destruction, converting even his "most inveterate enemies" to become successful advocates for his truth. Paul is a good example. "Sometimes, on the other hand, the reception of the truth, and renovation of the heart, goes on by slow and insensible degrees." The twelve disciples are good examples of a more gradual conversion. Also, the quality or intensity of the conversion is unpredictable from our human standpoint; the change and growth of the spiritual life can be quite remarkable, the greatest sinner becoming the most eminent saint. Remember the woman mentioned in Luke (7:36–50). Her many sins were forgiven, remarked Witherspoon, and "she loved her Redeemer much." But it could just as well be otherwise. The change could seem to be doubtful, at least for a time, and the believer's progress hardly discernible. The person might even be forced "to walk in darkness," the change being so confused and disorganized. Here is how Witherspoon sums it up: "The actual change may be wrought at any time, in any manner, by any means, and will produce its effects in any measure, that to infinite wisdom shall seem proper."[77] He allows for varieties of religious experience, but within the larger event of Christian conversion.

We should be aware that Witherspoon's emphasis on God's freedom and grace in saving sinners prevented him from resorting to graphic and frightening descriptions of an angry God and the horrors of hell in order to scare sinners into conversion. That strategy never occurred to him; he was too set on declaring God's mercy and forgiveness as fervently as he could, which in his judgment were quite sufficient to awaken sinners to the possibilities of rebirth. Also, the fact that Witherspoon wanted to uphold the divine initiative meant that he could not leave the experience of conversion completely in the hands of the sinner, to respond to a preacher's vivid picture of the place of terrible torment, or conversely, the place of infinite beauty and bliss.

Nevertheless, it is true that Witherspoon equivocated more than once on the issue of sovereign divine grace versus human response and effort. Further, when he pondered the extent of Christ's death in the doctrine of election, he was forced to admit that, logically, the effect of his death was limited. Jesus, in fact, did not die for everyone, only for the elect.[78] Nevertheless, much more often, with no apology for the apparent inconsistency, Witherspoon warned that it was up to each person to decide for or against the redemption offered and secured by Christ. In the sermon, "Christ's Death a Proper Atonement for Sin," he laid out three propositions, the second of which underscored election, and the third affirmed that Christ died for everyone. The propositions are summarized as follows:

1. The death of Christ has such power and value that it can "expiate the guilt of all the sins of every individual that ever lived or ever shall live on earth."

2. Granting this, not all are saved. Many do die in their sins, so in this sense Christ does not die for those who stubbornly reject him, and "who after all that he hath done, shall be miserable for ever."

3. Nevertheless, Christ's death is a sufficient foundation for preaching the gospel "to all without exception."[79]

To support his third proposition he reached for two New Testament passages, 1 Timothy 4:10 and 1 Corinthians 8:11. For him, these verses were authority enough to affirm "that there is a sense in which Christ died for all men, and even for those who perish." Indeed, how could he conclude otherwise? After all, the text for the sermon was that Christ is "the propitiation for our sins; and not for ours only, but also for the sins of the whole world" (1 John 2:2).

When preacher Witherspoon said that salvation through Christ should be announced to all, not only was he opening new theological territory beyond the idea of election and a limited atonement, but he was also providing a basis for foreign missions, an undertaking new to the eighteenth century. In a 1758 sermon, "The Absolute Necessity of Salvation through Christ" (Acts 4:12), he called upon the Society in Scotland for the Propagation of Christian Knowledge to send missionaries not only to the "unenlightened Heathen nations" but specifically to the American Indians "whom with a contempt equally impolitic and unchristian, we suffer to continue in ignorance of the only living and true God, and Jesus Christ whom he hath sent."[80] If God's call was to extend across the ocean to Native Americans, it should also stretch across the nave of his church in Scotland. At the end of one of his "action sermons," he kept conversion in God's hands but weakened the idea of election by expressing the hope that the harvest of redeemed souls would be bountiful beyond measure. "And my earnest prayer to God for you, is, that he would at this time, convert some, or (why should we limit him?) every prophane sinner in this assembly . . . that he would make it a joyful communion to many of you, and a profitable communion to all. Amen." At home or abroad the gospel was to be preached "indefinitely to all without exception."[81]

How did Witherspoon finally hold to the divine initiative and yet assert human responsibility? He sought out the famous passage in Paul's letter to the Philippians that unites both actions: "[W]ork out your own salvation with fear and trembling. For it is God which worketh in you both to will and to do his good pleasure" (Phil. 2:12, 13). To him this was a satisfactory way to balance human decision and effort with divine grace and action.[82]

On any given Sunday he might expand on these verses in the following way: God has aroused sinners from their sinful condition and extended to them his grace through Jesus Christ, calling on them to exercise their free choice in appropriating to themselves this ultimate goodness. An appeal would bring the sermon to a close, a shortened form of which might be as follows: Behold the Lamb of God! Your ransom has been paid, justice has been fully satisfied, by an Almighty Savior, "able to save to the uttermost, all that come unto God by him! . . . He is able to knock off the strongest fetters, and let the prisoners go free. Wherefore, I beseech you, my dear friends . . . that you do not sit still, and perish, but arise, and be doing, and the Lord will be with you."[83] He never tired of reiterating this generous divine grace as well as the plea to those in their lost and fallen state to reach out and take hold of their salvation.

Justification by the Imputed Righteousness of Christ

If the lost state of man by nature and salvation by the free grace of God are two elements of Witherspoon's piety, the third is the rather arcane and forensic phrase, "justification by the imputed righteousness of Christ." It is all about the atonement, and for Witherspoon it was the most important of the four truths. Justification was the concept that he treated only slightly in his "A Practical Treatise on Regeneration," but that he had already taken up in a serious way eight years earlier in the "Essay on Justification."[84] In the justification essay, Witherspoon explored the act of reconciling the unrighteous sinner with the righteous God (atonement), or in terms more congenial to the Confession, the pardoning of sinners and accepting them as righteous effected by Christ's death on the cross (justification).[85] In his sermons Witherspoon generally avoided the terms of atonement and justification and instead announced salvation through Christ, often in language descriptive of the kind of death he endured.

Justification he explained in this way: God wants to forgive sinners, but he does not introduce some righteous quality or virtue into sinful humans in order for them to be forgiven. Nor does he give any credit to human efforts toward holiness that might make women and men better people. Everything is done for Christ's sake, and by him, which means that because of his death sinners are forgiven and declared righteous by God. God sent his son that we might be forgiven, so justification is *God's* mighty act. Imputation means counting something for (or against) an individual to that person's credit (or discredit). So, it is *Christ's* righteousness, then, that is imputed to sinners to make them righteous and acceptable in God's sight. From the human side, it is through faith in Christ that sinners are made right with God. Sinners have received by faith God's gift of righteousness.[86] Witherspoon considered it necessary to underscore that the merciful God had from all eternity devised a plan to save sinners. He preached no single sermon explaining the doctrine of justification, but hearers and readers were reminded repeatedly of this astonishing act of God's love whenever appropriate. Whether he called it a plan, a scheme, a design, a transaction, even a contrivance (and he employed all these words), he was determined to make the point that this was not something God had lately thought up. From all eternity God was at his very best in offering this plan of salvation.[87]

For our part, we humans will never be able to comprehend the astounding love of God in Christ to save sinners. Our meager attempts even to talk about this are inevitably "swallowed up, in what is infinite and boundless." Yet immediately following such a confession, Witherspoon states emphatically that the plan of salvation can be deduced from scripture and appropriated by sinful persons for their everlasting good. Thus, the plan is not beyond the understanding of us ordinary mortals, for we are expected to comprehend it, make it our own, and communicate it to others. Witherspoon confidently takes the matter further in very understandable language by proclaiming what he deems to be the ultimate purpose of God in human history: "Does it not afford matter for adoring wonder, that the plan for redeeming lost sinners, and restoring them to the obedience and enjoyment of God, was the object of the divine purpose from eternity?"[88]

What is special in Witherspoon's reflections on justification is the change in the nature of God he sets forth. On the surface it might appear that he is guilty of eliminating God's sovereign will by reducing God's mighty and merciful action to a fixed plan or design, containing such juridical terms as justification, imputation, and satisfaction, but he does something different. In his admiration for the Deity who offers salvation to all sinners, he creates a new understanding of God, what he himself said was "the real nature of God."[89] It was not enough to quote the Shorter Catechism definition of God by describing God as "a Spirit, infinite, eternal, and unchangeable, in his being, wisdom, power, holiness, justice, goodness and truth." He improved this formal scholastic definition by announcing that the real nature of God was "the boundless mercy of the Father, and the infinite condescension of the Son, . . . and on the astonishing end of his appearance in our nature, that he might 'bear our sins in his own body on the tree.'" In effect, Witherspoon has gathered up all the named divine attributes and combined them into the justification of sinners by the imputed righteousness of Christ. That done, the doctrine does indeed become, he proclaimed, "the brightest display of all the divine perfections."[90]

The origin of the atonement lies in God's grace and mercy toward sinful humanity—and toward *all* humanity, as we have learned. Within the atonement is placed the need to satisfy divine justice, a need expressed in numerous sermons. The preacher reasoned that those who count on justification through Christ never deny "the obligation of the holy law of God upon every reasonable creature." Moreover, those who are justified have discovered in this "great transaction . . . the price paid for the purchase of our pardon: 1 Pet. 1:18." Justice is bound up in the atonement, but forgiven sinners no longer have to be afraid of it, they no longer have reason to despair. They can be confident and comforted. Because of what Christ has done, "justice being fully satisfied, seals the pardon, and adds to the comfort of the sinner." Parishioners were commanded to think upon the holiness and justice of God "as they shine in the sufferings and cross of Christ: that a righteous God required full satisfaction for sin; that 'the Lord laid on him the iniquities of us all'" (Isa. 53:6). Witherspoon was following closely the teaching of the Confession on satisfaction, which reads in part, Christ "did make a proper, real and full satisfaction to his Father's justice." Neither Witherspoon nor the Westminster Divines seemed to be aware that a satisfaction theory of the atonement is unbiblical, even though it has enjoyed a long history in the church. The word "satisfaction" does not appear in the Bible, and nowhere does the Bible say that if certain conditions are met or a price is paid, only then will God love us. But Witherspoon was adamant that Christ's death totally satisfied divine justice.[91]

He had recourse to terms other than satisfaction to describe Christ's work. They included sacrifice, ransom, propitiation, and even more often, substitution.[92] At times he let a substitutionary theory of the atonement stand alone—"Christ Jesus was substituted in the room [place] of sinners, and suffered, the just for the unjust, that he might bring us to God"[93]—but on other occasions he combined substitution with satisfaction. This meant that Jesus Christ, *on our behalf*, in his capacity as a human, bore the penalty for sin and offered satisfaction for it to God who demanded justice. Once more we have a forensic understanding of justification that precludes any personal union with Christ.[94] In explaining how Christ is a propitiation, Witherspoon viewed him as a "peace-maker" between God and humans, as he undertook his suffering and death. He explained, "he appeases him [God], rendereth him propitious or gracious to us, and purchaseth our pardon."[95] His references to Christ as Mediator were constant, though he also called him the Savior, the Redeemer, and the Lamb of God. In focusing on Christ's mediatorial role, he was following mainline Reformed theological formulations. A mediator, we know, assumes a position between two opposing parties and proceeds to reconcile them. In Witherspoon's theology, and that of other Reformed sources, Christ as Mediator reconciles humans to God. Witherspoon explains, giving Jesus a prominent place in the covenant of grace: "Jesus, the mediator of the new covenant, having finished his work, invites weary and heavy-laden sinners to come to him; and assures them, . . . that their debt is fully paid, and nothing is now to be laid to their charge: Rom. 8: 33, 34."[96] It must be understood that the Mediator is himself sent by God to do the reconciling work and as such is properly called God's Son. Yet, as both God and human, he only suffered in his human nature (more on his sufferings later). Those sufferings were so momentous and memorable that they secured our redemption.[97] Christ's mediation, thus, is centered in the way he unites the righteous God with the unrighteous sinner. Without Christ, there would be no avenue for the human to approach and make peace with the divine.[98]

In Reformed thought, Christ's mediatorial work ordinarily takes three forms. The Shorter Catechism summarizes these forms in the following question and answer:

> Question Twenty-Three: What offices doth Christ execute as our Redeemer?
>
> Answer: Christ, as our Redeemer, executeth the offices of a prophet, of a priest, and of a king, both in his estate of humiliation and exaltation.

This threefold function of Christ as Mediator had become a veritable fixture in Reformed theology from Calvin onward.[99] However, it is missing in Witherspoon's piety. He is content simply to name Jesus as the Mediator (intercessor, advocate, or reconciler), but in one discourse he does pay tribute to Jesus' work as priest. In the previously mentioned sermon, "Christ's Death a Proper Atonement for Sin," he quotes several passages from Hebrews, and then declares Christ to be the high priest who offered himself in the ultimate sacrifice.[100]

After all that he said about Christ's role in justification, it comes as no surprise to find that Witherspoon taught that Christ's humiliation is far more important than his exaltation.[101] There is the infrequent allusion to his exaltation: the resurrection, ascension, reign in heaven, or the second coming, almost always in connection with how these actions impinge upon the life of the believer. Witherspoon used Christ's exaltation to comfort and reassure the faithful. Christ, he proclaimed with confidence, having finished his saving work and entered glory, has given us the assurance that we also shall overcome in his strength. In the midst of earthly misery and sorrow, believers have every right to gaze ahead and imagine the happiness of heaven. He concluded, "Then shall our eyes see the glorious Saviour standing at the right hand of God, surrounded by ten thousand of his saints, who have been redeemed by his blood."[102]

The exaltation received brief notices of this sort, but the humiliation of Christ loomed far greater in Witherspoon's thought. The humiliation was not just the crucifixion; it extended from his lowly birth to his burial. It was not enough to portray Jesus as humbling himself, taking the form of a servant. Witherspoon painted Jesus' humiliation in far darker hues. "Remember him," Witherspoon lamented, "despised and rejected of men, a man of sorrows, and acquainted with grief. His life indeed was one continued scene of sorrow, from the cradle to the grave."[103] No sooner did he rise from his humble birth (Witherspoon said it was "contemptible," meaning pitiable) than "bloody tyrant" Herod sought to destroy him.[104] Because Jesus was a man of sorrows and acquainted with grief, Witherspoon decided that he had never laughed and that he wept often. He was "of a tender frame" which meant that he suffered intensely from his afflictions, so much so "that his body was wasted, and his strength melted and decayed."[105] His major afflictions, all severe, numbered four: he was destitute, was called terrible names, suffered distress from the devil's temptations, and endured the "sharpest pangs" by the suffering of others.

The worst suffering of all, however, was "bearing the wrath of a sin avenging God." Throughout his life he constantly drank from the cup of humiliation, but on the cross "he came to drink off [*sic*] the very bitterest dregs of it. The waves of divine wrath went over him, and he waded still deeper and deeper in this troubled ocean, till he was well nigh overwhelmed." We know for a fact that his suffering was horrendous, explained Witherspoon, when we hear him cry, "My God, my God, why hast thou forsaken me!" It makes no difference whether or not God merely withdrew his presence from the man on the cross, or if God inflicted on him the same punishment that was due to sinful humanity; Witherspoon states but will not choose between the two possible interpretations. He suggests a mixture of both. "One thing is certain" he avows, "in his life, and at his death, he suffered what was a full reparation of the dishonor done to God." In other words, he fully satisfied divine justice.[106]

Such a morbid assessment of Jesus will cause modern readers to shake their heads first in disbelief and then in disagreement. One immediately wants to put tough questions to Witherspoon about what full humanity means. Does it not signify the breadth of human emotions and feelings, joys as well as sorrows? Also, what about the parts of Jesus' life that Witherspoon has overlooked—his love of children, parables that have a humorous twist to them, a wedding at Cana? These do not portray a Jesus whose whole life was "one continued scene of sorrow."

If we want to comprehend why Witherspoon paints such a gloomy portrait of Jesus, we will have to start with the fact that he picked up the doctrine of Jesus as the Mediator and ran with it as hard and fast as he could. If a person like Witherspoon sees Jesus primarily, if not exclusively, as a suffering Savior, then it is not a great stretch to regard his years leading up to the cross as, in the phrase of the Shorter Catechism, "undergoing the miseries of this life," and full of suffering and sorrow. If an interpreter thinks along the lines Witherspoon chose, then there can be a consistent whole to the life and work of Jesus. His humiliation will last his whole life long, culminating in the dreadful crucifixion. We may not agree, but this is the way Witherspoon saw it.

He would not tolerate alternate interpretations of Jesus either. He denounced those nominal Christians (Moderates?) who presented Jesus as a teacher, who, in effect, placed him in the class of ordinary human reformers. Any understanding of Jesus as someone other than a savior is not an option. In our day, Witherspoon, standing firm in his Christology, would have been pleased to include in a hymnal, "Just as I am without one plea," and would just as quickly have turned down, rather angrily, any hymn that called Jesus a "guide divine," a "friend" or a "shepherd." His death was all that counted. Again we see how Witherspoon shortchanged a well-rounded interpretation of Jesus by ignoring important parts of his life and ministry.[107] A modern confession of faith, such as the Presbyterian "Confession of 1967" that depicts Jesus' humanity within the context of Palestinian Judaism and his concern for the many kinds of sinful people, would no doubt have been anathema to Witherspoon.[108]

In the judgment of Pastor Witherspoon, the doctrine of justification by the imputed righteousness of Christ held considerable practical devotional value for the lives of the faithful. Outlining this value consumed a major section of his "Essay on Justification."[109] The believer, he wrote, will first have a heightened sense of the evil and danger of sin and in order to deal with it sufficiently will recognize the need for an awesome atonement. Next the doctrine will restore the right order of relationship: Believers will appreciate more than ever the purity and holiness of God, and simultaneously their own unworthiness. They will come to see that they need a mediator in order to approach God. Third, the doctrine instills a sense of gratitude, which, in turn, inspires obedience to the will of God. Believers will embrace every opportunity of converting their thankfulness into "an entire consecration of their lives to their benefactor's service."[110] Lastly, those justified will be veritably consumed by a love for God. Quoting 1 John 4:16, 19, Witherspoon insisted that God's unspeakable mercies bestowed on us will excite our ardent love in return. His succinct summation? "We love him because he first loved us."

Is this not the foundational principle of piety? Is this not bound up with the first and great commandment of the law, "Thou shalt love the Lord thy God . . ."? Thus, Witherspoon has returned to the ground on which he builds his piety—"a supreme and superlative love to God."[111]

We began the exposition of Witherspoon's doctrine of justification by the imputed righteousness of Christ by describing it as arcane and forensic, recognizing that he taught that God had devised a plan or scheme whereby sinners who rightly deserved God's wrath for their sin were, in fact, forgiven and made righteous. It was noted further that he often resorted to juridical language in discussing the atonement: Christ's death did fully satisfy divine justice, and Christ did fully purchase our redemption. But we also learned that there was another side to Witherspoon's understanding of salvation that was not best explained by plan, scheme, or transaction; nor was this salvation effective only for the elect. He preached a merciful God revealed in the person of his Son and in the Son's atoning sacrifice—which applied to all humanity. Witherspoon directed his people to "wonder at the boundless mercy of the Father, and the infinite condescension of the Son." He told them that this was the real nature of God.[112]

A final word on justification needs to be entered. Witherspoon was loath to use the time-honored Protestant phrase "justified by faith." There is no question but he knew that faith was part of piety. He preached sermons that emphasized faith,[113] but he seemed reluctant to join faith with justification. In these sermons he discoursed as much or more on the content of faith as on the act of believing.

In the sermon, "The Nature of Faith," the first main section was "The object of faith," the second, "The actings of faith." Relying on his text, 1 John 3:23 (". . . that we should believe on the name of his Son Jesus Christ"), Witherspoon stated that the object of faith was none other than "Christ Jesus the Saviour." This led him once more to preach on the sinfulness of human beings; salvation freely offered by God; Christ, the Mediator of the new covenant "dying in our room, and purchasing our pardon"; and the renewal of our natures, or sanctification. He did not apologize for this kind of repetition, because for him, given his understanding of scripture, it was far more important to know *what* to believe than *how* to believe. For lack of a better definition he offered, "The simplest view of faith seems to be receiving 'the record which God hath given us of his Son.'" Against contemporary definitions of faith that emphasize trust in God and God's revelation, Witherspoon's concept of faith was much more a matter of cognition and proposition.[114]

In due course, he did treat three "particulars" of the act of believing. First, faith is "a firm assent of the understanding to what is revealed of Christ in scripture." There is no suggestion of trust here or that faith involves the whole person. He continues by contrasting the reliable understanding that faith provides us with the unreliable understanding of sense. Faith tells us that our true happiness is in the favor of God, that eternity is approaching, and that there is no time to be lost. Sense deludes us by trying to convince us that the world is good, that its delights are pleasant, and that our comfort is here and now. The first step, thus, is a strong cognitive assent to the reality of Christ and his work. The second step is "the consent and approbation of the heart to every truth with regard to Christ's person and character, and salvation through his blood." This is not the same as the first step, though it calls for consent to the truth of Christ. Witherspoon is now proposing that believers not only agree mentally that salvation through Christ is true, but by means of their will they will decide that it is "wise, reasonable, gracious, and necessary" for them. It is as if the person is now saying, "Christ is true *for me*."[115] The third and final stage is when the person of faith enjoys "repose of conscience and peace with God." The *how* of believing has just been reduced to a simple three-step process.

Witherspoon knew very well that a sovereign gracious God bestows faith; humans do not manufacture it. Yet his evangelical fervor got the better of him from time to time, and he preached as though faith is less a divine gift and more a human decision and an effort of one's will. In the present sermon under consideration, after he had outlined what to believe and how to believe, he appealed to his listeners with these words: "If you are truly and inwardly satisfied of Christ's power and mercy, you will close with [draw near to] him, as your Saviour, and say unto him, in the words of Thomas, when his doubts were removed, 'My Lord, and my God.'"[116]

He concluded his message with something approaching an altar call. The verbs signal human response and effort as well as understanding what God has done in Christ. He implored every sinner in church that day to "believe in [Christ's name] and merits for your pardon; rely on his grace and Spirit for your reformation; and return to God, through him, as your unchangeable portion."[117]

If he tended to put too much emphasis on faith as human endeavor, he never went so far as to assert that faith was the means by which humans earned their salvation. He may not always have been successful in his attempt, but he was trying to hold both ideas in balance, that faith was both a divine gift and free human response, the human response embracing a deep understanding of God's gracious action in Christ.

Sanctification by the Effectual Operation of the Holy Spirit

Sanctification is the last of the "truths of such unspeakable moment." Under the rubric of regeneration Witherspoon gave some attention to the truths of grace, justification, conversion, and sanctification. He wanted to keep justification and sanctification distinct yet linked, and further proof of that is that sanctification received substantial treatment in his "Essay on Justification." In that piece it seemed logical to him to set forth the effects of justification, which belong to the doctrine of sanctification, "the powerful and effective aid" provided by the gift of the Holy Spirit.[118]

The simplest definition of sanctification is being made holy, and this only becomes possible once Christ has completed his atoning work.[119] In Reformed theology justification and sanctification do belong together. Indeed, they have often been called the two dimensions of salvation, one being incomplete without the other. Justification provides God's forgiveness to the sinner, and sanctification insures renewal of life to the forgiven sinner.[120] Some have charged that in Reformed church life there is the temptation to emphasize sanctification at the expense of justification, but at its best Reformed thought keeps the two doctrines in balance.[121] Witherspoon himself affirms the close interdependence of the doctrines, stating that both are grounded in Christ;[122] nevertheless, a close examination of his sermons reveals that justification receives more emphasis than sanctification. What he does impart to his auditors on sanctification is both practical and consistent with the Reformed tradition.

The agent of sanctification is the Holy Spirit, who performs wondrous works. He penetrates believers with a sense of sin, prevents impiety and "supine sloth and negligence," prompts the faithful to do their duty with alacrity and vigor, invigorates their powers, leads them into all truth, and in time, enables them to become partakers of a divine nature. Sanctification *is* the work of the Holy Spirit, but Witherspoon's analysis of the Spirit's accomplishments, particularly in relation to one's duty, stresses human participation along with divine empowerment. One more time he quotes Philippians 2:12, 13 ("work out your own salvation").[123]

In "A Practical Treatise on Regeneration," Witherspoon inserted a whole section on sanctification as part of regeneration.[124] Here more benefits of sanctification are offered. The doctrine guarantees a new heart and new "apprehensions." Justified women and men are different now. Their knowledge, attitudes, insights, and feelings are enriched. Having overcome all degrees of disbelief, the sanctified are now acutely aware of God's presence, power, and providence. They truly know that God is great and God is good. They stand astonished yet saddened at their former conduct. Previously, they thought they were accountable only to themselves. Now they know better: They belong to God. They understand that they should shun worldly persons, even those of wealth and station, and instead have intercourse with the saints of this world. They know for a fact that "a Christian in a cottage appears more honorable and more amiable than a blasphemer in a palace."

The sanctified have new apprehensions of eternity, which put to flight "the shadows and vanities of time." Whereas before things unseen were of little importance, now they become "the great realities of another world." New views of Jesus the Savior belong to them too. Before, claims of Jesus as Mediator were denied as absurdities or ridiculed as emotional excess—"they were nick-named nonsense, cant, and unintelligible stuff," remarks Witherspoon. Now, however, Jesus becomes the great and only Savior of sinners. Even Sunday loses its "offensive gloom," its "confinement and restraint," and becomes a "delight." Believers now cannot get enough of the word of God. They "thirst after the water of life," and join the psalmist in exclaiming, "I was glad when they said unto me, Let us go into the house of the Lord" (Ps. 122:1).[125]

However, and this is a serious exception, the sanctified person does not find life easy going. Scripture and human experience, not to mention the Confession and the Pictet textbook, all declaim that sanctification is not perfection. Justification does not produce sinless saints, a fact that some Christians, past and present, tend to forget in their hope that the Christian faith will erase all wrongs and worries. Sanctification is at once a process or growth toward perfection, as well as outright war, a bitter struggle between flesh and spirit.[126] The Confession minces no words, describing the conflict as "continual and irreconcilable war." Witherspoon concurred. Do not forget, he remonstrates, that there is "much unsubdued sin remaining in the children of God." And, in the sermon "Yoke of Christ" he remarks that "It seems to be the mistake of some persons to think that so soon as they have truly embraced the gospel, and obtained peace with God, the conflict is over, they shall have an easy and slothful assurance, without opposition from affliction or temptation." Even the great figures of the Bible discovered that the life of faith was imperfect. Take King David's adultery and murder, Solomon's idolatry, and Peter's denial of his Lord.[127]

Because sin continues to assail those who are now justified, the struggle to overcome it is very real. It is a tough fight. Their aim, of course, must be "to obtain a victory over their corruptions," but on some days they find themselves unequal to the struggle. They become disappointed and are "ready to sit down in slothful carelessness," even murmuring secret complaints against God. This is deplorable. They have to realize that "Faith and despair are beyond all question inconsistent. Faith and hope are inseparable. Yet certainly the excellent ones of the earth may be sometimes involved in great perplexity and doubt. This is plain from scripture examples, from daily experience, and from the nature and reason of the thing."[128]

Witherspoon does not minimize the sanctification struggle. In exceptional cases it can be such turmoil and there will remain so much of that "unsubdued sin," that it is well nigh impossible to decide "whether the love of God or of the world hath the greatest habitual influence in the heart." Alas, the contest between grace and corruption may be so severe that we humans will never be able to determine the outcome right up till the last day.[129]

Because sanctification is so imperfect, the redeemed must live with care, vigilance, caution, always ready to repel the enemy within or without. Witherspoon calls up several Bible passages that advise simple vigilance and caution (Heb. 6:11; 1 Pet. 5:8; 2 Pet. 1:5–10), and others that, he argues, call for extra vigilance and timely effort on the part of the Christian. The Christian passage through life is one of striving (Matt. 7:13). It is also running a race (Heb. 12:1), fighting the good fight (1 Tim. 6:12), and it surely is "incessant labor" (Phil. 2:12).[130]

Incorporated into this vigilance and caution is the act of self-examination, for the sanctified need to determine what corruption still resides in their hearts. They have to be tough on themselves. It is not enough to mourn past sins; they must wrestle with the inherent evil that remains, they must ask and answer the questions, "Does your sense of the evil of sin not only continue, but grow?" and "Are you daily making new discoveries of the vanity, sensuality and treachery of your own hearts?" Such self-examination may indeed lead to discouragement. It should lead to a suitable humility and an abiding enjoyment of the gospel of peace.[131]

If sanctification entails striving, running a race, even fighting a war, it also means, thank goodness, progress and a final victory. Therein is the comfort and assurance of the doctrine. Of course the progress may be slow, along with times of regression, but progress there will be. In the sermon, "The Deceitfulness of Sin," Witherspoon maps out the progressive steps that mark the journey of the sanctified person growing in holiness. He contrasts the rise of a saint each step of the way with the downfall of the sinner (which he had already exhibited).

Ideally, the growth in sanctification occurs as follows: (1) New converts find it hard to withdraw from their sins but begin to do it. (2) After a time good persons find their way to be smoother. (3) They begin to associate with other saints and receive the benefits the association brings. (4) They discover now it is their very nature to love God and the life of holiness. (5) They have reached the degree of sanctification that prompts them to shun the world. (6) They are now filled with a driving desire for the things of religion. (7) These Christians are raised above the world; their hearts are in heaven.[132]

For most Christians, growth in sanctification does not follow this seven-step process evenly and smoothly. Witherspoon knows this, so he dispenses some advice to two kinds of travelers proceeding along the way. To those impatient for perfection or, at least, easy rapid progress, he scolds, you want too much comfort from the Spirit, so much so, that temptation would amount to no temptation at all, and suffering, which also is the lot of every Christian, would be no suffering. "Your improvement in the spiritual life is but very gradual," he reminds his readers and, in so many words, tells them to rid themselves of their impatience and their unreal demands of the Spirit's benefits. To those who tire of the struggle, he explains that progress *is* slow, duty *is* painful, doubts *will* assail. It is so tempting to stop trying, stand still, and finally to become despondent and inactive. You must not give in, he warns; this is exactly what Satan wants, so we have to resist him and his devices, which are so "unspeakably artful."[133] William Bouwsma once described Calvin's view of the spiritual life in the following way; he could just as well have put Witherspoon's name on it too:

> Therefore, through service, struggle, adversity, and pilgrimage, the spiritual life acquires a kind of dramatic unity as it proceeds through a series of ardent and strenuous moments from beginning to appointed end. A positive spiritual life means progress in realizing the purposes of human existence. It develops an increasingly close and confident relationship with God (faith), which finds expression in a more and more spontaneous and joyful conformity to God's will (sanctification) and in wholehearted glorification of God and appreciation of his works.[134]

Witherspoon's final advice to all who walk the road of sanctification is, "Endeavor, Christians, to preserve and increase your hope in

God, by further degrees of sanctification, by zeal and diligence in doing his will. The more the image of God in you is perfected, it will be the more easily discerned."[135] And victory is promised. The saints shall overcome. In the sermon, "The Object of a Christian's Desire in Religious Worship," Witherspoon reassures believers by proclaiming God's power and sanctification's final victory:

> I shall only add, that the divine all-sufficiency is to be considered, as regarding our sanctification as well as comfort. What distress does not the Christian often suffer from the treachery of his own heart, and from the power of surrounding temptations? Covered with shame for his past unsteadfastness, convinced, by experience, of his own weakness, he hath no other refuge but in God. And what courage does he derive from the fulness of divine perfection, the greatness of divine power and the faithfulness of the divine promise? "My grace shall be sufficient for thee, and my strength shall be made perfect in weakness." He then says, with the Psalmist, Psal. 71:16. "I will go in the strength of the Lord God: I will make mention of thy righteousness, even of thine only."[136]

Chapter Two

Pious and Useful Actions

> Now, we glorify God by cultivating holy dispositions, and
> doing pious and useful actions.
>
> *Works, 3:39*

The Christian's "After Walk"

With the awkward yet intriguing phrase, "after walk" (Witherspoon also called it "after obedience"), Witherspoon approached the
problem of depicting the person of piety, one who knows from both
head and heart the reality of sinfulness, God's grace, justification,
and sanctification.[1] He made a good faith effort to convey how the
pious person walks through life after being transformed by "holy dispositions," or in other words, he would tell of the works that faith
produces. He believed wholeheartedly that there should be no separation between belief and practice. "All moral actions must arise
from principle," he once declared.[2] When he portrayed religion as
practical, as he often did, he was asserting that salvation was not just
belief—though it surely was that—it was life as well. He did not
mean that religion was practical in the sense that it always guaranteed to a person some great material advantage or a prosperous life.
He was primarily concerned with how that person lived, not with
what he or she owned—the practice of piety, as it were, not the practical benefits of piety. In stating that good works follow faith, Witherspoon was being true to the Confession, in which the chapter on
good works follows the one on saving faith. There is no record of a
Witherspoon sermon based on James 2:14–26 (faith without works
is dead), though he was on record that good works were essential to
piety: "Whilst therefore you remember that faith in Christ is the
only source of new obedience, remember also, that faith without

works is dead."[3] The Bible taught it and he believed it, but there was another reason to emphasize good works. Certain Moderates and unbelievers ("infidels") of the day were criticizing the members of the Popular party saying they were serious only about doctrine and the salvation experience, not about Christian conduct.

In two sermons in particular, Witherspoon directly addresses this criticism. Throughout the first, "The Trial of Religious Truth by Its Moral Influence," based on the familiar words of Matthew 7:20, "By their fruits ye shall know them," he highlights the truth that the serious test of the validity of any religious idea or observance is "Will it make us more holy than before?"[4] This pragmatic test of judging religion by its results appealed to Witherspoon. "This is the best rule that could have been given," he exclaims.

The truths of the gospel do actually work. Every real Christian, he insists, has "inward and experimental proof of the gospel . . . stronger and more stable than any speculative reasoning." This conviction is contagious. These persons carry with them authority and an example, even more than those of brilliant intellect and powerful persuasion: "It is the piety and probity of the person that gives weight to his example, and force to his precepts." Before he reached the end of his sermon he had gone so far as to compare the pious Christian with the infidel, avowing that the works of the Christian's faith far surpass those of the unbeliever. He draws the comparison in the form of several questions: "Is it the unbeliever or the Christian, who clothes the naked and deals his bread to the hungry? Ask the many and noble ancient structures raised for the relief of the diseased and the poor, to whom they owe their establishment and support?—Which of these two classes of men are most remarkable for self-government?" Since the answer to each question is obvious, he quickly concludes, "We shall carry the comparison no further in this place."

In the second sermon, "The Nature and Extent of Visible Religion,"[5] whose text was Matthew 5:16 ("Let your light so shine before men"), Witherspoon reiterates one of his favorite themes, that every habit of the heart has a natural expression manifested by outward symptoms. "Natural affections of the mind, as sorrow, anger, and joy, do immediately discover themselves in [one's] countenance and carriage." To frame one's witness in terms of duties, shining one's light before others means a Christ-like forgiving of injuries and loving of enemies, upholding justice and integrity in all of one's dealings, showing mercy and charity to those in distress, and diligently meeting the requirements of one's profession or station in life (heads of families, magistrates, teachers of youth, ministers, and rulers). The social dimension cannot be ignored. The declaration, "True religion always enlarges the heart, and strengthens the social tie,"[6] almost attained the status of a maxim for Witherspoon. His concern was partly evangelistic; the light shining forth from a real Christian should convince and convert others. But his larger concern was the preservation of the public honor of religion in a time when, in his judgment, it was in a declining state, and there were far too few advocates of truth and righteousness. Later, in America, he was to push this point even further, pleading that piety was essential to a virtuous society and a republican government. The times cry out for Christians whose lives will be "shining example[s] of piety and usefulness of conversation," he announced.

What, we might well ask, is the criterion for a "shining example"? What is the look of the Christian's "after walk"? One way to learn about pious behavior is to apply a kind of shorthand, simply by delineating the opposites of the sins that Witherspoon condemned: Those opposites would be the virtues of love of others, humility, sobriety, chastity, pure and plain speech, honesty in business, justice, simplicity, self-restraint, and application to duty. The implication is that pious persons who live out these virtues, cloned many times, will form a healthy church and a strong nation. These are personal, family, and national values because, of course, they are biblical values! Some of these values are solidly grounded in "the second table of the law," prohibitions against murder, stealing, adultery, and the like. More virtues are to be found in other parts of the Bible, the preacher pointed out: the Old Testament prophets, the Sermon on the Mount, and Paul's letters. These sections of the Bible teach reverence for the name of God, self-denial, penitence, frugality, charity to the needy, care of the sick, and contempt of the world. The fact is, Witherspoon's sermons lift up a long list of virtues that comprise a pious way of life. Nevertheless, some virtues are more basic than others and receive more attention from him.

Humility, or meekness, is much to be prized and a prominent feature of one's piety. The sin of pride is to be shunned, while the virtue of humility is to be nurtured: "There is no disposition more the object of divine abhorrence and detestation, than pride; nor consequently, any more amiable and necessary than humility." When a confession of guilt is accompanied by deep humility, a person is ready for the grace of God, which not only forgives but furthers spiritual growth.[7] To rid ourselves of pride and gain humility requires constant effort and many prayers offered to the throne of grace. Christians cannot remain passive. Instead, "Serious, voluntary, deliberate humiliation, is the true way of promoting that steadiness in duty, and that peace with God, which ought to be the Christian's supreme desire. Whatever destroys self-sufficiency promotes the growth of true piety."[8]

In other contexts Witherspoon calls this quality self-denial or self-abasement, for it is the logical outcome of ascribing everlasting glory to God. To be fully aware of the fullness, sovereignty, power, and wisdom of the Creator and Redeemer compels one to humbly acknowledge his or her weakness and smallness. Indeed, Witherspoon once denoted self-denial and mortification to be one of two general characteristics of the disciples of Christ, the other being spirituality and heavenliness of mind. The "scripture-saints" prove the rule that "the more any person has made real improvement in holiness, he will think and speak in so much the humbler manner."[9] Imbedded in the whole scheme of redemption is the impulse "to abase the pride of man, and to exalt the grace of God."[10] Witherspoon takes denial of self to its limits, asserting that God is everything, the human nothing, even proposing that a person might undergo everlasting punishment in order to promote the glory of God.

The old story, no doubt apocryphal, of the candidate for ordination undergoing a rigorous examination by his presbytery, makes the point effectively:

> Demanding Interrogator: "Now then, young man, would you be willing for the greater glory of God to be damned to hell?"
>
> Harried Candidate: "Yes, sir, and I'd even be willing to have the whole presbytery damned for the greater glory of God!"

Would the story possibly have its origin in Witherspoon's thought? Hardly, but surprisingly, he took the query seriously for the purpose of discussing it. In "A Practical Treatise on Regeneration," he asks if the true penitent would be "willing, satisfied, and some say even 'pleased,' that God should glorify his justice in his [the penitent's] perdition?" He then answers his own question by concluding that while the question illustrates a vital truth, that is, acknowledging the awful sovereignty of God and the correct abasement of the sinner, the question itself is a strict impossibility. The true penitent can never be "separated from, and deprived of, the fruition [salvation] of God."[11] The real nature of God—"the boundless mercy of the Father and the infinite condescension of the Son"—would never allow such a thing. So no more worries for the candidate or the presbytery. But we must never forget the message for the growth of piety: The true Christian practices self-denial and exemplifies humble mien and bearing.

Next, humility itself bears fruit in self-control, or as Witherspoon names it, "self-government." Passion, or high feeling, indicates irresponsibility and unsteadiness. Excess of any type, in owning wealth, exercising power, tending to family, enhancing reputation, is not the mark of a pious person. All of us have greater cause "to guard against sins of excess and intemperance than of abstinence. The first are . . . more common and prevalent than the other," Witherspoon claims. If we are crucified to the world, as piety requires, then we will rein in our "idle fancies" and "romantic suppositions of happiness." Ministers and young persons are singled out for special advice. The former are to remember all pertinent principles found in scripture "for avoiding every dangerous extreme," and the latter, who have a great deal to learn about their feelings and handling temptations, are to be helped by parents and guardians who must teach them moderation and restraints. Witherspoon told the readers of "A Serious Inquiry into the Nature and Effects of the Stage" that they "ought to set bounds to, and endeavor to moderate [their] passions as much as possible, instead of voluntarily and unnecessarily exciting them [by attending the theater]," and he advised his Princeton students to get their "passions in due subjection" if they wanted success in life. Persons of "furious and ungoverned tempers, prone to excess in attachment and resentment . . . are seldom successful in their pursuits, or respected and useful in their stations." He wanted it understood that self-government, like all other aspects of piety, has its beneficial side.[12]

A central part of self-control is control of the tongue. If we control our passions, we will perforce control our tongue, but it is so integral to piety that it deserves "very particular attention, separately as a maxim of prudence." Witherspoon advised his students to "habituate yourselves to restraint" in matters of the tongue. Quoting

Solomon, he told them to "be swift to hear, and slow to speak." We know from his "Lectures on Eloquence" and "The Druid" [Essays] that, in general, words, language, verbal and written communication were to him weighty matters. For instance, he could not tolerate speakers who employed peculiar phrases, improper epithets, unnecessary words (a long list of examples is supplied), and vulgarisms.[13] Of course, he did not stand alone in such convictions. To name only one, Hugh Blair (1718–1800) among the Moderates, was famous for his instruction in speaking and accomplishments in rhetoric and belles lettres.[14] Exemplary speech was part of the equipment of both an Enlightenment figure and a pious Christian. But Witherspoon had a sound theological reason for upright speech: Revering the name of God was a serious obligation, and swearing and profaning God's name was downright reprehensible. God was the epitome of holiness, goodness, and truth. Love of God required reverent, God-like speech. Taking God's name in vain was tantamount to denying divine supremacy and sovereignty. It was, he said, "a direct violation of his sacred authority." Thus, piety demanded that the love of God should always be demonstrated by reverence for his name.[15] Government of the tongue covered more than swearing or blasphemy. It addressed all of one's talk, day in and day out. As Christians take their place in the larger world, others in the world have a right to know who they are and what they stand for.

> As to the government of the tongue, the world must know whether your conversation is pure and inoffensive at all times, and profitable, as opportunities present themselves; or if it is frothy, unprofitable, peevish, passionate, unchaste, censorious. As therefore, in the language of our Saviour, a city that is set on an hill cannot be hid; so a Christian, in these cases cannot be concealed.[16]

These words make his position clear. He denounced profanity and offensive language, and extolled the virtue of speech pure and undefiled. He was especially angry with the British soldiers during the Revolution for profaning church buildings and shocking good colonial Christians with the "horrid sound of cursing and blasphemy." Not only vile but excessive talking was a black mark on one's piety. If a young man rambled on, Witherspoon commented, "I shall hardly be brought to have a good opinion of him."[17] The watchwords were moderation, restraint, caution, and honesty in one's conversation. He offered some final advice: Avoid saying anything "that may have a tendency to insnare the unwary, or conform the wicked in an evil course."[18]

Seriousness of purpose and application to duty were additional features of a pious Christian. Sloth? A dangerous enemy! "Fear it, hate it, and despise it." Never make the mistake of taking God's promise of grace and strength as "a warrant or excuse for sloth." Application to duty is *our* responsibility; divine promises of succor and strength are to be understood as encouragement to diligence, not to laziness.[19] Former president Jimmy Carter spoke the same truth when he testified to his own responsibility to do his Christian duty: "My faith *demands* that I do whatever I can, wherever I can, whenever I can, for as long as I can with whatever I have to try to make a difference."[20]

Witherspoon developed further this theme of diligent industriousness in his sermon, "The Security of Those Who Trust in God" (text: Prov. 18:10, "The name of the Lord is a strong tower; the righteous run into it, and is safe"). One of his main points was that "the righteous runneth into the name of God as a strong tower by diligence in his duty." He reassured his hearers that the strong tower of God's strength is constant and sure as long as Christians adhere to their duty, no matter what gets in their way: "We may be tempted to impatience under calamity, to resentment of injuries, to taking wrong and sinful methods of redress. In opposition to all those, the servant of God will be particularly careful to avoid those sins which his situation invites him to, and to discharge those duties which the aspect of Providence seems to ask of him."[21]

He pled with those under his care to read the useful instruction found in the book of Proverbs. There, he says, you will find all you need to know about application to duty; you will read how sluggards should imitate the industrious ant (Prov. 6:6–11); you will read about the field of the slothful overrun by thorns and nettles (Prov. 24:30–31). Even if poverty strikes, apply yourselves to the duties of your calling, that you may uphold your honesty and integrity. Later, in America, he dispensed additional advice: "Cherish a love of piety, order, industry and frugality," if you want your new nation to be strong and upright.[22] By urging a pious application to duty, Witherspoon was merely reiterating what the Reformed tradition had always proposed. Reformed Christians were known for their industry and determination. An apocryphal story from the seventeenth century exaggerates the truth: A man declared that he would rather see a whole regiment of soldiers with drawn swords coming at him than a single Calvinist convinced that he was doing the will of God! And it was Charles I who is supposed to have said that there was no one more dangerous than a Presbyterian "fresh off his knees."[23]

Finally, persons who apply themselves to their duty are not to be noisy or boastful, but quiet and subdued, advised Witherspoon. This is the style of faithful Christians. They serve God and do their duty with a quiet resolve, disregarding the esteem or approval of others. They will be active and zealous wherever they are called to serve, and will leave the pattern of larger events to God. In the end, their reward will be "unspeakable consolation."[24]

Another quality of a genuine Christian is a dedication to truth. Witherspoon never stopped to say exactly what he meant by truth, but frequently he talked about it as though he meant sincerity. Never did he capitalize the "t" in truth or engage in anything like a theological discussion of the term. For him the word took on more the meaning of honesty or integrity. His several exhortations to truth are bold and basic. He urged "an invariable adherence to truth," while confessing that he truly did not know where to begin or end in "speaking of the excellency and beauty of sincerity, or the baseness of falsehood." He lauded sincerity, calling it "amiable, honorable and profitable." Acquire such a high reputation for telling the truth, he added, that while your enemies may accuse you of abusing them by your words, they will never get the chance to say that you deceived them.[25]

It might surprise modern readers to see where on this list of virtues Witherspoon places the love of one's neighbor. Whereas today's Christians might place that obligation at the head of the list of ethical demands, Witherspoon actually preached more about other marks of piety than about the love of others, even though as the second commandment of the law it stood right next to the first and greatest. Still, love of the neighbor is included in his group of virtues, and he does occasionally bind it with the first commandment.

In "A Practical Treatise on Regeneration," Witherspoon took up the second commandment of the moral law and stated that loving others was an important part of practical religion.[26] To explain how this command of Jesus might apply, he told his hearers that they would have to divide humanity into two classes, what we would call the "good guys" and the "bad guys." He began with the obvious, that it is easy to love good people. Goodness attracts goodness, Christians attract Christians. He cited the admiring comment made by pagans in the early centuries when Christians were being persecuted: "Behold how these Christians love one another." The tougher part of love, he said, was to love bad people. Their sin must not call for an angry response on the part of Christians. He asked the pious to be kind to sinners, "instructing them" in goodness, "admonishing them" when appropriate, and "pleading for them at the throne of grace." To put it bluntly, Witherspoon thought the best way to love others was to try to save them from their sins. As for hating bad persons, it is out of the question. He did not say it, but it catches his intent, that one should hate the sin but not the sinner. Because Witherspoon knew his Bible, he knew what Jesus had said to his followers, that they were to love their enemies, bless those who curse them, and pray for those who despitefully use them and persecute them. These are hard words, Witherspoon acknowledged, but we must take them at face value and do what Jesus ordered. After all, if forgiven sinners receive full pardon from God for all their "innumerable and aggravated offences," they should be quick to forgive the "far slighter trespasses" of bad people. All believers have to do is recall Jesus' words from the cross: "Father, forgive them, for they know not what they do."[27]

This represented Witherspoon's finest statement on loving others. His other directives to love one's neighbor could be grouped under the heading of charity. He was specific in what the pious should do: feed the hungry, clothe the naked, care for the poor, widows, and orphans. Scripture dictated such charity, namely, Matthew 25:34–36, "For I was an hungred, and ye gave me meat." The preacher could be jarring when he challenged his parishioners by asking, "What have you done for the good of others? How often have you relieved the necessitous, comforted the distressed, instructed the ignorant, admonished the negligent, punished or restrained the profane?"[28]

If we are tempted to ask why Witherspoon did not show more compassion, and on more occasions emphasize the need for believers to love their neighbor, the answer is both theological and scriptural. Briefly stated, his theology was directed to the glory of God, not ministry to others or to society. He read Jesus' words about the moral law literally. It stated that the *first* commandment was, "Thou shalt love the Lord thy God." Witherspoon had already made this point, loudly and clearly. The second commandment could not be ignored, but it does follow the first.

The last aspect of the "after walk" is how persons of piety should cope with the world outside the circle of faith. Witherspoon had already observed that piety by example is highly effective because it makes a statement of faith to those of no faith. He had also, figuratively speaking, identified the last stage of sanctification as somehow leaving the world and lifting one's eyes heavenward. In two successive sermons, both bearing the title, "The World Crucified by the Cross of Christ" (Gal. 6:14), he made his fullest statement of Christ's recommendation to show "contempt for the world."[29]

First, though his heart was not in it, he tried to demonstrate that there is some good in the world. The natural world is good; the "whole frame of nature," he goes so far as to say in a burst of hyperbole, is "perfectly faultless." One wonders how he can overlook storms, floods, droughts, volcanic eruptions, and other natural disasters. But he does. He continues by stating that the world is good because it is the locus for God's providential acts and mercies. Lastly, the world is good, or good enough, for Christians to live and do their duty in it. Therefore, it is a serious error to run from the world, "to place religion in voluntary poverty, in monkish austerity, or uncommanded maceration of the body. This is not doing, but deserting our duty . . . not overcoming the world, but flying from it."[30] Nevertheless, if Christians are to remain in the world, they are to hold it, so to say, at a long arm's length. Of course, Witherspoon hungered for the ideal Christian society. Yet despite the efforts of individual believers or the established church to try to accomplish it, and he never said that they should, the ideal remains unattainable. He never advocated measures or invented strategies by which society as a whole could be redeemed. The natural world might be perfectly faultless and God's providence might prevail, but human society was unredeemed. For Witherspoon, that was a given. It was this kind of a world that Christians must shun, casting their eyes heavenward.

What is wrong with the world? Plenty. First, there are those despicable temptations, three in particular: *riches*, which engender "oppression of others, sensuality of temper, and forgetfulness of eternity"; *honors*, including power, that "tends to intoxicate the mind" and downgrade humility; and *pleasures* with their dangerous appetites, which, one should beware, steal upon one secretly and at last enslave one absolutely! Witherspoon brought the message home to Paisley, for he admitted he was beginning to worry about the increasing population and improving economy of the city, that this apparent good fortune would bring with it the "danger of the introduction of a worldly spirit by the rising generation." The lesson was that temptations could be found almost anywhere.[31]

Another reason to shun the world was its spirit of vanity. He returned for a moment to the sin of vanity, but developed the idea further by associating vanity with the acquisition of worldly goods as the means of assuring human happiness and peace. Clearly, this kind of vanity must be avoided, though Witherspoon is forced to admit that "the world, *in a certain proportion* [italics mine], is indeed necessary to us." His answer to the question of how much that proportion should be is unsatisfactory. On the one hand, he seems to give approval to the idea that God will decide for each person what the correct proportion of worldly goods will be. Just leave it to God, and do not give it another thought. It almost goes without saying that this is an amazing justification for never moving from one's place on the social scale or the economic ladder. On the other hand, in the same sermon Witherspoon recognizes that each person will have to struggle to determine the proper amount of goods that strikes a balance between shunning the world yet living in it. There is no easy answer.[32]

At last the preacher proposes some positive steps that true believers could adopt to keep from selling out to the world. He advises continual vigilance so that they would be able to identify worldly temptations when they saw them, and continual prayer for strength to resist them. Ponder the temporality of material things, and the fleeting nature of the "schemes of ambition," "political struggles," and "contests for power." These, like the frivolous amusements of children, shall soon pass, he opines. His final advice is to have low hopes and expectations of the world, and then we will not be disappointed when we discover that "it hath little comfort to give." Church members might still have hoped for more precise directions on how to live in and yet not be of the world, but they could not fault their minister for refusing to take on the problem and not passing on some advice, a portion of which at least might prove useful.[33]

The Exercises of Piety

Princeton University sociologist Robert Wuthnow has observed that practice-oriented spirituality is different from seeker-oriented spirituality in that the former provides "a more orderly, disciplined, and focused approach to the sacred." He continues by noting that spiritual practices prompt individuals "to take responsibility for their own spiritual development by spending time working on it, . . . seeking to understand the sacred through reading and the counsel of others, and seeking to have contact with the sacred through personal reflection and prayer."[34] In this view the "exercises of piety" become matters of great moment. Witherspoon thought so too. He had three names for those religious activities associated with piety: religious duties, exercises of piety, and ordinances. The first two were broadly conceived, and included both public and private worship, while ordinances were restricted to the several parts of public worship.[35] In his sermons he had little or nothing to say about such items of public worship as the reading of the Bible and the singing of psalms, but much about the sermon and the sacraments. Incidentally, we are limited in what we know about his thoughts on worship, either public or private. He left no treatises on worship, manuals, diaries, prayers, or poetry that might serve as guidance or models for others to follow. All we can assume is that he followed the general outlines provided in the Westminster Directory for the Public Worship of God (1645).[36] What he does convey is the importance of both public and private worship. Worship followed naturally, logically, from one's inner disposition. If Christians truly loved God above all, they would from that love burst forth into praise and thanksgiving. Knowing themselves to be dependent creatures, they would honor their Creator. As sinners redeemed and renewed, they would worship God unceasingly with hearts grateful for their salvation. Worship was no "add-on"; it was fundamental. It was inextricably linked to the other parts of piety, and was the means of undergirding and sustaining a life of piety.

The Sabbath

Worship in the Church of Scotland was a function of the Sabbath. Ministers and lay people who read the Confession knew that from the beginning of the world to the time of Christ, the seventh day of the week was called the Sabbath. After the resurrection of

Christ, the day of rest and worship, the first day of the week, was to be called the Lord's Day or the Christian Sabbath. Witherspoon was merely adhering to the custom of the time by naming the Lord's Day the Sabbath. He knew the biblical basis for the Sabbath—the Creator resting on the Sabbath (Gen. 2:3) and the commandment to keep the Sabbath holy (Ex. 2:8)—and he assumed his parishioners did too.

Sabbath observance may have been somewhat relaxed among the Moderates, but the general observance of the day for most of Scotland required a cessation from all work, from normal activities and forms of recreation. The time was to be spent in public worship, quiet walks, family talk, and private devotion (in Witherspoon's phrase, "duties of the closet"). He can rightly be called a Sabbatarian if the word is limited to one who holds to the Christian Sabbath and complies with strict rules of behavior. He was not a Sabbatarian if the word means an obsession with strict Sabbath observance and much scolding about it. He never laid down rules for keeping the Sabbath, though he had some in his head when on a few occasions he denounced Sabbath-breaking in Scotland and America.[37] He was sensitive to criticism in his day from those who thought strict Sabbath observance was boring, dreary, and repressive. So he seized the opportunity to praise the attitude of new converts who might "from their heart, call the Sabbath 'a delight, the holy of the Lord, and honorable.'"[38]

Witherspoon came close to proscribing one activity for the Sabbath in his "Letters on Education," articles that he wrote in 1775 on religious education of children for the *Pennsylvania Magazine*. There he advised parents not to weaken standards in dealing with their children and to be sure to make religious practices habitual. An issue had arisen requiring his advice: the legitimacy of visiting friends on the Lord's Day. He advised against this kind of gadding about and paying private visits, citing two dangers. First, such visits would interrupt family time and private devotion, and second, it would be difficult "to guard effectively against improper subjects of conversation." He regarded these Sunday social conversations as powerful diversions, trivial at best and corrupt at their worst! "The vain and unprofitable, and sometimes sinful conversation, that prevails in such cases, must greatly weaken, or entirely obliterate any serious impressions, made upon your mind, during the [morning] service of the sanctuary."[39]

The Church

Witherspoon thought the church was essential, but he designed no ecclesiology, no theology of the church, in his sermons and essays. Indeed, he had little to say about the church. He appeared to concur with the Confession in the distinction between the universal invisible church, consisting of the elect and known only to God, and the catholic visible church, made up of true Christians throughout the world.[40] In his few statements about the church, his interest in the visible church focused on the established Church of Scotland. In a sermon on prayer, he entreated his hearers, "Be earnest in your supplication, and importunate in your pleading for the church of Christ, and the glory of his kingdom, especially in your native country. . . . The languishing state of religion in this nation, and the threatening aspect of Providence, should press us to this duty." Nevertheless, the eventual fate of the church lies not in the hands of ordinary mortals but "in the power of God." He observed that the emblem and motto for the Church of Scotland comprise a forceful symbol: a burning bush that is not consumed (Ex. 3:1–6). The truth buried in that symbol is that God's power is never undone.[41]

The church—"Christ's mystical body," Witherspoon once called it—is a vital aid to piety. It is where very good things happen to good and pious people. He remarked, "Even as members of the visible church we are servants of God, born in his house, baptized in his name, favored with the light of the gospel, blessed with clearness and fullness of instruction, animated by eminent and shining examples."

A further point, obvious to most Protestants, is that the church is composed of laity as well as clergy. The reason for declaring this truth is that in his judgment there was too much favoritism being shown to the clergy in the Church of Scotland. He alleged that when the word church (*ecclesia*) was used in the New Testament, it hardly ever meant the church leaders exclusively. It was an inclusive term, bringing together clergy and laity.[42]

Public Worship

Witherspoon may have failed to develop a theology of the church, but that did not mean he regarded the church as incidental to the life of a Christian. Its existence was essential, a sine qua non for piety. It is the only place where regular public worship can be celebrated— and vital public worship is critical to the growth of piety.

Humans were not created to live in isolation, contended Witherspoon. Individual worship is acceptable and necessary, but "social worship" is even more appealing to God (see Matt. 18:19, 20; Ps. 87:2). God has established his church and created an ordered ministry. It is through the church that he communicates his will and guarantees his presence; his people, therefore, must attend instituted worship where God's word will be read and heard. It bears repeating that the sermon was the central act of public worship, and that Witherspoon's biblical sermons were crucial for building up the piety of those in the pew.[43]

Public worship afforded the author of piety to look away from this world to the one above. More than once he viewed public worship on earth not as a final expression within itself, but as a beginning, a preparation for eternal life with God—as he phrased it, "the earnest of our future inheritance [preparing] us for his immediate presence hereafter." Worship in heaven, beginning here on earth, encompasses four distinct acts—adoration, gratitude, desire (desire of "the glory and excellence of God"), and trust and subjection, in a word, obedience.[44]

In Witherspoon's judgment, religion was languishing in Scotland. He continued to be concerned about this condition, and he knew what was causing it: "careless, formal, heartless worship," "indifferent, slothful, disdainful hearing the word," and "the neglect of prayer." This national spiritual malaise nagged at him and sorely tried his patience. He confessed that he had tirelessly hammered home criticism of lifeless worship, but he said every one of the warnings was needed. He complained, "I have often . . . put you in mind of the fatal effects of a heartless, customary, formal worship: it is provoking to God, pernicious to others, hardening to the heart, and ruining to the soul."[45]

He could be sharply censorious in his denunciation of impious worship and worshipers. In a sermon on obedience and sacrifice, quoting John 4:23, 24 ("God is a spirit; and they that worship him, must worship him in spirit and in truth"), the preacher lashed out:

> Are there not some who rest in the form of worship, and are strangers to the spirit of it? . . . How many sinful motives may bring us to the house of God! If you come to avoid the reproach of men, is that a real sacrifice to God? If you come from ostentation, to be seen of men, is that an offering acceptable to God?

If you come to gratify your fancy, by hearing the performance of man, you are offering the incense to the creature that is due only to God. Consider further, how often we may be sinfully employed in the house of God. Are careless inattentive persons offering acceptable sacrifices to God? Are those who indulge vain, proud, sensual, covetous thoughts in worship, offering sacrifices to God? Are those who come to censure or admire the speaker, offering sacrifice to God?[46]

Many, perhaps most of the congregation, must have felt thoroughly shamed. In order to amend their ways, these inattentive irreverent worshipers must come to church and bring to the work of worship all that attention, reverence, and love that "the sacred and important truths of the everlasting gospel" altogether deserve! Further, such recalcitrants must concentrate on the infinite glory and majesty of God, and equally on the unspeakable condescension of that God in bestowing the unsearchable riches of his grace on the sinner. Then, only then, will they begin to worship God in the way they should, in spirit and in truth.[47]

Sacraments

Once more Witherspoon followed the custom of the time and the wording of the Confession in designating the sacraments of Baptism and the Lord's Supper as "seals of the covenant." This seventeenth-century Reformed theological term states that Christ and the benefits of the covenant of grace are, in the sacraments, communicated and made real, sealed as it were, in the lives of believers. We can be reasonably certain that the Shorter Catechism definition of a sacrament ("A sacrament is a holy ordinance instituted by Christ, wherein, by sensible signs, Christ and the benefits of the new covenant are represented, sealed, and applied to believers") would be familiar to Witherspoon's parishioners, which would explain why he never supplied a definition.[48] What he does offer is his appreciation of the sacraments, especially the Lord's Supper, as building blocks for constructing personal piety. The sacraments make Christ and his saving work real to worshipers; the sacraments draw worshipers close to God and deepen their love for God.

The references to baptism are few and brief, and only one of them touches directly on theological concerns. Witherspoon supported infant baptism on the grounds that children belong within

God's covenant. After baptism they become members of the visible church and as such are "relatively holy," he explained, until they attain full church membership. For biblical evidence he went to the Old Testament to find occasions when children were given a blessing: There was circumcision, a sign of God's grace, administered to male infants. Also, he argued, the influence of pious parents upon their children brought them within the reach of the promise. And one must not overlook the record of the patriarch Jacob formally blessing his grandsons (Gen. 48:8–20). As we might expect, Witherspoon failed to find any direct evidence for infant baptism in the New Testament.[49]

His one complaint about how infant baptism was practiced in the Kirk sounds strangely modern. Witherspoon lamented the fact that among many persons baptism took on a semimagical quality, namely, that some parents who "have not a credible profession of faith in Christ" wanted their children baptized nonetheless. Criticism of the minister often resulted when he refused to baptize the infant of unbelievers; it was said that he could thus be the cause of "an injury to the child, besides other bad consequences sometimes pretended." Witherspoon responded by explaining carefully that sacraments were not grace by themselves, only the means of it and they belong to believers alone. It is a remnant of "Popish superstition," he commented, "to look upon the sacraments as spells, or charms, which have some effect independent of the exercise of faith in the receiver." He concluded the matter by pointing out that infants have a right to receive the sign of baptism and will gain real benefit from it only if they are the children of "those who believe sincerely."[50]

The Lord's Supper was far more effective than baptism in helping to turn sinners into forgiven sinners and (re)uniting humans with the divine. Even so, Witherspoon fell short of composing anything like a comprehensive theology of the Lord's Supper. Two emphases do stand out in the seven "action sermons" so labeled (and the two that are not so identified) in his *Works*.[51] The first is the atonement, the ultimate sacrifice of Christ, and the second is the benefits received by those who have faith in Christ and receive the sacrament.

In a long rhetorical plea bringing to a close the action sermon, "Redemption the Subject of Admiration to the Angels," Witherspoon highlighted the richness of divine grace shown forth in the sacrament: "Think, with humble amazement, on the boundless

mercy of God, which reached even to you. . . . Dwell on this impen-
etrable mystery of 'Immanuel God with us'—'God manifested in the
flesh.' Think on this awful proof of divine justice and holiness, the
wrath of God poured out upon his own Son. Think on the perfection of that atonement which is made for the sins of the world."[52]

Witherspoon was not unique in his estimate of the importance of
the Lord's Supper in the life of a Christian. Large impressive out-
door Communion festivals, usually lasting several days, were a feature of church life in eighteenth-century Scotland. Called "the
Action," they often attracted several thousand communicants who
might have traveled great distances to hear sermons from visiting
ministers that began on Thursday and concluded on Monday, and to
receive the sacrament on Sunday. The considerable literary output
on the subject of the Lord's Supper by John Willison (1680–1750),
an evangelical minister from Dundee, is yet another example of the
significant place the Lord's Supper occupied in lay piety of the
period.[53]

It will be valuable to mine for theological and devotional truth
one sermon in which Witherspoon preached directly on the sacrament, "The Believer Going to God as His Exceeding Joy."[54] His
first point is that worshipers ought to go to God in the Lord's Supper as their exceeding joy because in the sacrament they will receive
the fullest assurance of forgiveness and peace with God: "His blessed
body was broken, and his precious blood was shed, for the remission
of sins." In true Reformed language he did not state that in Communion Christ's sacrifice was repeated; he did say that it was com-
memorated, that is, to be called to remembrance, and that the
elements of bread and wine were "the visible signs and the appointed
seals" of that sacrifice.[55]

Another reason for believers going to God in the sacrament is to
appreciate divine love to the fullest extent. Be aware of all that God
is, but be aware that God's love is "the most conspicuous of all." And
that love, as Witherspoon repeats what he has said so many times
previously, is what makes possible God's greatest gift to us, his Son
(John 3:16; Rom. 5:8; 8:32). There was only one way to express an
uncommon degree of love, and God chose that way. In the Lord's
Supper we are captured and held by that love.

A special reason for going to God in this ordinance is to understand what God's providence means. In this dimension we can
express our gratitude for favors already received and be bold

enough to ask for more. There are, Witherspoon stipulates, two kinds of blessings that we need and that God will supply. These are the wonderful benefits that the sacrament provides, and the list is a long one. First, there are spiritual blessings—hearts inflamed with the love of God, sins mortified, faith strengthened, the conscience pacified, lusts deadened, and sanctification realized. The last spiritual blessing communicants receive at the Table is a victory. Believers "confident of their Saviour's power, get their feet upon the necks of their enemies, and say, 'I can do all things through Christ strengthening me.'"[56]

A second set of blessings are the material ones. Here Witherspoon might have considered the physicality of the bread and wine and how they are put to a sacred use in the sacrament, symbolizing how the earthly can be transformed into the spiritual. He never thought this way, however, concentrating instead on the providence of God. The communicant is to see providence in the bread and wine, and then to acknowledge that it is from God's hand that we receive food, clothing, and all necessary provisions for sustaining life. Additionally, God's care will enable us to withstand suffering when we are beaten down by "the blows and buffets of adverse fortune," and even to escape from the suffering itself if God wills it.

There is one final blessing, the ultimate one. Witherspoon sees believers' joy extending right through death to heaven itself. Thus, he affirms the eschatological dimension of the Lord's Supper—for the community and for the individual. The sacrament is a lively foretaste of that eternal happiness in heaven that God has prepared for the pious. It is the logical and glorious conclusion to the salvation that God has provided, and the fulfillment of that communion with God that has begun for the faithful here on earth. What is heaven? Witherspoon ponders. He answers his query by accenting the spiritual blessings to be enjoyed rather than any physical ones: freedom from sin; freedom from the earthly plane where misery, sorrow, and wretchedness are often to be seen; freedom to contemplate the glory of an infinite God, to see "the glorious Saviour standing at the right hand of God, surrounded by ten thousand of his saints"; and finally, freedom to "serve our God and Redeemer with the same spirit and joy as the angels do in heaven."[57]

Witherspoon is little concerned with how the presence of Christ in the bread and wine can be explained. It was as if the sixteenth-century Protestant-Catholic contest over the doctrine of transubstantiation (the belief that the very substance of the bread and wine are changed into the substance of Christ's body and blood) had long been settled and did not need to be repeated. He was content to accept the Reformed teaching that Christ was "really, but spiritually" present in the sacrament, and then preach on the Lord's Supper with a personal devotional intention. His chief aim was to bypass theological refinement in the cause of enriching the lives of Christians and making them truly pious. The practical benefit of the sacrament was of first importance.

That said, Witherspoon lifted up the sufferings of Christ for those coming to the Communion table. This was the way he chose to make Christ immediate and real:

> The sufferings of Christ, then, ought to be ever present to the mind of the believer. . . . The institution of the Lord's supper had the remembrance of Christ's sufferings as its direct and immediate intention; I Cor. 11:24, 25, 26. . . . Remember his agony in the garden. . . . Remember him seized by the treachery of one of his own disciples; . . . dragged to the tribunal of an unrighteous judge; . . . severely scourged; blindfolded, buffeted, and spit upon; . . . Remember that spotless victim, the Lamb of God, stretched upon a cross, and nailed to the accursed tree.[58]

It is the suffering Christ that one must meet at the Table with open eyes and open heart, to be received by faith. Witherspoon's exhortations are all directed toward a deepening and strengthening of faith as one attends and then departs from the celebration of the Lord's Supper. Faith, of course, is accompanied by gratitude. We ought to "surrender ourselves to God, at once to increase our present gratitude and promote our future steadfastness in the paths of obedience."[59]

As the communicants departed from the sacrament and reflected on God's mercies, Witherspoon challenged them with words that suggest a kind of litany:

> Take him for your portion; place your happiness in his favor. . . . Resolve to serve him with your body and spirit which are his, serve him sincerely. . . . Serve him with zeal, espouse his interest, plead his cause[s] . . . promote his glory. Put your trust in his providence. . . . Let him dispose of you freely.[60]

Witherspoon's devotional interest in the Lord's Supper corresponded with his evangelical understanding of Christianity. The Lord's Supper was a seal of saving grace, and as such incorporated the basic doctrine found in the everlasting truths of the gospel, the substance of the faith of each Christian. It was no wonder, therefore, that he could claim that "no one circumstance has contributed more to preserve the pure uncorrupted doctrine of the gospel, than the sacrament of the Lord's Supper."[61] High praise, indeed!

Private Worship

In a sermon in which he dwells upon the worship of the saints in heaven ("The Happiness of the Saints in Heaven"), Witherspoon criticizes those saints on earth who neglect the worship of God, especially in their homes. Unless these earthly saints mend their ways, they may never have the privilege of engaging in heavenly worship, he warns. Those who knew Witherspoon intimately testified to his own "daily devotions of the closet," alone and with his family. At other times, too, there were occasions of fasting and prayer within the home.[62]

The responsibility for conducting family worship fell to the male head of the household, so he was guilty of the greater sin if he omitted or slighted private religious exercises. Witherspoon regarded family worship to be so central to a life of piety that a neglect of it called for an imprecation: "Wo shall be to that man, who is too busy, too proud, or too modest, to worship, in his family, the King of kings, and Lord of lords."[63] Not only did the head of the house have a responsibility; both parents were expected to pray for the temporal and spiritual well-being of their children.[64] Family worship in eighteenth-century Presbyterian Scotland was generally thought to be so vital to a life of piety that both for lay people and for ministers, the "duties of the closet" were obligatory. In many country homes and city flats there was a small room or closet where the head of the family and others could go for private devotions.[65] Family worship, consisting of Bible reading and prayer, possibly some psalm-singing, was usually held twice a day. Other religious activities in the home included instructing the children in the Shorter Catechism, and Bible reading by everyone. Witherspoon advised extensive Bible reading because, as he said (quoting in part 2 Tim. 3:6), scripture is profitable for doctrine, reproof, correction—and necessary for conviction. Only real Christians, he remarked another time, those who are mature in their spiritual life, know the "promise of strength and assistance contained in the scriptures."[66] Family members should engage in meditation too, but this activity was not as high on his list of religious exercises as some others. Christ's sufferings should not be "strangers to your meditations," he wrote, nor should you fail "to seat yourselves, in the immediate presence of God."[67] This is good spiritual advice, of course, but he had no suggestion of a discipline by which one reached the immediate presence of God. He knew that there was value in solitude for the life of the spirit. In our day, Catholic writer Henri Nouwen has stated that it is virtually impossible to be a person of piety without solitude. He admits that developing a discipline of solitude is not easy for modern men and women, so he proposes, as did Witherspoon, that concentrating on the words of the Bible can help in focusing our attention on the divine presence. Scripture can form a safe anchor when we are caught in a stormy sea of wandering thoughts and distractions. Likewise, after spending time in residence at a Benedictine monastery, Presbyterian poet and writer Kathleen Norris reported that she had incorporated her own routine of *lectio divina* (monastic holy reading of the Bible) into her daily exercises of piety.[68]

"It seems plainly an essential character of true piety, to be given to prayer." This was Witherspoon's way of saying that prayer, like Bible reading, was indispensable. He even committed a surprising grammatical error by resorting to a double superlative to make his point, saying that prayer was "a duty of the most absolute necessity." To expound the meaning of prayer and the place it should hold in the life of piety, he wrote two sermons on the topic and treated prayer directly in three others. He started with the basic assumption that piety needs prayer![69]

His admonitions commence with the general and practical advice to be often and diligent in secret prayer. Secret prayer has a direct benefit because the more you converse with God in secret, he asserts, the more powerfully and profitably you will be able to speak to people in public. At first glance, this seems like a crass instrumental reason for praying. What he wants to stress is that there is no need to burden others with personal needs, problems, and weaknesses. Instead, take them to God, who can do something about them. God will hear you and make you strong. God "can effectually help you."[70] His pragmatic emphasis continues. Prayers do not always have to be framed in high-flown phrases or contain lofty sentiments. They can be simple and concrete. It is "lawful" to ask God's blessing on your labors, or for recovery from illness, or for deliverance from other forms of distress.[71] However, while your prayers may be simple, sincere, and specific, do not expect that God will always grant your petitions "in hand, or in your own time and measure." God is God, an infinitely wise God, who knows best what is for your good and who may have valid reasons for not answering your prayers when and how you would like. In this matter it is quite enough to put your trust in God.[72]

Overall, Witherspoon views prayer as activist and intensive, not as a quietist or passive occupation. Prayer is neither a tranquil waiting nor a solitary silence. If the kneeling supplicant comes up against spiritual blocks, he or she must go to work and overcome them. Some of these may be a sense of guilt, calamities or the "rod of correction" inflicted by a "frowning Providence," strong temptations, a weak faith, spiritual laziness, and impatience with God's answers to prayers. These roadblocks should never cause spiritual wayfarers to slow their journey or turn back. They are to take as their model Jacob wrestling with the angel of God (Gen. 32:24–30). As the two sermons entitled "Fervency and Importunity in Prayer" unfold, it is plain that when Witherspoon advocates wrestling with God, he does not mean an angry, literal, verbal wrestling. Christians are not to have an actual knockdown fight with God. Rather, he makes two points to those listeners in the pew: First, prayer is no easy pastime. It draws on the will, it demands effort to overcome obstacles, it is a struggle if it is true prayer. Even the minister in the Sunday morning service was to demonstrate wrestling in his long opening prayer. Prayers are not made up of a string of words that the petitioner rattles off hoping that the Deity will pick up a few here and there. Prayer is serious business, hard work. The other point he wishes to make is that wrestling with God is not only allowed but encouraged, as long as believers keep in mind that they are inferior and God is superior. Wrestling with God means baring one's soul, even arguing with God, but always addressing the high and holy One with integrity and respect and no undue familiarity. In this way, wrestling is a form of talking back to God—with fervency and importunity, but with respect, as difficult as this may be to uphold. Some biblical commentators might interpret Genesis 32 as a struggle between Jacob and God, or God's representative, as equal combatants. Not

Witherspoon. He refuses to upset the divine-human imbalance by offering such an interpretation. God's sovereignty must remain inviolable.

Having said that, it was necessary for Witherspoon to clear up some misunderstandings. First, those who say it is wrong to wrestle with God must be corrected. They have forgotten that God wants genuine intercourse with his people, and at the right time, in the right way, and in the right situation even wants them "to offer a holy violence to him."[73] At first glance, "holy violence" would seem to be an oxymoron, but this is Witherspoon's unusual way of counseling respectful back talk to God. Next, he has more to say about a respectful approach to God. Indecent familiarity is forbidden, as is "any trifling, slovenly, or ridiculous manner of addressing . . . the throne of grace." He will abide no familiar "Hey God now listen here" form of address in wrestling with the divine. There are certain conventions that must be upheld. An acknowledgment of the glory and majesty of God comes first, followed by "plain and ardent expressions of the very temper of the soul." Finally, the preacher tells his people to pray fervently for the right things—for the improvement of their own spiritual life, for the church of Christ and the Church of Scotland, for the power of God to inform the approaching communion, and for all ministers of the gospel.[74]

Today, far removed from Witherspoon's time and experience, Jewish writer and Holocaust survivor Elie Wiesel has captured the spirit of faithful wrestling with God. He denies the accusation some have made that as a result of his Auschwitz experience he has renounced his faith in God. He supplies his own understanding of "plain and ardent expressions of the soul":

> I have risen against His justice, protested His silence and sometimes His absence, but my anger rises up within faith and not outside it. I admit that this is hardly an original position. It is part of Jewish tradition. . . . Abraham and Moses, Jeremiah and Rebbe Levi-Yitzhak of Berdichev teach us that it is permissible for man to accuse God, provided it be done in the name of faith in God. If that hurts, so be it. Sometimes we must accept the pain of faith so as not to lose it.[75]

Witherspoon would have understood that.

"Nothing can be said stronger on the benefit of wrestling with God, than that we shall assuredly prevail." This is Witherspoon's affirmation that prayer works.[76] It worked for Jacob; he got his blessing. It will work for latter-day Christians too. Even before we ever get to the question of how God answers prayers, fervent prayer puts us in the proper mental and spiritual frame. It prepares us for the reception of God's mercies. And God *will* answer prayer. Success is promised. The Bible tells us so.[77] The way Witherspoon reads his Bible, every command to pray in the Bible contains within it a promise of an answer from God. God will answer, but it is God who decides how and when the answer will be forthcoming. Lastly, to preserve and improve one's spiritual life Witherspoon recommends intercessory prayer. Prayer for others "has the most powerful influence in warming the heart, and enlivening the affections." We can do no better than imitate Jesus on the cross, who even prayed for his executioners.[78]

Summary

We have gathered more than enough evidence to conclude that the piety Witherspoon preached to his congregations was a doctrinal one contained in the four doctrines, which he called the everlasting truths of the gospel. What this meant was that to become a pious person, a true or real Christian—and he was constantly making that distinction—was in the first instance to agree, perhaps even unconsciously, that theology was important. To be pious meant that on some level one had to think theologically, to know the meaning of those four doctrines. The next step, following hard on the first, was to believe those doctrines with one's intellect, of course, but even more, with "the consent and approbation of the heart." Outward assent to the beliefs amounted to very little if not accompanied by inner conviction. The Faith needed the "lively exercise of faith."

As we have discovered, these core beliefs were rooted in the federal theology of the Westminster Confession of Faith, in the Shorter Catechism, and in the *Christian Theology* of Bénédict Pictet. Those sources were the immediate theological predecessors of Witherspoon, albeit largely unacknowledged by him. His theology, embodied in the special truths he named, belongs to a longer tradition, that of Calvin and even back to Augustine in the fifth century. In Witherspoon's treatment of human sin, God's grace, predestination, and justification, he owed a debt not only to Calvin but to Augustine, though he hardly mentions either. He did not seek authority for his doctrines in the ideas of great theologians but in the Bible itself. Scriptural proof was sufficient, which explains the multitude of biblical references in each sermon and the paucity of quotations from or references to some of the great Christian thinkers of the past. The four great truths, standing on the authority of the Bible, were, Witherspoon reminds his hearers and readers, "to be clearly explained, strongly inculcated, and frequently repeated."[79] These truths, he asserted repeatedly, constituted the essence of the Christian faith and the very heart of piety.

If his was a doctrinal piety, it was a selective doctrinal piety. Only a few doctrines were thought to be essential. There were, in fact, several key doctrines in the Confession and in Pictet's theology that were preeminent in their own right and belonged legitimately to a full expression of the Christian faith but that received short shrift in Witherspoon's rendition of piety; to name several: decrees, adoption, perseverance of the saints, or for that matter, inspiration of Bible, Trinity, creation, resurrection and the final judgment.[80] This is not to say that these were insignificant, that he said nothing about one or more of them, or that he did not deal with some of them in his "Lectures on Divinity," for instance. It is to say that in his estimation these were not the eternal truths basic to the formation of Christian holiness, that is, the making of a pious person.

Piety for the pew was also evangelical—in the sense that each Christian must experience a new birth, that profound transformation from the state of sin to a life of faith, in a word, regeneration. We have seen how Jesus' death on the cross was believed to be the means by which salvation occurs. It bears repeating here that in the sermons under study Jesus is portrayed almost exclusively as a savior, whose life, as it were, began on Maundy Thursday and ended late on Good Friday. Witherspoon himself phrases it best: "But as every thing else was only introductory and preparatory to his atonement, or consequent upon it, I shall direct your attention to him as a Saviour."[81] Jesus is not depicted as Example, Teacher, Healer, or even Miracle Worker; his birth, boyhood, journeys, interaction with individuals, and many of his sayings receive little or no attention in Witherspoon's sermons. His earlier life and ministry, as well as his resurrection, postresurrection appearances, and ascension, are but prelude and postlude to his saving work on the cross. Surely Witherspoon can be commended for his unfailing concentration on Jesus the Savior, for such is the core of the Christian religion. At the same time, however, he has to be criticized for limiting so severely the person and work of Jesus, for excluding the richness of his earthly life, his ministries of teaching and healing, the auspicious beginning to his life, and its triumphant ending. Witherspoon should have reread some of the sixteenth-century Reformers such as Calvin and Luther; in so doing he might have been prompted to develop a richer Christology.

It is worth reiterating that Witherspoon's piety was practical, not that it guaranteed direct material benefits to the believer, but that the truly pious person exhibited an "after walk" and a lifestyle that was the outward expression of the person's inner disposition.[82] Witherspoon went straight to the two commandments of the moral law when he once tried to say what practical religion was: "Love to God, and love to man, make up the sum of practical religion."[83] Christianity was a practical religion, for it made a difference in the way believers lived their lives, treated other persons, and conducted their business in the world. Theology matters, both in personal spiritual journeys and in the way believers behave in public. Witherspoon was, of course, repeating what other Reformed thinkers have said. Theologian Brian Gerrish has noted that the "Reformed habit of mind has always been unabashedly practical," and he quotes Calvin on the duty of a theologian, which "is not to tickle the ear, but confirm the conscience, by teaching what is true, certain, and useful." Centuries earlier, the famous John Chrysostom struck the balance between inner disposition and outward practice when he noted that "nothing is so important as to keep an exact proportion between the interior source of virtue and the external practice of it."[84] In a passage perceptive of the way he viewed the interaction between faith and works, Witherspoon wrote:

> It is a fatal, though a common error to separate them; entirely to confine religion to the times and places of immediate worship, and suppose it hath nothing to do with the maxims of trade and commerce, or other worldly callings. On the contrary, your impressions of things spiritual and eternal, will direct and regulate your views as to the present life; and your success or misfortunes in worldly schemes, will have a certain and visible effect upon your Christian conversation, and the state of your souls.[85]

Witherspoon's piety was outward looking, not inner-directed. Christians were to live by faith, knowing what and in whom they believed, being in the world and yet not overcome by the world. Their piety was not to be informed by some spiritual rule or discipline, nor was the goal to escape from or shut out this world in order to dwell in the ineffable presence of the divine. It was very much a down-to-earth piety.

It might seem as though Witherspoon's piety for lay people is a finished product, a complete document that needs no codicil, no "declaratory statement" to keep it up-to-date. He has defined piety at some length. One has the impression that if he were somehow to appear in our day, he might feel constrained to make a few changes in wording, but not in the constituent elements of his piety. Those remain; those are everlasting. However, as final as it might seem, he has not actually spoken his last word. He had more to say about piety, this time about the piety that belonged not to those sitting in the pew but those who stood in the pulpit. In Scotland, but even more so in America, Witherspoon found himself thinking about piety for the preacher.

Part Two

Piety for Those in the Pulpit

Chapter Three

Real Religion for a Minister

> One of the most essentially necessary, and most exten-
> sively useful qualifications of a good minister, is, that he
> have a firm belief of that Gospel he is called to preach, and
> a lively sense of religion upon his own heart.
>
> *Works, 2:286.*

On at least two occasions, at Largs in 1748 and Paisley in 1758, Witherspoon was asked to preach at the ordination of a young man to the ministry of the Church of Scotland.[1] The most important advice he could give to new ministers was to look inward to make certain that they were "born again." Everything else they might do or become would hinge on this one fact, that they were "united to Christ by faith." This was basic to a minister's calling and integrity. He stated it concisely: "It is a difficult thing, and it is a dreadful thing, to preach an unknown Saviour." Although he would later advise that ministers know much theology and the several branches of literature and science, the initial virtue that must be possessed was the "inward persuasion of the great truths of the everlasting Gospel." If nothing else, the text for the sermon, "Ministerial Character and Duty," affirmed that one of the essential and most useful qualifications of a good minister was that "he have a firm belief of that Gospel he is called to preach, and a lively sense of religion upon his own heart."

To make this truth vivid, Witherspoon goes to sea for his illustration. To undertake a dangerous voyage, he explains, any sensible person would, if there were a choice, board a vessel commanded by an experienced captain, not by one who had just finished a navigation course on shore. By analogy then, laypersons worried about their souls will choose a minister "who appears to have the wisdom to save his own."[2] But the truly pious cleric had better have more than "appearance" as a recommendation; he had better make sure that he has the real thing. Witherspoon warns, "A minister is as much liable to self-deceit as any other, and in some respects more so." Therefore, ministers should not be fooled into thinking that they possess true religion because they are frequently thinking and speaking of holy things. Piety for the person in the pulpit requires, first of all, that the preacher have an authentic inward conviction of Jesus as the Savior.[3]

The next thing, coming hard on the heels of the first, is a belief in and proclamation of the four gospel truths. Readers of the *Works* should not expect otherwise, for if these truths were basic for lay piety, they are downright critical for the clergy. For emphasis, Witherspoon lists each of them in the "Charge" to the new minister in 1748, and then complains forthwith that he has heard reports that among some clergy these great doctrines were being "either flatly contradicted, or kept entirely out of view, and something else substituted in their place." He hopes that this is not a universal problem, and of course it should not be, he declares, since these doctrines are clearly stated in "the Confession of Faith, which every minister in Scotland has subscribed." Now his anger begins to boil and the reader senses that in Witherspoon's judgment, these truths are, in fact, being compromised. These doctrines are so crucial to a minister's work and to the life of the Kirk that his anger spills over at last and he is moved to declare to the ordinand and to the congregation and clergy present at the service of ordination: "If, therefore, there be any one among us, who doth not preach [them], he is guilty of perjury of the worst kind, for which I know no excuse. Such a person is not only chargeable with departing from the faith, but with an absolute prostitution of conscience, and a whole life of hypocrisy and deceit."[4] Harsh words these, but they signal the importance he attributed to the truths as essential for ministry and clerical piety.

Pondering this outburst even for a minute makes it obvious that Witherspoon's concern is both doctrinal and ethical. It is his way of getting into the subject of professional integrity in a minister's preaching. To preach these truths, especially to announce to sinners, who would be prone to stop their ears, that they are wicked and need to be saved, takes courage and requires integrity. Witherspoon actually calls it "faithfulness." Sadly, the unfaithful preacher will seek "the favor of the great, or the applause of the multitude." The faithful parson will not. He will refuse to preach "*smooth things*" and he will not *"prophesy deceit"* (Witherspoon's italics). One is tempted to think that Witherspoon would quickly offer a similar warning to modern televangelists and heads of megachurches. Faithful pastors, he continues, will assume two specific responsibilities, "which can only flow from true piety," further insuring integrity: First, the faithful minister will preach sermons that are not general or vague, but are "very particular, and close, in application." Second, the same pastor will not shirk the responsibility to administer "private admonition, and personal reproof" to parishioners when they need it.[5]

Witherspoon practiced what he preached. He became entangled in the infamous Snodgrass case in 1762, which in due course captured the attention of both church and civil courts. Witherspoon had publicly condemned the behavior of several irreverent young men who allegedly had held a mock Communion service near Witherspoon's church on a Saturday night. He became so incensed at this sacrilege that he wrote a sermon, "Seasonable Advice to Young Persons" (text: Ps. 1:1), which was printed and widely circulated. The sermon was so persuasive and the misbehavior deemed so scandalous, that many sided with the author. The young men were ostracized and even physically attacked. However, Witherspoon apparently had gone too far, for one of the delinquents, Jack Snodgrass, successfully sued Witherspoon for criminal libel. Witherspoon eventually had to pay a fine and costs,[6] literally paying a price for his public admonition.

Thus, he knew firsthand what could happen when a sermon "hit home," so he was able to declaim from personal experience what could happen when accusations by wicked persons were directed toward faithful pious servants of God. If the preacher is preaching with integrity, he pointed out, attacks of this sort are inevitable. Self-deceived persons who are self-satisfied will resent even the slightest reproof, whether by word or example. The minister's temptation will be to soften the message in order to please the congregation. Of course, the greater temptation is to please persons of standing and privilege. "If I am not mistaken," he opined, knowing full well he was not, "fawning and servility hath been the road, in which ambitious and corrupt churchmen have traveled to preferment in every age." Beware of the great and wealthy, he charged: "though they live in open defiance of the laws and ordinances of Christ, yet will be much offended" if the preacher's message is pointed though truthful. Ministers must live and work by a far higher principle than to court "the favor either of great or small, good or bad." The sum of the matter is that the clerical calling by its very nature will induce criticism and resentment. "Faithful ministers of Christ, for instance, are the lights of the world, and, by their piety and diligence, are a standing reproach to the world lying in wickedness." Even away from the world and inside the church as a whole, the pious preacher's lot is not always a happy one. No matter how cautious and circumspect he may be, if he works hard at his preaching and is "assiduous in the duties of his function," he cannot help "excite the resentment of the lazy, slothful part of his profession." The fact is, attacks may come from all sides, inside the church or outside, from procrastinating clergy as well as disgruntled laity.

Then there is the matter of attitude. Real religion or true piety in a cleric will produce cheerfulness and readiness to serve. There is a world of difference between "a truly pious man [who] undertakes the office of the ministry from love to God" and "an unholy Minister [who] undertakes this employment only as a trade" and whose highest aim is "to promote his own worldly advantage." The former gets real pleasure in carrying out the duties of the office and is able to remain cheerful even when fatigue overtakes. The latter complains that the requirements of ministry are "tedious and burthensome," "toil and drudgery."[7]

Witherspoon himself seems to speak from much parish experience when he observes: "It requires no small attention and labor, to seek out fit and acceptable words, as the preacher expresses it, to stir up the attention of the inconsiderate, to awaken secure, and convince obstinate sinners, to unmask the covered hearts of hypocrites, to set right the erring, and encourage the fearful." With this litany of responsibility Witherspoon is making the point that the pious minister has to be as diligent as possible for one simple reason: The minister must answer to God. A pastor's burden is not a light one. "If he is truly pious, as he loves God, he loves his brother also." That love will impel the diligent pastor to stop at nothing "to prevent sinners from going to that place of torment."[8]

There is more. The preacher is an example and the preacher needs to be in prayer. Witherspoon utterly rejected the notion, held in certain church circles even in his day, that the minister only fulfills a function. Like every other Christian, the minister is a sinner, though a forgiven one, of course. In this view the minister's morals and manners need not be qualitatively different from those of the laity. The minister stands in need of the gospel on the same level as everyone else. This is a view of the ministry that Witherspoon would have quickly rejected. Instead, he would have asserted that the minister's example is vital. What the preacher proclaims from the pulpit *must* be embodied in the preacher's personal life. He noted, "The example of a pious minister, is a constant instruction to his people. It ratifies his doctrine, while he not only charges them to do what he says, but to be what he is." If the minister's morals are lacking, for example, "loose and careless persons, think themselves quite at liberty to despise the reproofs of their pastor, if, while he teaches others, he teaches not himself." All this means is that the most important qualification of a good minister is to be "*a believing preacher* [Witherspoon's italics], and that, if he saves his own soul, he will be the probable mean [*sic*] of saving them that hear him."[9]

What he says about prayer is predictable. His admonition is brief and direct: "Be much in earnest prayer to God, that he would fit you for your work, and crown your labors with success. Prayer is absolutely necessary to the stead-fastness and growth of every believer, and especially to a minister."[10]

Earlier we noted the commotion that resulted from the publication of Witherspoon's "Ecclesiastical Characteristics." Written to reveal the hypocrisy of ministers of the Moderate party in the Kirk, the thirteen maxims denounced the characteristics of the Moderate clergy. To locate the features of true ministerial piety, according to the author, the modern reader has simply to take note of what Witherspoon scorns as components of Moderate piety. The following table illustrates the differences. On the left are several items of Moderate piety that he explicitly ridiculed; on the right, by inference, are the unwritten opposites, those marks of Popular party or orthodox piety:[11]

Moderate or False Piety	Orthodox or True Piety
1. Moderates honor and defend heretics. (Maxim I)	1. The Orthodox reject heresy by preaching the everlasting truths of the gospel.
2. Moderates protect as much as possible libertines whose conduct is marked by "good humored vices." (Maxim II)	2. The Orthodox renounce the world and those acts the Bible calls sins.

3. Moderates sneer at the Confession of Faith and hint that they do not believe all of it. (Maxim III)

3. The Orthodox subscribe to and honor the entire Confession.

4. Moderate ministers must acquire polish and good manners, and behave like fine gentlemen. (Maxim V)[12]

4. The Orthodox will speak simply and truthfully, associate with virtuous persons, live modestly, and be examples of Christian piety.

5. Moderate ministers need only study such writers as Shaftesbury, Leibniz, Collins, Hutcheson, and Hume. (Maxim VI)[13]

5. Orthodox ministers must have an extensive education in the Bible, church fathers, theology, church history, as well as the several historic heresies.

6. Moderate ministers call their Orthodox adversaries "knaves" or "fools" because they try to please the common people. (Maxim XI)

6. Orthodox ministers preach plainly in order to reach the common people.

7. Moderate ministers must "put off any appearance of devotion, and avoid all unnecessary exercises of religious worship, whether public or private." They must show disdain for those who "have a high profession of religion, and a great pretence to strictness in their walk and conversation." (Maxims VII and XII)

7. Orthodox ministers are exemplars of public and private piety; they practice self-denial and they decry vanity, social position, power, and wealth.

Maxim IV dictates four basic rules that a Moderate preacher must follow. In the following quotation the Orthodox responses are presumed and placed in brackets:

1. "His subjects must be confined to social duties." [The Orthodox minister would choose biblical themes, especially the "everlasting truths of the gospel."]

2. "He must recommend them only from rational considera-

tions, viz. the beauty and comely proportions of virtue."
[The Orthodox minister would preach on topics derived
from revelation, the Bible, not simply from reason or
"rational considerations."]

3. "His authorities must be drawn from heathen writers, *none*
[italics in original], or as few as possible, from Scripture."
[The Orthodox minister would appeal as much as possible
to scripture as his authority.]

4. "He must be very unacceptable to the common people."
[The Orthodox minister will try hard to reach and be
understood by all classes in society.]

The modern reader of the "Ecclesiastical Characteristics" quickly
recognizes that Witherspoon is exaggerating Moderate ministry,
even as he ridicules it, but there is a certain measure of truth imbedded in the exaggerations. Of course, Moderate ministers did not
make a habit of honoring or defending heretics or protecting lib-
ertines; nor did they base their sermons on "heathen writers" rather
than the Bible. However, in their sermons they did not emphasize
the doctrines found in the Confession, and they did emphasize
morality over belief. Furthermore, they generally upheld lay patronage as the best method of filling pulpits, and they were eager that
ministers of the Kirk should fit easily into polite society with their
advanced learning, good manners, and refined taste.

The last sermon that Pastor Witherspoon preached to his Paisley
congregation in May 1768 before setting out for America bore the
title, "Ministerial Fidelity in Declaring the Whole Counsel of God"
(text: Acts 20:26, 27).[14] The word *piety* scarcely appears. The whole
sermon, forceful but irenic, lengthy but substantial, has to do with
the probity of the preacher. If piety includes probity—and it surely
does—then this sermon says much about clerical piety even if the
term itself is missing. The preacher will be sure to hold forth, not on
a partial list, but on *all* the truths of the everlasting gospel, "in their
full and just proportion," with conviction, and finally, he will preach
on them "honestly and boldly, without respect of persons."

It was apparent that the departing minister wished to pass along
some advice to his Paisley parishioners as they sought a new minister. As he left to go to Princeton and as his former congregation
chose a new pastor, he wanted them to give serious thought to the
requisite qualities of ministers. He did not seemed worried that they

might choose a Moderate for their new pastor. Confident that they would not, he remained silent on this point. Instead, his advice is straightforward and down to earth. Never does he boast of his own record, although reading between the lines of the sermon a careful reader might detect a trace of boasting.

In this sermon, the first piece of advice to the congregation is never select a pastor who is lazy or worldly. Witherspoon is only too aware of how easy it is for a minister to become lazy. The ministry is a multifaceted profession, and as the minister undertakes his many responsibilities, "he may apply chiefly to what is most pleasant to himself, or what gives him the greatest opportunity to shine in the eyes of others, while he neglects those parts that are more burdensome to the flesh." Witherspoon then turns sarcastic: "Indeed, it is wonderful to think what ingenious excuses men will invent for the neglect of those duties, which they have no inclination to perform." He selected a particular duty of a minister, pastoral visitation, and became quite sharp with those pastors who failed to call on their people:

> I have often heard ministers endeavor to prove, that visitation of families, which doubtless is very fatiguing, was also a very unprofitable and unnecessary piece of service, than which, I think, there never was any thing more manifestly false. It is not only, when executed with fidelity, of great immediate use, in itself, but, by giving a minister a thorough knowledge of his people, enables him to perform every other part of his work with the greater propriety and success.[15]

Next, he warned the congregation to get rid of their several prejudices and mistaken notions, else they can expect correction from a new minister. Apparently, during his Paisley pastorate Witherspoon had not been altogether successful in helping to remove all of these prejudices. Some still remain, so if the new pastor is going to minister the way he should, he may rightly reprove a sin or a harmful practice of longstanding "with severity, and especially if he will not tolerate it without censure, he may expect no little difficulty and opposition. There are many who will complain of him as too rigid, and impute to ill-nature, and indiscretion, what arises from the dictates of conscience and a sense of duty." Just let him condemn directly "fashionable amusements, or conformity to the world,"

Witherspoon observed, and "he will often incur not only the hatred of the profligate, but the disapprobation of those prudent compliers." The departing pastor concluded the matter with a piece of timeless advice to both ministers and congregations: "As no congregation can expect to meet with a perfect minister; so no minister should expect to meet with a faultless congregation."[16]

Lastly, no pious pastor doing his duty "can expect to be without enemies." It is possible, grants the preacher, for a minister by "great prudence" and "particularly by silence and forbearance" to escape the resentment and rancor of certain wicked folk. However, that should not be the aim of the minister of integrity: "Neutrality, as to the interest of religion, is commendable in none, but it is unpardonable in him. He must bear testimony openly and resolutely against vice and wickedness. . . . A faithful minister will not suffer Satan's kingdom to be at peace."[17]

Witherspoon preached another memorable sermon on the ministry in 1768, this time in Princeton shortly after he arrived: "The Success of the Gospel Entirely of God" (text: 1 Cor. 3:5–7).[18] It is appropriate to consider it as part of his understanding of ministry developed in Scotland, even though, technically, it belongs to his American period. The sermon does reveal that he had something more to say to congregations about clerical piety; he had not spoken the last word a few months earlier in Paisley. What he said deserves special consideration and analysis.

He commences his three-part sermon, first, by examining the text and concluding that the principal teaching of the three verses is that ministers should think of themselves, and be viewed by their people, as entirely subordinate to God. Whatever they are and do, their assistance and eventually their success in ministry derive solely from God. Next, in the central part of the sermon Witherspoon develops this theme by making three points. First, repeating his introductory statement, he declares that ministers must realize that they are entirely subordinate to God, who not only calls the person to ministry but "imparts the ability to discharge the trust." That said, Witherspoon then describes two distinct kinds of qualities of great significance in the Christian ministry, both of which are bestowed by God. The one is called "gifts," the second "the effect of the gracious and sanctifying influence of the Holy Ghost." The gifts are the natural and acquired endowments of the mind, perfected by education and exercise. This means that the person may be blessed with the knowledge and comprehension of the sacred truths, but also will be able to speak well, and will have the ability to communicate these truths effectively. God not only bestows these gifts initially, but divine providence makes possible the refinement of the gifts as time passes. Witherspoon made the point negatively and tersely: "Let human efforts be what they will, if God do not smile upon them, they will infallibly be blasted."[19]

The second kind of quality, the influence of the Holy Spirit, is nothing more or less than "holy and gracious dispositions," which direct a person's talents to a good end and give them "force and influence in the application." Here Witherspoon means the love of Christ dwelling and reigning in a pastor's heart. When that happens, "it gives such attachment to his cause, so much love to his people, so much clearness and comprehension in understanding his truths, so great willingness, or rather desire to communicate them, as cannot fail to have the greatest influence on a minister's diligence, and at the same time gives reason to hope that he will speak from faith to faith."[20]

To whom is a minister indebted for these holy dispositions, for this love of Christ in one's heart? The answer, of course, is predictable. It is the power of God that regenerates the preacher, and God's indwelling spirit that daily sanctifies and enables the preacher "to adorn the doctrine of God . . . in all things." Witherspoon, however, is a realist. He knows very well that not all ministers are pure in heart and completely under the influence of God's spirit. So he allows for the possibility that a hypocritical cleric can to some degree be a successful minister. He even admits that it is possible for some parishioners to arrive at the heavenly gates "who were converted and edified by the ministry of those [pastors] who themselves have taken up their abode in the place of torment." This is a rather striking statement on the surface of it, but it is consistent with Witherspoon's claim that the preacher, pious or not, does not convert. God alone has this power.

With a measure of insight into ministerial psychology, Witherspoon admits that in some cases clerical hypocrisy may be more accidental than intentional. It becomes so easy for pastors to deceive themselves, readily mistaking their responsibility "in thinking and speaking of holy things" for the actual evidence of gracious dispositions in their lives. In the second main part of the sermon the author addresses this matter.

For the purpose of the argument, he theorizes, let us not select a hypocritical pastor but a talented devoted leader of the highest order, one who has "the most acute and penetrating genius, the most lively imagination, the most solid judgment, the most charming and persuasive eloquence," even one who possesses "an eminently pious and devout heart." Witherspoon is at the point of overdrawing the illustration when he begins to make his case. One would naturally suppose that this kind of a minister would bring untold converts into the fold. Not necessarily, warns Witherspoon, explaining that that will happen only when God is "pleased to open the way by his divine grace into the hearts and consciences of the sinner." If this is hard for some people to fathom, they had better go straight to the text on which the sermon is based and reread it: "I have planted, Apollos watered; but God gave the increase."

Witherspoon now moves easily, and predictably, to invoke a drawn-out gardening illustration, which concludes with the truth that ministers sow the good seed of God's word, but it is God who places in the seed "a regenerating and sanctifying efficacy" and makes it "productive of faith in the heart, and good works in the life."[21]

After quoting two New Testament passages, John 6:44–45 and Matthew 28:19–20, Witherspoon closes the argument by turning to Acts 16 and the conversion of Lydia, "a seller of purple." Here, indeed, was a promising case, he observes. She had renounced idolatry and was worshiping the true God. She wanted to be instructed in the faith of Christ. She had met with Paul and could not have had a more qualified counselor. Yet "the great apostle of the Gentiles" could not succeed on his own: "The Lord must by his own good Spirit, open the heart of Lydia." Divine grace had to complete the work. The moral? "A Paul or Apollos in the pulpit will be altogether unsuccessful without the almighty power and grace of God."

The final point in the main section of the sermon prompted Witherspoon to reiterate the idea of the sovereignty of God. It is, in fact, ever so easy to overlook the divine dimension in the call and work of ministers, he confessed. For God's part, he sometimes manifests his sovereignty by working without means, or the least of means, to accomplish his ends. That said, we had better be prepared for some surprises. The choosing and fitting of the twelve disciples for their work was in itself a miracle: "They were originally poor illiterate fishermen, quite unequal in themselves to the astonishing undertaking of producing a revolution in the state of religion." But they succeeded. "I have often considered this matter," admitted Witherspoon, "with a mixture of reverence and admiration." The point? "Sometimes those of very moderate, or even of the weakest natural abilities, have an unction from the holy one, and by their piety and diligence become workmen, that need not be ashamed, rightly dividing the word of truth."[22] The truth is that God sometimes blesses the labors of the "humble pastor of meaner rank, who loves his master, his work, and his people," and withholds his blessing from the parson of "superior parts" whose ministry is marred by unwholesome ambition and worldly contest and faction.

Finally, what should ministers, especially younger ones, learn from this text and the sermon itself? For one thing, remembering the truth imbedded in the text—God gives the increase—will preserve them from trusting in themselves and will force them to look upward and "engage them to maintain a continual intercourse with the Father of lights, and the author of every good and perfect gift." Further, it will preserve them from two dangerous extremes—ostentation and sloth. It is despicable to see a minister "burning incense to his own vanity, and preaching himself, when he is called to preach Christ Jesus the Lord." It should come as no surprise if God sees fit to pour down disgrace on that kind of ministry. That is what it deserves.

If ostentation is displeasing to God, so also is negligence or sloth. It is much more than just laziness. It amounts to "disobedience, presumption, and precisely what the scripture calls tempting God." One of the worst things preachers can do is "to rush into a pulpit unprepared, and disgrace their honorable calling, by rude, undigested, disorderly effusions, or such mean, slovenly, indecent language as lays the hearers under the strongest temptation, to treat it with an insolence of indignation and contempt."[23] And one of the best things ministers can do is unite "the simplicity of the gospel, and the dignity of the pulpit."

At the very end of the sermon, Witherspoon does something uncharacteristic: He offers his personal thoughts on moving to America. As we have observed earlier, he regards his departure from Scotland and arrival in Princeton in theological terms, viewing the move as a new form of service in the larger Church of Christ, in the "oneness of his body," as he calls it. Compared to the greater journey we all take from this life to the one beyond, "the change of our scene of service from Europe to America, would appear altogether unworthy of notice," he admits. What does worry him, he confides, is that he will not be able in terms of achievement and service to justify all "the respect and affection," "the testimonies of joy and satisfaction" that have been poured out on him since his arrival. At the very end, he implores the prayers of the Princeton congregation, townspeople and students:

1. "Pray that an all-sufficient God . . . may pour down his blessing on the public institution in this place [the College of New Jersey]. . . ."
2. "Pray that success may attend the ministry of the gospel in this place. . . ."
3. "Once more, pray that my beloved charge, whom I left in Scotland, and will never forget, may . . . be supplied with a faithful pastor, who may feed them with knowledge and understanding."[24]

At the point when Witherspoon arrived in America and assumed responsibilities in addition to the pulpit, it is legitimate to pause and raise the question of whether his views on the ministry took final form in Scotland or whether they were in the process of changing, especially in light of what we shall discover shortly in his "Lectures on Divinity."

Judging from the several statements he made and the views expressed in the four sermons that we have reviewed, Witherspoon would seem to be presenting a predictable pastoral piety, characterized by such features as a firm belief in the gospel, humility before a sovereign God, adherence to the four everlasting truths and to the Confession, integrity, courage of one's convictions, outspokenness, modesty, willingness to be an example of piety, hard work, and "holy and gracious dispositions." But, a person is wont to ask, is this all? Is this the sum of Witherspoon's piety for the preacher?

In my judgment, there is sufficient evidence to suggest that while Witherspoon was opposing the Moderates during his years in Scotland, he was also inadvertently absorbing some of their spirit and their way of thinking, and that he carried these Moderate tendencies with him to America. In Princeton, he was not content merely to repeat the admonitions on the ministry that he delivered to his Scottish congregations and clergy. I believe, in fact, that Witherspoon's relation to the Moderates may be more complex than simple opposition in the ecclesiastical courts on such matters as the Confession, lay patronage, and the theater.

In the first instance, when he was a student at Edinburgh University, Witherspoon shared a common learning and background with several individuals later to become Moderates, classmates such as William Robertson, Alexander Carlyle, and Hugh Blair. Though apparently not close to any of them, he seems to have been on somewhat friendly terms with all of them. As time passed he made it his business to know what the Moderates stood for, as is clear from a careful reading of the satirical "Ecclesiastical Characteristics." He knows the authors they read, their church politics, their attitudes toward the Confession and to the common people, and the sources for their sermons. He chose a style of writing, that of ridicule, recommended by one of the intellectual heroes of the Moderates, Lord Shaftesbury. And, of course, the title of Witherspoon's own essay was an attempt to ridicule Shaftesbury's *Characteristics of Men, Manners, Opinions, Times.*

Further, Witherspoon was not above using other Moderate stratagems in the Moderate-Popular party struggle. John Rodgers reported a conversation between Witherspoon and Principal William Robertson of Edinburgh University that occurred in the General Assembly when for once the Popular party members had won a skirmish with the Moderates. Robertson conceded to Witherspoon, "[I]n a pleasant manner, I think you have your men better disciplined than formerly.' 'Yes,' replied Witherspoon, 'by urging your politics too far, you have compelled us to beat you with your own weapons.'"[25] The story is difficult to verify, but it does suggest that in studying the enemy, Witherspoon may unconsciously have absorbed more of the Moderate approach and ideas than he ever intended.

Also, we have his own admission that he was not restricting his reading as a minister of the Kirk to just British and Continental divines. In a 1772 advertisement on behalf of the college, addressed to boys and their parents in the West Indies, Witherspoon boasted that an American college such as his would ensure a more effective instruction and a higher standard of morals for boys than a British university. He continued by claiming that "not many have a more thorough acquaintance with, the means of Education, at present, in Great Britain, than the author of this address, who was born in the neighborhood of Edinburgh, educated in it, and spent the greatest part of his afterlife *in constant intercourse and great intimacy with the Members of the University of Glasgow* [italics mine]."[26]

To which members is he referring? It would hardly be Francis Hutcheson, who died in 1746. Perhaps he was thinking of Adam Smith (1723–1790), author of *Theory of Moral Sentiments* (1759), who was at Glasgow from 1752 to 1764, or Thomas Reid (1710–1796), who had an even longer tenure at Glasgow (1764–1796) and was the author of *An Inquiry into the Human Mind on the Principles of Common Sense* (1764). Witherspoon recommended both of these authors and titles to the Princeton students who took his course on moral philosophy.[27] In the end, we are left to speculate who these members of the university were and exactly how much and what kinds of intercourse and intimacy Witherspoon enjoyed. Even if we charge him with exaggeration and subtract something from his boast, he may be disclosing a broadening of his mind and the means by which he prepared himself for writing his "Lectures on Moral Philosophy" and "Lectures on Divinity" after reaching America.

Soon after 1768, Witherspoon became a self-acknowledged advocate of liberal learning in the process of acquiring a reputation as a leading minister and educator in the middle colonies.[28] But even in Scotland, he began to urge a more liberal education for ministers. In his farewell sermon to his Paisley congregation, we find him criticizing a worldly way of life for the Christian, but then adding what almost seems a contradiction: "While I say this, I would not be understood as being against a liberal education, and elegant manner of life, or anything that is truly becoming in an advanced rank. There is no more religion in being sordid, than in being sumptuous. But I think the spirit of the gospel is such, that it will dispose a truly pious person to be rather late than early in adopting new ornaments."[29]

He is hedging his advice, but the sentiment is unmistakable. Liberal learning in a minister is to be admired and encouraged. In his mind there is no contradiction between subscribing to the Confession on the one hand, and wide reading in theology and beyond on the other. Even a few years earlier, he had advocated a broad education for ministers, stating, "It is a great mistake to think, sound learning is an enemy to religion, and to suppose that an ignorant minister is the best or safest. There is no branch of human knowledge of which a Divine may not be the better, or which a good man will not improve to the glory of God and the good of others."[30]

As we have observed, Witherspoon was recommending to his ministerial compatriots that they should look inward to be certain they were "born again," that they should have a firm belief of the gospel, and carry a lively sense of religion upon their hearts. Belief of the gospel, of course, meant holding fast to the four foundational truths. Such was the basis for "real religion for a minister." By the end of the chapter we have discovered a new note: Sound learning needs to accompany the everlasting truths. And apparently there is no conflict between the two. Has Witherspoon succumbed to Moderate demands of a learned and polite clergy? Was it a slip of the tongue, or did he mean every word when he used the phrase an "elegant manner of life" and spoke of what was "truly becoming in an advanced rank"? Was Witherspoon, in fact, now trying to make room for liberal learning in that clerical "real religion"?

The conclusion that one reaches is that while he has not converted to Moderatism, he has demonstrated that he is a friend of an evangelicalism that will live under the same roof with a broad education. He apparently has reached the point where he sees no contradiction between proclaiming the everlasting truths of the gospel and reading broadly in areas theological and secular. More than that, he is at the point of insisting that if one is going to preach the truths successfully, one must come to the task armed with what we today would call a liberal education. Real religion, then, will not be narrow or circumscribed. It will be enriched by wide experience and learning. Simultaneously, real religion will supply a focus for a minister's studies in "literature and science," Witherspoon avers. It will direct and "turn into its proper channel" the broad knowledge the minister acquires.[31]

This conjunction of real religion or piety and broad learning in the work of ministry raises questions that need to be confronted. The next chapter will attempt to answer some of these questions by discussing how piety and broad learning not *can* be but *must* be joined in the life of the minister.

Chapter Four

Piety and Learning /
From Proof to Promise

I would therefore begin, by earnestly beseeching you, to keep clear views of the importance, both of piety, and literature, and never suffer them to be divided. Piety, without literature, is but little profitable; and learning, without piety, is pernicious to others, and ruinous to the possessor.

Works, 4:11

John Witherspoon did not often reveal his inner personal thoughts and feelings. However, once when in Princeton he looked back with nostalgia to his years in Paisley when he had preached "to a crouded [*sic*] audience of from twelve to fifteen hundred souls." He then pondered his new situation in which the congregation was "such a thin and negligent assembly" but the opportunity to educate future ministers a very welcome one. "Nothing would give me a higher pleasure," he confided, "than being instrumental in furnishing the minds, and improving the talents of those who may hereafter be the ministers of the everlasting gospel. The hope of it, is indeed the chief comfort of my present station."[1] So spoke Witherspoon in his very first divinity lecture, justifying to himself that his new challenge would be "an ample recompense" for the loss of a large congregation.

Witherspoon appeared on the American scene at a time when there were no divinity schools or seminaries to train ministers.[2] Education for the ministry usually took the form of an experienced and acclaimed minister acting as a mentor to several aspiring ordinands. Often living in the manse with the minister and his family, the theologues-in-training would read, recite on, and discuss theological topics under the supervision of their pastor-professor. They could also observe firsthand the duties of the pastoral office and the professional activity of the minister, thus combining the practical with the theoretical in their education. Such close contact between mentor and novice also meant that proper attention could be paid to the students' growth in personal piety as well as in theological acumen. In the best sense it was a successful scheme of apprenticeship, or in more modern terms, an internship.[3] It was expected that the ministerial candidate would have acquired a classical pretheological education at one of the few colonial colleges, such as Harvard or Yale, before undertaking his theological training. In some cases, if a student did not choose to study theology in the manse of a working pastor, he might arrange to do so with a college president or professor of divinity. Indeed, in eighteenth-century America the first step toward separate formal theological education in an academic setting was taken when a student, having finished his baccalaureate course, would remain at his alma mater to be tutored in theology on a non-degree basis. The period of time was flexible, from a few months to a year or more, depending upon the student's aptitude and finances. When the candidate for the Presbyterian ministry felt he was prepared, and the mentor or professor judged him qualified, following the procedure established in Scotland, he then notified the presbytery, which had previously taken him under its care, that he was ready to be examined. Upon successful completion of the required examinations, he was first licensed and then later ordained to the ministry.[4]

Witherspoon was not the first at the College of New Jersey to tutor theological students. Prior to his arrival, presidents Jonathan Dickinson, Aaron Burr, and Samuel Davies had found time to teach a small number of candidates.[5] However, quite soon after 1768 Witherspoon began to tutor graduates of the college, mostly in theology, for one or two years. One of his earliest divinity students was his future son-in-law, Samuel Stanhope Smith, who studied theology following his graduation from the college in 1769. Another of Witherspoon's postgraduate students was James Madison, who studied Old Testament Hebrew with Witherspoon after graduating in 1771.[6]

Witherspoon's divinity lectures prove that he took seriously his responsibilities as a professor of theology and that he had a clear idea of the kind of minister the young American Presbyterian Church needed. Even in the 1780s, when Princeton was graduating fewer students going into the ministry, Witherspoon was still promoting a comprehensive and exacting regimen for preparing future clerics.

What was immediately apparent as Witherspoon began his divinity instruction at the college is that it is not nearly enough for the minister to have a vital religious experience, know the Confession forward and backward, or be able to quote long Bible passages on demand. However defined, piety by itself is insufficient. Secular knowledge, what Witherspoon calls "literature," must be the handmaiden of piety. Thus, Witherspoon's ministerial ideal combines both piety and literature, a point he makes emphatically in the introductory divinity lecture: "I would therefore begin, by earnestly beseeching you, to keep clear views of the importance, both of piety, and literature, and never suffer them to be divided." He continues by warning, in a memorable phrase, of the dangerous outcome if they ever are divorced: "Piety, without literature, is but little profitable; and learning, without piety, is pernicious to others, and ruinous to the possessor."[7] The balance between the two, of course, is the goal; the extremes are to be shunned at all costs. The excessively pious who think "that religion is better than all the learning in the world," who in modern terms vociferously claim that the godly minister preaches the Bible, the whole Bible, and only the Bible, are as much to be condemned as those would-be intellectuals who have become "too much enamored with human wisdom" and turn each sermon into an erudite tour de force.[8]

Piety

We already know that Witherspoon accepted as foundational for ministerial piety those everlasting truths of the gospel that were so vital for the layperson. While he did not repeat them in the opening lecture on divinity, he did make it clear that ministers, as well as laypersons, need to have the full religious experience embodied in those truths. "Whatever be our calling and profession," he declaimed to his divinity students, "the salvation of our souls is the one thing needful."[9] Should the minister's salvation experience be quantitatively or qualitatively different from that of others? He dodges the question, repeating what he has said before: It is neither the converted nor the unconverted minister who converts the sinner, but the grace of God. Nevertheless, the minister neglects true religion or piety at his own peril because, at bottom, a lively piety is crucial for the discharge of his trust. "It will," he promises, make a cleric "active and diligent, upright and impartial, happy & successful."[10]

Of particular concern to ministers, however, are certain problems that are peculiar to them, such as doubt. Witherspoon knows his students and has noticed that at least some of them, beset by doubts, have relinquished their vocation. The truth is, and all must recognize it, that a mixture of faith and doubt is the lot of every believer. Not every Christian believes everything, every hour, every day! Both pastors and people, therefore, must take comfort in what the author of Hebrews calls the assurance of hope.[11] All true believers, Witherspoon teaches, have some degree of hope, which compels them to rely on Christ for salvation. Holding fast to Christ is the minimum; beyond that, doubting is possible. "There are not very many," he sagely observes, "who have such a degree of steady, and firm assurance, as to exclude all doubting."[12] That apparently settled the matter for the professor, but one wonders if the issue did not excite further discussion between professor and students, a few of whom at least might have been seriously troubled by their doubts.

Witherspoon continues with his prescriptions of piety for future pastors. His admonitions are nothing if not simple and down to earth: A wise minister, of course, will shun what is recognized as sin. More than that, he should avoid what might be technically lawful but would appear to others to be sin and thus somehow offend them. In this matter the virtue to be cultivated is "strictness and tenderness of practice."[13] And the way to cultivate such a virtue is to be faithful in the "exercise of piety, and the duties of the closet." To carry out those exercises might be easier if one belonged to a liturgical tradition, but since "there are no forms of prayer with us [Presbyterians]," Witherspoon explains, it is all the more important to acquire and cultivate "the habit of closet devotion" as the only way to improve the minister's spiritual life. The earlier one begins these pious exercises the better. Some Christian virtues—humility, prudence, sensitivity to providence, purity of principle—can improve over the years, Witherspoon thinks, but "fervour in devotion must be begun early, while the passions are strong, and continued by the power of reason and habit."[14] To begin these exercises of personal piety early in life and then be punctual and regular in their practice is to insure and enhance the spiritual life of the minister.

Next, what Witherspoon calls the "principles of study" are part of the minister's equipment. Again, the aspiring cleric should begin early in life to determine and internalize these so that throughout his ministry he will be able to keep "the whole system of revealed truth in view" and uphold its importance. In the process of studying to become the best minister possible, the temptation to succumb to pride and "to shine" before others is ever present. "Real excellence" in ministry grows from doing all to the glory of God and not from enhancing one's standing or reputation. If self-denial is a necessary part of lay piety, it becomes no less a part of clerical piety.

Lastly, once more we see Witherspoon's practical, down-to-earth orientation. He knows the theological student mind and, one might remark, even the current student mind. He knows very well how judgmental, even censorious, divinity students can become once they discover the distance between "what is" in the ministry and churches and "what ought to be." They become impatient and tend to make the "exercises of piety, and the ordinances of the gospel, matter[s] of science and criticism, rather than the means of edification." The solution to the problem is not to ignore the gap between theory and practice, but to "let it not carry you so much away," that it might diminish your work in ministry.[15]

Learning

Learning, for Witherspoon, is what we would call secular knowledge, though he omits some subjects, such as natural philosophy or science, art, music, and of course, drama. Such learning is essential for two reasons. First, stated negatively, presenting the sacred truths without learning exposes the ministry to contempt and turns away persons of "literature and taste." Second, learning is necessary in order to repel the attacks of the enemies of the gospel, specifically, to grasp their arguments and be able to refute them. The apostle Paul is the best example of one who successfully joined learning and piety, declares Witherspoon.

He does not advocate that a minister be a renaissance figure, ranging over the many areas of human knowledge, nor one who has a thorough knowledge of a subject far removed from theology. "Extensive knowledge" is his recommendation. Even though he seems to propose more than that, once remarking that a minister "ought to be well furnished with literature of every kind," Witherspoon clarifies his recommendation by advising that the particular areas of competence should be those somehow related to the ministerial vocation. There is no need for competence in a whole host of disciplines; in many of these a general knowledge will suffice.[16] The four subjects a person of the cloth should master are languages, moral philosophy, history, and eloquence.[17]

Languages

One might expect Witherspoon, a Reformed professor of divinity, to recommend routinely the mastery of Latin, Greek, and Hebrew, not only to facilitate study of the scriptures but to be able to read the classics since, he observes, they are still "the standard of taste." What is unusual is his additonal recommendation of French and his rather extravagant opinion that the French language embodies a greater purity, simplicity, and precision than English. French is useful to ministers because they will be able to read important French authors in "calvinistic, reformation divinity" as well as some "admirable practical treatises" by Roman Catholic divines.[18] Later we will see which authors Witherspoon recommends.

Moral Philosophy

In short Witherspoon blesses moral philosophy by calling it "a good handmaid to the Christian" inasmuch as it deals with principles and issues. Some of these would include themes that he discusses in his "Lectures on Moral Philosophy," such as the moral sense resident in every human being ("really a principle of our nature," he explains); duty to God, to our neighbor, and to ourselves; the social contract; and the nature of virtue. In this matter, more recent thinkers are to be preferred to ancient ones, although Plato and Cicero, especially the latter, will be of assistance to those in the pulpit.

History

He offers three reasons of greater or lesser importance for a prospective minister to study both sacred and secular history. First, it is currently fashionable to do so. (Witherspoon is obviously aware of the general awakening interest in historical study as part of the Enlightenment.) Second, knowing history will form one into a person of liberal knowledge, able to hold his own with those of rank and letters. Finally, and the best reason, a study of history will enrich critical study of the Bible and increase a minister's comprehension of the ways of the world and its people.

Eloquence

Finally, the future minister must pay attention to eloquence, or belles lettres. Rather than argue the necessity of excellent speaking and writing at this point, Witherspoon refers theological students to his own course on eloquence. The "Lectures on Eloquence" are replete with advice on how to fulfill the demands of pulpit, courtroom, and public assembly.[19] In those lectures Witherspoon reiterated the importance of extensive knowledge. An eloquent minister "ought to be well furnished with literature of every kind." However, the first recommendation to insure eloquence in a minister is piety, "to have a firm belief of that gospel he is called to preach, and a lively sense of religion upon his own heart," advice he has issued before. Yes, piety means acquiring valuable "experimental knowledge" that will aid in one's choice of studies and encourage diligence, benefits Witherspoon has previously enumerated, but to which he now adds "unspeakable force"! We can imagine him raising his voice when he declaims to his students that piety has power; it generates "a piercing and a penetrating heat . . . which flows from the heart." A few lines later Witherspoon again pleads for passion and feeling. "Another quality of a minister's eloquence," he announces, "should be force and vehemence." If the preacher will only think of the message that is his to proclaim, he cannot help but be forceful. Simplicity is important, as are accuracy and judgment and propriety, qualities that Witherspoon tends to repeat. But power and force and feeling are even more the marks of eloquence. "There is no speaker who has a greater right to exert himself to the utmost, or who may properly interest his hearers more, than a minister of the gospel." One is tempted to remark that this is ironic instruction coming from one whose own preaching was described as clear, sensible, graceful, earnest, even solemn, but never powerful or forceful. We can recall that John Rodgers made a point of noting that Witherspoon was "not a fervent and animated orator." One is prone to cite the old proverb, "do as I say, not as I do," and apply it to Witherspoon's homiletical instruction, though it is conceivable that he actually imagined himself to be preaching forcefully and vehemently.

Witherspoon culminated his advice on eloquence and learning by referring his divinity charges to a bibliography he had prepared, "a list of the principal and most valuable writers in every branch of science." The list was supposed to be appended to the "Lectures on Divinity," but because the lectures as published are incomplete, the list was omitted and does not appear in any edition of his *Works*. However, in the New York Historical Society Library, New York City, I have recently discovered what is surely a copy of the list. It is reproduced in appendix B. The original is bound with William Beekman Jr.'s student copy of Witherspoon's "Lectures on Moral Philosophy," and the title on the cover page reads, "A List of Books of Character—as collected by Dr. Witherspoon—1773—Transcribed at Nassau Hall by William Beekman Junr." The title on the first page of the list is "List of Books of Character in different Branches of Science to direct Students, especially in Divinity, either in the Course of their Reading, or furnishing their Libraries."[20]

The bibliography deserves a more careful analysis than is possible in the present study, especially if a modern reader wishes to have a firm grasp of the titles that ought to undergird the piety and learning of an accomplished late eighteenth-century Reformed pastor. However, a few observations are in order. First, the list supplies specific items, not only for piety, but for three of the four categories of learning that Witherspoon recommended in his second divinity lecture—moral philosophy, history, and eloquence. We now know what writers he deemed worthy of study. Second, it is an extensive list of approximately two hundred items, either a title or an author, far more than the thirty-three on the recommended reading list at the end of the "Lectures on Moral Philosophy." Admittedly, several of the two hundred are repetitions as Witherspoon moved from one area of study to another. Third, both the areas, or categories, and the authors listed within each, underscore what Witherspoon advised elsewhere: Ministers should be widely read. They should know, or at least know about, authors of many persuasions and viewpoints, religious and secular; orthodox and heretical; ancient and modern; Reformed, Anglican, and Roman Catholic; Latin, English, and French; British, Continental, and American. As noted earlier, Witherspoon's recommendations of secular literature did not extend to such subjects as natural science, economics, medicine, art, music, or drama. The five main headings within the list hold only one surprise ("Controversy"); otherwise they correspond exactly to the four most important courses Witherspoon taught. The five groups are: "Theology," which includes "Biblical Studies"; "(Theological) Controversy"; "Moral Philosophy"; "History"; and "Belles Lettres and (Literary) Criticism." Clearly the subheadings and individual authors demonstrate Witherspoon's eclecticism and breadth of outlook. While there are more authors sympathetic to Witherspoon's beliefs and positions, notably in the main sections of "Theology" and "Controversy," overall the variety is obvious and something of a balance is struck. There are few surprises.

A quick inspection of the titles under "Systems," the first category under "Theology," discloses Witherspoon's preference for mostly moderate Continental Reformed theologians, with Calvin's *Institutes* at the top of the list. Closer to home, two Scots are included, John Cameron (1579–1625), who preached and taught in the French Reformed Church, and John Forbes (1593–1648), an early ecumenist. Witherspoon reached out to two Anglican bishops for their views that transcended narrow denominational boundaries, Gilbert Burnett (1643–1715) of Salisbury, a former Church of Scotland minister, and John Pearson (1613–1686) of Chester, author of the widely read *Exposition of the* [Apostles'] *Creed* (1659). Absent are any sixteenth- and seventeenth-century Puritan divines, such as John Preston, William Perkins, or William Ames, as are, with the exception of Bénédict Pictet, more orthodox Reformed system builders, such as Johannes Wollebius (1586–1629) of Basel and François Turretin (1623–1687), whose major theological work was so influential at Princeton Theological Seminary during the nineteenth century.[21]

The second category under "Theology" is that of biblical studies, termed "Commentators and Criticks." British divines predominate, including three Anglican episcopal scholars—Bishop Simon Patrick of Ely (1625–1707), who wrote a ten-volume commentary on the Old Testament; Thomas Sherlock of London (1678–1761), whose *The Use and Intent of Prophecy* (1725) was a collection of six sermons preached against the deists; and Bishop Edward Stillingfleet of Worcester (1635–1699), whose *Origines Sacrae* (1662) dealt with the divine authority of the Bible. A number of non-Anglicans are on the list, including Philip Doddridge (1702–1751), whose famous biblical work was the six-volume *The Family Expositor, or a Paraphrase and Version of a New Testament, with Notes* (1739–1756). Witherspoon obviously liked Doddridge. He was also listed under "Systems" and, later on, under "Practical Writers in English." Continental writers include Calvin (his commentaries and the harmony of the Synoptic Gospels), the Dutch Biblical Exegete Compegius Vitringa (c. 1659–1722) (his commentary on Isaiah and his study of the relation of the primitive church to the Jewish synagogue), and several French Reformed scholars. The one surprise is Sir Isaac Newton (1642–1727), famous mathematician and scientist, whose *Observations on the Prophecies of Daniel and the Apocalypse of St. John* (1733) Witherspoon apparently liked, even though Newton otherwise denied the doctrine of the Trinity. Witherspoon also approved of George Benson's (1699–1762) three-volume work on the book of Acts in spite of the fact that Benson was an early Unitarian.

However, when Witherspoon drew up his main section on "Controversy," he was not quite so evenhanded. Again, a variety of authors was offered, but in the "Popish" controversy only two Catholic writers were cited as opposed to five Protestants, and in the next controversy only one who might be called Arian, John Taylor (1694–1761), and another who might be accused of Unitarianism, Samuel Clarke (1675–1729). Lined up against them were such heavyweight opponents as Jonathan Edwards (1703–1758), John Wesley (1703–1791), and Isaac Watts (1674–1748). In the "Deistical" controversy, Witherspoon mentions well-known deists by name only, including two he plainly dislikes, Lord Shaftesbury and David Hume. He showed his disdain for the deists by recommending to his students that they not bother reading from their works; it would be sufficient if they read what English nonconformist divine John Leland (1691–1766) thought they said![22] To counter the deists, Witherspoon supplied the names of seven orthodox writers and their works, which students were expected to read firsthand.

Finally, illustrative of Witherspoon's "practical" orientation and his knowledge of French, there were two sections called "Practical Writers," one containing English writers and one French. Surely he had *The Saints Everlasting Rest* (1650) in mind when he recommended Richard Baxter, and *The Rise and Progress of Religion in the Soul* (1750) when he cited Philip Doddridge one more time. Isaac Watts is again mentioned, this time perhaps not so much for his hymns and psalms as for his poetry and religious educational manuals. Other writers, both Anglican and nonconformist, are noted mainly for their collections of sermons. This would be even truer of the French authorities Witherspoon cites, all Protestants except for

Catholic Bishop Jean Baptiste Massillon (1663–1742) and Father Louis Bourdaloue (1632–1704), both of whom were considered to be outstanding preachers.

Witherspoon's breadth of outlook and his concern that theological students should be widely read becomes ever clearer when one scans the remaining categories on the list, those that comprise learning in the piety/learning duality: "Moral Philosophy," "History," and "Belles Lettres and Criticism." For instance, Hume and Shaftesbury were "outside the pale" as deists, but Witherspoon could recommend the former as a historian and the latter as a moral philosopher. A Moderate leader in the Scottish General Assembly, William Robertson, is another historian worth reading. Witherspoon surely would not have countenanced many of Voltaire's religious ideas, but he thought him an acceptable French historian. A wide selection of moral philosophers was offered, but there were, after all, some limits. For instance, Witherspoon refrained from recommending to theologues *The Leviathan* by Thomas Hobbes (1588–1679) or *The Prince* by Niccolo Machiavelli (1469–1527), both of whom, incidentally, were on Witherspoon's short reading list attached to his "Lectures on Moral Philosophy."

Occasionally, Witherspoon produces a surprise. He wanted no flowers in his speeches or garden. In the pulpit he was reckoned to be clear and sensible, graceful, and earnest. The bits of humor of which we are aware are buried in the acerbity of *The Ecclesiastical Characteristics*. But at the conclusion of his reading recommendations for divinity students we find a section on poetry and, surprisingly, one given over to "Wit and Humour"! The persons listed would fail to make today's TV comedy hour, but a reader with some historical sense, and a certain understanding of wit and humor, might begin to see why Witherspoon included, for instance, Miguel Cervantes's *Don Quixote*, with its humorous yet pitiful exploits of Don Quixote and Sancho Panza, or playwright Molière's display of the hypocrisies of his time by means of humor in his comedies. Even today we can recognize the humor in the remark of one of Molière's characters: "Good Heavens. For more than forty years I have been speaking prose without knowing it," or the whimsical truth in one of Pascal's *Provincial Letters*: "I have made this letter longer than usual, because I lack the time to make it short."[23] Or perhaps Witherspoon was recalling with a smile the character of Falstaff in Shakespeare's *Henry IV*. A minister's learning, we now can conclude, had to be, above all, serious and cerebral, but at the same time Witherspoon allowed for an occasional light note.

Where and how was a young minister encouraged to apply all these works, theological and nontheological? If the aspiring cleric were to follow Witherspoon's example, he would not clutter his sermons with literary or historical allusions, or even quotations from respectable Reformed theologians and biblical scholars. Preaching plain-style did not permit that. It would be proper, however, to insert quotations and references in other types of writing, and occasionally Witherspoon did so. In the "Lectures on Divinity" he noted some of the authorities on his "List of Books of Character," referring when appropriate to writers such as moral philosophers Cicero and Shaftesbury, French historians Louis Dupin (1657–1719) and Antoine-Yves Goguet (1716–1758), and literary celebrities Jonathan Swift (1667–1745) and Joseph Addison (1672–1719). He followed the same practice when he produced his "Lectures on Moral Philosophy" and "Lectures on Eloquence." These authors were almost exclusively mentioned in the lectures themselves and not in any footnotes.

At this point, it may be best to correct the impression that for Witherspoon gravity was all and that life was a serious matter. As we have just seen, he did permit some "wit and humour" in a minister's reading. The truth is that at times he could relax, and there were diversions and lighter moments, even if he never did unwind that much. John Rodgers reported that when Witherspoon was not engaged in serious business he was one of "the most companionable" of persons and a good storyteller. "Furnished with a rich fund of anecdotes, both amusing and instructive, his moments of relaxation were as entertaining, as his serious ones were fraught with improvement," observed Rodgers. Ashbel Green has recorded that Witherspoon rarely drank hard liquor, but sometimes, due to his feeble and nervous condition, made a breakfast (!) of "a glass of Port Wine and Biscuit." Green said that at dinner with friends, he "was in the habit of taking a glass or two of wine," and offering toasts to "absent friends," America, and either "the President of the United States" or "the prosperity of the college." In 1774, John Adams sampled some of Witherspoon's wine on his visit to Princeton. After inspecting the orrery and attending evening prayers, he related that he and Witherspoon "went into the Presidents House, and drank a glass of wine." Apparently, Witherspoon liked to have a ready supply of wine on hand, for there is the record of one local merchant selling Witherspoon twenty-seven *gallons* of wine in 1793, a year before his death.[24]

Sir Henry Raeburn made the Reverend Robert Walker famous by painting him ice skating on Duddingston Loch on the outskirts of Edinburgh. But minister Witherspoon went ice skating too, at least while he was in Scotland, where he was known as an active curler. Collins has reported that "he had the reputation of being the best curler Beith had ever seen," and even today the researcher can find manuscripts reporting two incidents revolving around Witherspoon's curling activities on Lochwinnoch ice near Beith.[25]

From Proof to Promise

The "Lectures on Divinity" ably demonstrate that part of a cleric's piety should include the ability to defend the faith. The underlying assumption of Lectures 3–8 is that Christianity must be shown to be true in the face of its attackers. As such, these lectures comprise an apologetic for Christianity—a defense of the Christian religion—a true possession that every minister worth his calling in the latter half of the eighteenth century should own and treasure. As Witherspoon engaged his students in this enterprise, he went beyond merely showing Christianity to be true; he aimed to demonstrate that it was superior to all other religions. He advised his charges to be wise and judicious in defending the faith—the threat was real—but told them that they should not expend every ounce of energy in confounding the enemy. They should assume that congregations are full of believers, not "infidels" (atheists), so preachers should not be guilty of inserting refutations of objections to Christianity into every sermon. Nevertheless, the adversaries are out there and from time to time they must be confronted, atheists and deists alike.

Witherspoon knew very well what the Enlightenment was doing to traditional religion. His head was not buried in the sand. He was aware that many tenets of faith—reliance upon supernatural power, submission to external authority, belief in revelation, a personal sense of sin and cosmic evil that could only be met and overcome, not by human effort, but by divine grace and power—were under attack in his lifetime. He was keenly aware of the revolt by many against historic creeds and time-tested traditions, and the emergence of autonomous reason and conscience as the standards of truth and conduct.

Proof

Of the two chief enemies of the Christian faith that Witherspoon identified, the deists were more to be feared than the atheists, though, as he once remarked, the "boundless scepticism" of a David Hume should not be written off.[26] It was the deists who especially evoked his wrath, "those pretended friends of revealed religion, who are worse if possible than infidels." We can almost hear him grinding his teeth as he accuses them of setting "the reasonings of man, independent of revelation, above the testimony of God, and revelation itself."[27]

Therefore, the first line of attack, which Witherspoon used to combat both atheists and deists, was to show that reason and revelation are not antithetical. There was no need to spend much time arguing the case for reason; revelation required and received most of his attention.[28]

He first tried to prove that reason by itself was insufficient. Unaided reason leads to distortions as any inspection of heathen religions will reveal—absurd anthropological notions of God, impious and shocking rites, and so forth. Reason by itself cannot cope satisfactorily with the seriousness of human evil and guilt. Describing humans merely as imperfect does not answer the charge that "the history of the world is little else than the history of human guilt."[29] Nor can reason alone furnish the knowledge of God's mercy and compassion. It can only teach that God is kind to those who are good. It takes revelation to teach that mercy and forgiveness can actually be offered to the guilty. In no time, Witherspoon was sure he had shown the inadequacy of reason as the sole source of ultimate truth.

> I confess it is agreeable to me to shew, that the truths of the everlasting gospel are agreeable to sound reason, and founded upon the state of human nature; and I have made it my business through my whole life to illustrate this remark. Yet to begin by making the suggestion of our own reason the standard of what is to be heard or examined, as a matter of revelation, I look upon to be highly dangerous, manifestly unjust, and inconsistent with the foundation-stone of all revealed religion, viz. that reason, without it is insufficient to bring us to the knowledge of God, and our duty.[30]

Next, and at some length, Witherspoon attempted to show that revealed religion, in this instance, Christianity, is rational. He summoned what he judged to be a number of telling arguments: first, the superiority of the doctrine taught—its sublimity, purity, efficacy, plainness, and consistency; second, the force of him who is author and subject of faith, that is, Jesus Christ—his admirable, blameless character, his role as a suffering savior rather than proud prince, his message of self-denial and service, and the loyalty and devotion of his disciples; and finally, the circumstances surrounding the publication of the gospel.[31] In this last instance, Witherspoon cited the relative ease of transportation and communication within the Roman Empire and the Pax Romana that insured the political stability, both of which Jesus' followers needed to transmit the good news to distant peoples. Witherspoon has nothing but praise for the "great design of Providence," which planned the circle of disciples and inspired them to carry out their mission. Calling them "a handful of illiterate mechanics," he declared that they did the most amazing things. Therefore, do not even the disciples prove the validity of Christian revelation?

> [They were] able to overthrow the whole system of Heathen theology, that had continued so long, and spread so wide. . . . Strange indeed, that these successful agents, should come from an obscure corner, and from a nation, that was of all others, not merely despised, but execrated, and abhorred. That they should, notwithstanding, succeed by preaching the divinity of a crucified man, a fact that carried in it the highest idea of baseness and ignominy. Finally, that they should do this without the parade or form of worship to engage attention; without secrets or mysteries, to excite veneration; but by the simplicity of that truth, which the worldly man despises and the strictness of that law which the sinner hates.[32]

Witherspoon continues his effort to demonstrate the veracity and rationality of Christianity by addressing the problem of miracles. At the outset he states, without any qualification, that biblical miracles are direct proof of the truth of the Christian religion. Passing over customary definitions of miracles as (1) either a suspension or alteration of the laws of nature, or (2) doing what is above the power of any finite being (how can we say, finally, exactly what is and is not within the power of any finite creature?), Witherspoon chooses a definition that is really an adaptation of the second but that for him contains a necessary distinction: doing what is demonstrably above the power *of the immediate agent* in the particular situation.

With this definition established, Witherspoon proceeds to assert that the worth of both Old Testament miracles and those of Jesus is in their sanctioning and validation of revelation. What annoys Witherspoon are the skeptics who dismiss a miracle not because it is scientifically improbable or impossible (a modern view), but because the truth it sanctions appears to be contrary to reason to begin with. This is surely wrongheaded because it makes our own reason the standard of what is admissible or not, and he concludes that that is "mad work indeed." Miracles are in no sense window dressing or "add-ons"; they have serious work to do, which in the case of the Messiah is to be "the evidence of his divine mission." The Pharisees foolishly asked for a sign from heaven. Jesus could easily have dazzled them with "the appearance of some extraordinary meteor in the airy region." He refused. Instead, he chose the "plainest subjects" for his miraculous proofs: "the winds—healing the sick—feeding the multitude—raising the dead."[33]

There are more proofs, those that come after Jesus' appearance on earth.[34] Repeating what he has previously stated, Witherspoon recites once more the amazing spread of Christianity as a proof of its validity. He is just as enthusiastic about the way the gospel has increased knowledge and improved human behavior as he is about biblical miracles and other proofs. Not only has it produced a more refined religion, but also it has helped to advance secular knowledge, at least up to a point. He turns critical of those writers who affirm that all human knowledge—physics, astronomy, chronology, for example—is to be found in the Bible. They go too far. Modest claims about increased knowledge, thanks to the Christian religion, are justifiable.

Finally, Witherspoon turns to the conduct of Christians as proof of the worthiness of their religion, what he calls "the effects of the gospel." He, of course, has made this point in other contexts—that Christianity is practical, it works, it "improves" the behavior ("the manners") of women and men. Now he uses Christian piety to show the superiority of the faith itself and to explain how Christianity succeeded in spreading throughout the ancient world.

> A Christian's heart is possessed by the love of God, and his will subjected to the order of his providence. Moderation and self-

denial is his rule, with respect to himself, and unfeigned good will, proved by active beneficience, with regard to others. . . . The visible and eminent piety of the first ministers of the New Testament, and the earliest converts, had the greatest effect in procuring reception to the principle that produced them. The general integrity of their lives, and the eminent appearance in some of them of the illustrious virtues, charity, fortitude and patience, was what subdued all opposition.[35]

One has to admit that some of Witherspoon's statements on the superiority of Christianity are excessive. He is no disinterested observer of the rise of Christianity. He passionately contrasts the virtues of the early Christians with the "ferocity and barbarity" of their pagan neighbors, not to mention their "sottish idolatry, . . . lust, pride, ostentation." He does not have to force himself to conclude that thanks to the gospel, general human behavior ("the manners of men") has "greatly improved." Of that he is certain. One wonders what Witherspoon would say if we could somehow transport him to the year 2000. Even if, in the latter half of the eighteenth century, there were some basis for such a positive assessment of Christianity's influence, would he not at the end of the twentieth century have to be rather less exuberant about any improvement in human "manners"?[36]

We would do well to pause and remember that Witherspoon had a clear purpose in delving so deeply into the many proofs of the truth of Christianity. Even when in Lectures 9–11 he turns to the explication of the doctrine of the Trinity, with the attendant beliefs in the divinity of the Son and Spirit, he does so within the framework of proofs. And he does so by design. It was imperative to answer both those who advocated the superiority of human reason and those who criticized Christianity for being unreasonable. We have already seen how adamant he was that the gospel truths were reasonable. But he found he had to go further than that. Even though Witherspoon would stoutly reiterate the old medieval saw that true religion consists of "nothing contrary to reason," he found that he had to insert into the discussion another category, one that also had a long history: There are some truths that are above reason, which means, he pointed out, they are "beyond the power of reason to discover, and above the reach of reason to comprehend." In fact, when we pause to consider that God is divine and we are human and therefore limited, "it is consonant to reason and the analogy of nature that there should be many things in the divine nature that we cannot fully comprehend." There is not even a suggestion of weakness or defeat to admit the limitations of the human mind and turn over the final solution of a problem to the overpowering wisdom of God. We are human and limited; God is divine and omniscient. We have absolutely no right, therefore, to demand that God conform to our kind and level of reason. The implications for piety are obvious. It does have its limitations, humanly speaking. It can never claim to have all the answers.

Take the doctrine of the Trinity, for example. Our best course is to leave it in the realm of mystery and admit that it is above our comprehension. Every attempt to explain it, Witherspoon announces, will be unsuccessful. The way of wisdom is to receive it as revealed and leave it at that.[37] Again, on the matter of God's sovereignty and how this impacts the truth of human freedom, Witherspoon passes out some advice: Do not torment yourself, as John Milton (1608–1674) imagined those damned in hell do, with trying to solve unsearchable questions.[38] The better part of wisdom and humility is to take comfort in the fact that there are a vast number of questions, not just Christian doctrines either, which we can only place in the hands of God. According to Witherspoon's interesting ruminations, some of these questions would include such puzzlers as: Why was the gospel given to such a small number of persons? Why was so much of the "howling wilderness" of America left for so long before being settled? Why is one person born a slave and another a monarch? Again, and more profoundly, why are so many advantages bestowed upon one person and so many hardships on another?[39]

Yet Witherspoon does not leave Christians altogether empty-handed when trying to resolve the dilemma of God's sovereignty versus the "free agency of the creature." He directs them to the Confession. The ultimate resolution, of course, is in the mind of God, but for now he advises us to try to believe both truths. "My being unable to explain these doctrines [does not] form an objection against one or the other." And so, he advises, we had better be suspicious of anyone who claims to be able to solve this puzzle.

Because Witherspoon assumes that reality consists of the qualitative distinction between the superior mind of God the creator and the inferior mind of the human creature, he can easily conclude that, in fact, it is entirely reasonable for us poor mortals not to be able to

Yester Parish Church, Gifford, near Edinburgh, built in 1702. Witherspoon's boyhood church. The church bell dates back to 1492. *(Permission to reproduce granted by the minister and Kirk Session of Yester Parish Church.)*

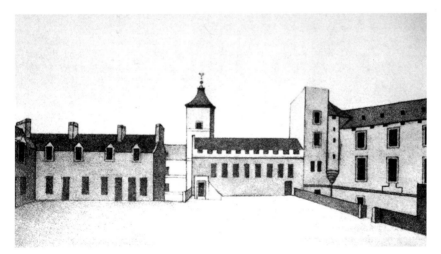

The University of Edinburgh in Witherspoon's day. Two libraries (1617, 1642) are center and right, student chambers to the left. *(Reproduced by permission of Edinburgh University Library.)*

St. Giles' Cathedral, High Street, Edinburgh, where the Reformer John Knox preached in the sixteenth century and where Witherspoon would have worshiped. *(Permission to reproduce granted by the minister of St. Giles Cathedral.)*

Edinburgh's Tolbooth (town hall, jail) in Witherspoon's day. *(Reproduced by permission of Edinburgh University Library.)*

Edinburgh Castle in the early eighteenth century. *(Crown Copyright: reproduced by permission of Historic Scotland.)*

The house of John Knox, High Street, Edinburgh. *(Drawing courtesy of George Olson, The College of Wooster.)*

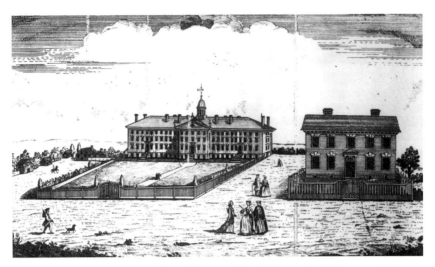

A 1764 view of Nassau Hall and the president's house in Princeton. Nassau Hall was an all-purpose academic building, containing classrooms, chapel, student rooms, refectory, and offices. *(University Archives. Department of Rare Books and Special Collections. Princeton University Library.)*

A modern view of Nassau Hall, Princeton University, which houses administrative offices. *(University Archives. Department of Rare Books and Special Collections. Princeton University Library.)*

An eighteenth-century view of Tusculum, Witherspoon's country home, near Princeton. *(University Archives. Department of Rare Books and Special Collections. Princeton University Library.)*

A modern view of Tusculum, now privately owned. *(University Archives. Department of Rare Books and Special Collections. Princeton University Library.)*

An artist's sketch of the Continental Congress meeting at Princeton in 1783. *(University Archives. Department of Rare Books and Special Collections. Princeton University Library.)*

The signature of John Witherspoon as it appears on the Declaration of Independence.

The title page of Witherspoon's May 17, 1776 sermon, in which he announces he is introducing politics into the pulpit.

John Witherspoon's grandfather clock. *(Permission to reproduce granted by the Presbyterian Historical Society.)*

16

solve all problems, religious or even secular. "I may say," as he concludes the matter, "it is consonant to reason and the analogy of nature that there should be many things in the divine nature that we cannot fully comprehend. There are many such things in his providence, and surely much more in his essence."[40] If one argues this way, it can be said that Christianity is indeed rational, and not so incidentally, Witherspoon's piety remains intact.

Douglas Sloan has summarized Witherspoon's position on the larger question of reason and revelation by describing it as "Presbyterian supernatural rationalism." What Sloan means is that Witherspoon met the challenge of the Enlightenment by avoiding the extremes of a purely rationalist understanding of religion on the one hand, and on the other, a virulent skepticism.[41] Within the Westminster Confession, Witherspoon took pains to place religion in a middle position, allowing for both reason and revelation, making it conform to reason as much as possible—thus his appeals to reason and experience—while leaving abundant room for revelation or the supernatural.

Sloan continues by suggesting that as a supernatural rationalist, Witherspoon was less an original thinker, creating new categories or solving old problems in new ways, than he was a synthesizer and interpreter of accepted positions. His gift was to grasp some major lines of thought in the eighteenth century and make them intelligible, especially to his theological students, equipping them for ministry at a time when revealed religion was under attack. He was to extend this effort in his "Lectures on Moral Philosophy," a course covering a wide range of topics required of all seniors at the college.

Promise

As Witherspoon continued his "Lectures on Divinity," proofs gave way to exposition, an attempt to explain the doctrine of the Trinity, at least to Witherspoon's satisfaction, and then exposition on several doctrines in the Confession—the decrees of God, the fall of human beings, and sin. The doctrines of the fall and sin bring Witherspoon to the subject of the covenant, that of works and that of grace, and finally, to promise. He does not concern himself overmuch with the covenant of works. He states that the term "covenant" has wide use in the Bible. He recognizes that the term is not applied in Genesis to God's ways with Adam, but is suitable to describe God's relationship to humans beginning with Adam. "As far as there can be a covenant relation between God and man, it evidently took place here. . . . It [also] appears that Adam in the covenant of works, was to be considered as the foederal head and representative of the human race, as he was then the natural head."[42] Thus, when Adam sinned, he brought down the whole human race with him: "As to the effect of Adam's sin upon his posterity, it seems very plain that the state of corruption and wickedness which men are now in, is stated in scripture as being the effect and punishment of Adam's first sin." The terrible evil of sin is to be found throughout the Bible ("The evil of sin appears from every page of the sacred oracles") and just as plainly in the world about us ("One can scarcely have a clearer idea of the evil of sin than by comparing the effects of piety and virtue . . . with the effects of universal corruption and depravity in any society").[43]

What can be done about this terrible human predicament, the pervasive evil of sin throughout human existence? Since we have already studied Witherspoon's sermons we have no doubt what the answer will be. In answering the momentous question for his divinity students, the professor proceeds to the covenant of grace, because "nothing is more plain from scripture or better supported by daily experience, than that man by nature is in fact incapable of recovering without the power of God specially interposed."[44] In short order, Witherspoon announces that this second covenant does nothing less than encompass "the whole plan of salvation through Jesus Christ," which in his purview includes discussing at some length such matters as the satisfaction of divine justice, the propriety of substituting "an innocent person in the room of the guilty," and whether such a "mediator should be a divine person." We know Witherspoon's thoughts on these issues, for he has already disclosed his positions in his discussions of piety for those in the pew.

He wants it clearly understood, however, that the second covenant is a *covenant of grace*, so-called because salvation is not by works but by God's free grace. It can, deservedly, be described in other ways, he admits, as long as one returns to what we might call the "base of operations," that is, grace. It can be termed a "covenant of peace" and described as "everlasting," for it surely is both of these. Finally, however, it can and should be called simply "the promise," because it is the one great promise God has made and fulfilled in Jesus Christ.

Rather than presenting the covenant of grace as one all-encompassing promise, Witherspoon informs his students that he will enumerate five separate promises so that they will be privy to "the way most proper for preaching the gospel." What he wants them to do, of course, is to proclaim what he has previously called "the real nature of God."

The covenant of grace promises:

1. Christ the mediator to make satisfaction to divine justice, by his sufferings and death.
2. The full and free pardon of all sin through Christ.
3. The spirit of sanctification to renew our nature, and form us for the service of God.
4. The favor of God, and all its happy fruits, while in this life.
5. Eternal life.[45]

If these promises remind us of the everlasting truths of the gospel that, according to Witherspoon, comprise the substance of lay piety, we should not be surprised. Witherspoon has just finished explaining to his future preachers that these promises, in the exact order he has offered them, are to be preached to their congregations as the very substance of the covenant of grace. And, one might add, the very message of salvation.

Part 3

Piety That Makes Politics Possible

Chapter Five

Providence

> Believe it, Christians, a personal application of the truths relating to Divine Providence, would reveal as it were a new world to you, and would make the paths of God towards you every day more intelligible, every day more profitable, and shall I not add, every day more comfortable.
>
> *Works, 2:52.*

Those of us who freely admit that we are historically conditioned will have no difficulty in understanding that theology never exists in isolation. It is impossible to think through and articulate the Christian faith inside some intellectually antiseptic bubble, free from the influences of the surrounding environment. Theology is always shaped by a number of factors, not the least of which are the social and political features of the culture in which theologians believe, think, and write. More than their predecessors, modern theologians are more sensitive to and candid about all those personal and external influences bearing upon them.[1]

It never occurred to John Witherspoon to explain that his piety was taking on a new dimension once he came to America and a war between the colonies and Great Britain was brewing. Yet his thinking about God and how God acts in history was changing. A more exact way of explaining this metamorphosis is to note that his understanding about the divine presence and activity in the world shifted from an almost exclusive focus on God as Redeemer to the same God as Creator, Sustainer, and Governor of all things, events, and persons. In America, Witherspoon's doctrine of God expanded to encompass a vital belief in God as Providence as well as Redeemer. He continued to preach his sermons on sin and salvation, but his new situation and the unfolding events leading to war with Britain prompted him to stretch his theology to emphasize an understanding of God's oversight of and care for all of creation and all of God's peoples.[2]

Witherspoon's doctrine of providence did not appear new and full-blown after 1768. One can find the term "Providence" in a number of his pre-1768 sermons. The careful reader of chapters 1 and 2 of the present study will already have observed that Witherspoon spoke of the "omnipotence of Providence," God's "sovereign providence," how the world is the locus of God's providential acts, and even how the believer can see providence as part of the significance of the Lord's Supper.[3] Frequently, Witherspoon simply invoked "Providence" instead of employing the usual name for the Deity, particularly when considering divine power and sovereignty.[4] He would speak of Providence the same way he would use the term "Creator" or "Maker." Even the phrase, "the dispensation of Divine Providence," was little more than an elegant way of speaking of God's mighty acts.[5] More significantly, Witherspoon did occasionally preach on the subject of providence as he ministered to his Beith and Paisley congregations even though providence was not one of the "truths of such unspeakable moment." For Witherspoon, providence was more than a run-of-the-mill topic for sermonizing if for no other reason than it highlighted the omnipotence and goodness of God, the same God who redeemed sinners.

In two sermons, both probably first preached in Scotland, Witherspoon successfully conveyed to his parishioners the truth that God was good and that God truly cared and provided for all that believed. In what was for Witherspoon a remarkably short down-to-earth sermon (only eight and one-half pages), he preached from Proverbs 30:8 ("Give me neither poverty, nor riches; feed me with food convenient for me"), using the title, "Seeking a Competency in the Wisdom of Providence."[6] A summary judgment of the sermon would be that Witherspoon brought God close to each person in a direct and practical way. "God," he announced, "is the real and proper giver of every temporal, as well as of every spiritual blessing." Therefore, it is lawful, and certainly not unworthy, for each Christian "to ask of God, what is necessary [for] support and preservation in the present life." The Bible is replete with examples of how God has cared for those who believe, Witherspoon continued, so remember that "He holdeth your soul in life, and guards you by his providence in your going out and in your coming in."

At the same time, Witherspoon issued a warning against being too greedy and expecting too much from God. The believer's prayer should always be "give me neither poverty nor riches." More to the point, Witherspoon wanted our prayer to be something like, "O God, put me 'in a safer middle between the two.'" That way we will "neither be urged by pressing necessity nor over-loaded with such abundance as we may be in danger of abusing."

Witherspoon admitted that it was easy to advise the safe middle but harder to define it. There are, he observed, "many intermediate degrees between the extremity of want, and the countless treasures of the wealthy." So what is a believer to do?

The answer, Witherspoon believed, is in three parts, and one must heed all three. The first part opens a veritable picture window on Witherspoon's understanding of the structure of society, its fixedness and stability. At the time he preached this sermon he obviously saw no need for any reform of the structure of society. How much one needs in life and what one prays for are really very simple: One's station in life, "in which God hath thought fit to place us," determines what a person requires and where the safe middle lies. Persons who are deemed important in our society and bear larger responsibilities deserve more of this world's goods, and vice versa. Anything approaching a classless society would have been inconceivable to Witherspoon, as he explained further: "Therefore, what would be plenty and fulness to persons in inferior stations, would be extreme poverty to persons placed, and called to act, in higher and more exalted spheres." However, before those who are rich and important can lean back and ease into their comfortable way of life, Witherspoon issued a warning to rich and poor alike. Christian piety dictates that firm brakes be applied to the acquisitive urge (he calls it "a sensual inclination") no matter how much or how little we own. All of us "should be modest in our desires after temporal good things" and ask only for "what is really necessary or useful to us." Piety demands a statement like that, but one wonders if it would offer much solace to the poor or corresponding discomfort to the rich. The idea that society would be composed of rich and poor was not unique to Witherspoon. In the Reformed tradition, that notion went straight back to Calvin, who claimed that providence had ordered a "varying mixture of rich and poor."[7] The idea of a society of providentially ordered classes lived on after Witherspoon. In the nineteenth century, Protestants of many varieties cheerfully sang a verse to the well-known hymn, "All Things Bright and Beautiful," that has since been dropped quietly but decisively from modern hymnals:

> The rich man in his castle,
> The poor man at his gate,
> God made them, high and lowly,
> And ordered their estate.[8]

In another connection, Witherspoon did recognize that there were, in real life, wicked rich people who thought only of feeding their appetites, and by misusing their wealth made the rest of humanity miserable. His hope was that rich people would use their wealth responsibly and morally, "contributing to the happiness of multitudes under them, and dispensing, under God, a great variety of the comforts of this life."[9]

If the first part of the answer to how much should rightly be ours is one's station in life, the second is, simply, to put the matter in God's hands. Infinitely wise, Providence is definitely "the best judge of what is most fit and convenient for us." We think we know what is best for us, but in truth we do not. We think we deserve more than we have, but in truth if we had more we would not necessarily be better persons nor handle more wealth and power honestly and responsibly.

To make his point Witherspoon lays out a few questions to all those who "secretly murmur" at their present state. And we can be certain that he intends a resounding "No" as the answer to each:

> Are you sure, that if you were advanced to a place of power and trust, you would be able to carry [on] with prudence, resolution and integrity? Are you sure, that if you were supplied with riches in great abundance, you would not allow yourselves to wander in pleasure, or swell in pride? Are you sure, that if you were raised to high rank, surrounded by flatterers, and wor-shipped by servants, you would, in that standing, behave with humility and condescension; or that pressed on all hands by business, company, or amusements, you would still religiously save your time for converse with God?[10]

The point of this in Witherspoon's thinking is not social control, keeping everyone in some predetermined place or role, but the very integrity of one's piety. Witherspoon knows that God knows what is best for each of us. We do not know what is best.

Therefore—and this is the third part of the answer to how we must live between poverty or riches—since God is the best judge of what is good for us, our stance must be that of utter resignation. Every selfish desire is an act of rebellion against God. "Every impatient complaint is an impeachment of Providence." On the other hand, we affirm the wisdom and goodness of God "in the most authentic manner, when his holy and sovereign Providence is humbly submitted to, and cordially approved." And to prove that this is not merely a personal bias, Witherspoon ends his sermon with the apt quotation from Jesus' Sermon on the Mount: "Seek ye first the kingdom of God, and his righteousness; and all these [material] things shall be added unto you."

For a second sermon on Providence, with the rather ponderous title, "The Christian's Disposition under a Sense of Mercies Received," Witherspoon chose Psalm 16:7 as his text ("Return unto thy rest, O my soul, for the Lord hath dealt bountifully with thee").[11] This extended discourse is less an account of how God provides earthly goods and more of how the faithful should respond to the providence of God. The whole psalm, Witherspoon explains, is an expression of thanks for deliverance from great sufferings and cruel enemies.

If we have learned to "count our mercies," including simple things like food and clothing; if we have been brought to a new awareness of "the great Atonement," freeing us from a burden of guilt; if we have been cured of an illness; or if God has awakened us to the power of his presence and excited our "affections in his worship"—then we have the greatest reason to say, along with the psalmist, "for the Lord hath dealt bountifully with thee."

But think some more about what Witherspoon calls "the footsteps of Providence." Providence is present when the means by which any mercy comes is unusual, when the timing of the mercy is exceptional, and when the mercy fits the need and character of the person concerned. If God gives humility to the rich, resignation to the poor, strength to the weak, fortitude to the besieged, then it cannot be denied that God has "dealt bountifully."

Next, the preacher would have his listeners discern God's ways in their troubles, have them put away their grumbling and complaining, and "make a sanctified use both of their trials and mercies."

Those mercies especially remind us of the times when the Lord has dealt bountifully with us:

> When in general mercies have not led to security or pride . . . ; when great abundance of outward possessions has not led to sensuality . . . but, on the contrary, to humility, usefulness, liberality; when a numerous or growing family, children springing up as olive plants round about the table, only fill the parents with a tender concern to train them up in the fear of God . . . ; when you are favored with the esteem and affection of others, and God enables you to improve your influence by zeal and diligence in doing good.[12]

All these are sanctified mercies, serving "to confirm and strengthen every holy disposition, and lead us in the paths of truth and righteousness."

The remainder of the sermon deals for the most part with the believer's "disposition" when recognizing and acknowledging God's providential work. The preacher wants his hearers to ponder the meaning of the phrase, "Return unto thy rest, O my soul." "Return," he directs, "and . . . humbly acknowledge God as the author of thy mercies." This, in truth, is far more than some kind of formal thanksgiving. God's providential kindness calls for a veritable outpouring of praise and gratitude. The amazing truth is that while our thanksgiving makes us find our rest in God, God's mercies rest all the more with us. Thus, our praise "increases the sweetness of every comfort;—it purifies its nature;—it prolongs its duration. . . . The more we return our mercies in praise to the giver, the more we possess them, and the greater richness we discover in them."[13] This is indeed the rest of the gracious and grateful soul, claims Witherspoon.

If a belief in providence brings comfort and enriches one's life, it might also encourage a false complacency ("I need to do nothing; I'll just leave everything in God's hands"). Activist Witherspoon will have none of that. Providence should compel the believer to *do*. "Be public-spirited and useful," Witherspoon commands. "If the Lord hath dealt bountifully with you, commend his service, and speak to his praise." What better "disposition" than that "under a sense of mercies received."[14]

The two sermons represent part of Witherspoon's understanding of providence as defined in the Westminster Confession: "God, the great Creator of all things, doth uphold, direct, dispose, and govern all creatures, actions, and things, from the greatest even to the least, by his most wise and holy providence."[15] Witherspoon's achievement was to take this formal statement of divine activity and present it to his parishioners in a form they could understand and incorporate into their piety. In that way, he truly "improved" the doctrine of providence. Witherspoon was preaching plainly, as he intended, to make the point that God was upholding and governing each believer, "even to the least," in such areas of their lives as personal wealth or lack of it, status in society, their trials and blessings.

While he usually viewed providence as kind and caring, he knew that the Bible and experience also taught that we can expect from time to time "a frowning Providence." We may be at a loss to interpret "the language of Providence" when we are afflicted, or we may have trouble discovering "the cause of God's controversy with [us]." Nevertheless, we must never forget that our "trials have a peculiar direction, and are capable of a spiritual improvement." We must not rebel, only try to understand, and then rejoice when, finally, "it pleaseth God to reconcile our minds to the will of his providence." Before that, however, we may have to have our "corruptions mortified by suffering," "the spirit broken by contrition and penitence when the body is broken by sickness," and our attachment to the world weakened. Yes, the doctrine of providence may have to include "the rod of fatherly correction."[16]

There was yet another dimension to Witherspoon's belief in providence. A particular interpretation of providence became critical when, as a pilgrim and a minister-in-politics in America, he thought about the flow of history; of the rise and fall and the health of nations; of war and peace; and of God's direction and governance of all people, not just Christians. For the record, even while he was a parish minister in Scotland, he thought and preached about this larger view of providence, the more so, however, when he transferred his person and loyalty to America, when he sensed that war with Great Britain was imminent and he decided to put politics into the pulpit. So it was, when Witherspoon preached a jeremiad on February 16, 1758, on a national day of prayer in Scotland. He took his text from Isaiah 51:9, and, as was noted earlier, the full title signaled the preacher's intention to treat in some detail the relation of providence to the Scottish nation: "Prayer for National Prosperity and for Revival of Religion Inseparably Connected."[17]

He wasted no time in calling down the sinful state of the nation, noting that previous public fasts had been celebrated with a "shameful coldness and indifference." In the past, what had been lacking was true repentance followed by genuine reformation; this time Witherspoon hoped there would be an outpouring of fasting and prayer alongside a wholesale acclamation of the power and providence of God. In the past, there had been "no question but the flood of impiety which has overspread this nation, solicits divine vengeance, and prevents the efficacy even of the sincere prayers that are offered up for deliverance and mercy"; this time, on this special day, Witherspoon called for a renewed belief in God "as the Almighty Creator, and righteous Governor of the world; the supreme Disposer of every event, and sovereign Arbiter of the fate of nations. How were it to be wished, that there was a just sense of this truth on the minds of all of every rank! And that, in all who are in any measure sincere on this occasion, the impression may not be transient and partial, but lasting and effectual!"[18]

The preacher did not immediately plunge into his jeremiad; in fact, he spent a large portion of the sermon discoursing on the text and the truths to be learned from taking to heart the words from Isaiah: "Awake, awake, put on strength, 'O arm of the Lord.'" He called to mind certain theological and biblical truths: "The constant superintendency of Divine Providence" is a given, but we have no business quickly falling on our knees, asking for God's blessing and assuming we will receive it forthwith. Just say No to such self-serving! Our prayers for deliverance from public want and calamity must ever be directed to the glory of God. Yes, there is a legitimate place for the judicious use of worldly means and outcomes, but we should expect ultimate deliverance from God alone. The honor to God must be preserved inviolate; we must ever resist the temptation to put our trust in human ability and power. Next, temporal mercies are always welded to spiritual ones, which is why in the Bible the Savior of sinners is represented as great in his power, observes Witherspoon. What this means is that we have no right to pray for any kind of national prosperity without simultaneously praying for a national revival of religion. "What," Witherspoon asks, "is temporal to eternal happiness?" "What is peace at home to peace with God? Security from an earthly oppressor to deliverance from the wrath to come?" The answers to these questions point to the following truth: "Though temporal deliverance were granted to a nation, in any measure, without a dispensation of the Spirit and revival of religion, it would be no blessing but a curse, and could not be of any long duration."[19] The text of the sermon and these religious reflections lead to the conclusion that trust in providence is utterly reliable. In and out of the Bible instances of extraordinary providential deliverances guarantee divine power. Never doubt that God will support and preserve his people, Witherspoon reassures his hearers.

Until he reached the "improvement" part of his sermon, Witherspoon had not followed the format of the jeremiad with much care. Now he does. He submits the prolonged lamentation of the nation's sins (and misfortunes), the first part of a jeremiad, by introducing the question, "Is not our state, both as a nation, and as a church, exceedingly fallen and low?" and then exclaiming, "Every class and denomination of men among us, every party and faction . . . is yet willing to acknowledge that we are at present in a distressed, and in a contemptible state." What follows is a whole catalogue of what he calls "public strokes," specific examples of national delinquencies and suffering. Some of these refer to France and the Seven Years' War (1755–1763):[20]

- "Threatenings of scarcity and famine."
- "War with a powerful and politic enemy, . . . [causing] an obstructed trade, a loss of territory, a loss of honor, and expence of treasure."
- "A pliant and fashionable scheme of religion, a fine theory of virtue and morality, . . . [replacing] the cross of Christ, and doctrine of the grace of God."
- [The public notice of] "pompous details of armaments, . . . and [the premature celebration of] the characters of military leaders, while they are only putting on the harness, and going into the field."
- The want of public spirit, in those who retain any sense of religion, an evidence of its low and languishing state.[21]

Recounting national sins and shortcomings is but one part of this kind of public discourse. The other part is a prescription of a remedy to cure those ills and restore God's favor. As Witherspoon explained, "It may sometimes please God to make use of desolating judgments or alarming public strokes to awaken a secure and thoughtless generation; but dutiful, acceptable and successful prayer for their removal, can only be the work of his own children."[22]

However, not all in the present situation is "doom and gloom." There is hope. It will, of course, require the effort of every serious committed Christian. The faithful must begin by earnest prayer for a revival of religion, that God will not only convince and convert sinners, but in his own good time bestow a blessing on all corners of the land, on persons of every class and rank, on every station and office, civil and sacred. Let us pray for and strive for the elimination of all the unhappy divisions among us, Witherspoon further proposes, so that the only "strife" remaining will be between those "who shall love our Redeemer most, and who shall serve him with the greatest zeal."

Witherspoon would not have called this a political sermon, but he does go so far as to express hope in and thanks for kings and princes. Christians should give thanks and pray for King George II, that God will bestow wisdom on him, protect his person and direct his councils. As well, thanksgiving should include God's providential work on the Continent, where, Witherspoon asserts, God has raised up "an eminent prince in Germany [Frederick the Great, 1712–1786] as the head of the reformed interest"; our supplication should ask for divine help to "encourage his heart, and strengthen his hand, and fight his battles."[23] Reference to these two rulers indicates clearly Witherspoon's belief that divine providence extends to governments and matters of state, a view that was to have special significance during the American Revolution.

Finally, in a brief uplifting conclusion to his sermon, the preacher anticipates a time of restoration and calls his hearers to action: "Let no Christian give way to desponding thoughts," he orders. Enmity to religion presently abounds, he points out, and we have even seen a minister of Christ leave the pulpit for the stage (!). But that is not the end of the matter, for "religion shall rise from its ruins." There can and will be a revival of true religion. All that is required of us is to be diligent in our own spheres and in our proper duty, "earnestly pleading for the revelation of the arm of the Lord; let us recollect his favor and protection to the church in every time of need, and his faithfulness which is to all generations."[24]

In his farewell discourse at Paisley in May 1768, he credited providence for directing him to leave Scotland to take up his new responsibilities in America. He noted that not he alone but "every Christian ought to be an observer of providence," for nothing will more effectively promote a Christian's holiness and comfort, he promised. This last sermon preached in Scotland is a mixture of practical advice on the choice of a new pastor and an admonition to his people to pray for God's guidance: "Take notice of every step of his providence, whether of mercy or trial," he counseled.[25]

At Princeton, Witherspoon was to continue and expand his views on providence that he had proclaimed from his Paisley pulpit. When he preached his first sermon in Princeton, he acknowledged that it was "that dispensation of providence, which, though contrary to all human probability, hath brought me this new charge."[26] Others also decided providence had had a hand in Witherspoon's removal to America. One such was Witherspoon's ministerial friend, Thomas Randall of Inchture in Perthshire, who wrote to him,

> When I heard, some time ago, of your being called to the Presidency of N. Jersey College, I judged it a matter of thankfulness to GOD; as I have long thought it the intention of Providence (after our abuse of our great mercies, and our dreadful degeneracy from real religion) to fix the great seat of truth and righteousness in America; and that N. Jersey seemed to promise fair for being the *nursery* of the most approved instrument, for carrying on that great design, in that wide continent.[27]

At the end of that first Princeton sermon, a brief backward look to Paisley caused him to ask his new parishioners if they would pray that his old congregation would "by the special conduct of divine providence, be supplied with a faithful pastor."[28] We have no record of his ever saying it, but as he moved to America he must have pondered it in his heart: it was surely God who was guiding him in his going out and his coming in.

There is convincing evidence that Witherspoon, once he was in America and had begun to take up the cause of the colonists, now conceived of providence more on a corporate than on an individual or personal level. It was as if he picked up in America where he had left off in Scotland, convinced that God's providence ruled over nations and peoples as well as pious persons. But now he was to enlarge this understanding of the work of God. Before and during the War of Independence we find Witherspoon describing, sometimes at length, God's hand in political and military affairs. He even reached the point in May 1776 of stating publicly that he was compelled to bring politics into the pulpit and explain how God was involved in current events.

There is some indication that even one year earlier, in May 1775, Witherspoon introduced politics into the pulpit, and that he did so under the rubric of providence. In that sermon,[29] preached on May 11 and based on Isaiah 26:9 ("For when thy judgments are in the earth, the inhabitants of the world will learn righteousness"), the preacher began with the truth "that God is the cause of every event whatsoever" and, according to one of his listeners who took notes on the sermon, Witherspoon "concluded with some directions to those who may stand forth in defence of their country." We lack the record of what those directions might have been, but the sermon does at least testify to Witherspoon's desire by 1775 to link religion and politics in his preaching.

In Scotland, Witherspoon had not been so certain that politics belonged in the pulpit. Indeed, at one point he advised ministers to refrain from "intermeddling in civil matters." As long as they had an adequate income, they should shun "worldly employments," he advised, else they will acquire a "bad fame [reputation]." Even worse and more sinful would be "for them to desire or claim the direction of such matters as fall within the province of the civil magistrate." True, this is not an actual proscription against introducing politics into preaching, but there is no question that in 1758 Witherspoon thought ministers should put themselves at considerable distance from actual affairs of state.[30]

Obviously, he changed his mind once he came to America and made the patriot cause his own. "New occasions teach new duties," poet James Russell Lowell once noted. They may also require putting aside old convictions and adopting new ones. The new situation in the America of the 1770s would seem to require a new position on preachers and politics, and Witherspoon responded by revealing how the hand of God was directing current events. By 1775, Witherspoon the minister was ready to speak out on the events at the start of the Revolutionary War.

We have already noticed that in May 1775, a month after Lexington and Concord, Witherspoon was asked to chair a committee of the Synod of New York and Philadelphia to write a letter to ministers advising them on attitudes to hold and steps to take now that war with Britain had commenced.[31] The wording of this pastoral letter, which in format is a minijeremiad, reminds one of the phraseology and constructions found in Witherspoon's sermons. It is quite probable that as chair of the committee he drafted the letter. Presbyterians of every sort were advised to humble themselves before God and confess not only general and personal iniquities, "but those prevalent national offenses which may be justly considered as the procuring cause of public judgments." The faithful were told that God in his providence would hold back the punishment and would "interpose for our protection and deliverance," providing there were a "thorough endeavor after personal and family reformation." There are six specific "advices" mentioned to guide pastors and people during the conflict and toward the time when the war would end. Witherspoon and his committee do not guarantee victory in the struggle, and even remind their readers that "for the wise ends of his Providence, it may please God, for a season, to suffer his people to lie under unmerited oppression." Still, God will prevail, for the divine promise has never "failed of its full accomplishment; *the Lord is with you while ye be with him, and if ye seek him, he will be found of you*" [Witherspoon's italics] (2 Chron. 15:2).[32] Leonard Trinterud is correct in remarking that the letter shows a conviction that whatever lies ahead, "the event is in God's hands," and that the directive itself is marked by calmness and sincerity.[33]

Witherspoon's further commentary on the controversy over independence appeared in his famous sermon of May 17, 1776, that day "being the General Fast appointed by the [Continental] Congress through the United Colonies." Entitled "The Dominion of Providence over the Passions of Men," the discourse was based on Psalm 76:10 ("Surely the wrath of man shall praise thee: the remainder of wrath shalt thou restrain").[34] Hostilities had begun a year earlier, and a consensus for independence was mounting. Clearly it was time for a political sermon, yet in the final analysis this notable discourse was actually a sermon on providence, as the title announced. It has been called a jeremiad, and elements of that genre are present, but it lacks a key component, namely, the lengthy lamentation on the sins of the colonists. Some necessary components are present: the sovereignty of God, the activity and direction of providence, and the several pieces of advice which if carried out will assure God's blessing.[35] Two factors make the sermon so important in understanding Witherspoon's piety and his role as a Presbyterian minister in current affairs: the timing of the sermon (only a few weeks before he signed the Declaration of Independence) and the manner in which he developed the doctrine of providence in his discourse and then applied it to the war between the colonists and Great Britain.

Witherspoon's main point is a familiar one: God's power is absolute and human passions are ultimately under the control of divine providence. Divine providence, he explains, extends to things of "great moment" as well as to "things the most indifferent and inconsiderable," to "things beneficial and salutary" as well as to "things seemingly most hurtful and destructive." Make no mistake! God "over-rules all his creatures, and all their actions." In one short paragraph Witherspoon succinctly states his intention before developing the announced text:

> That all the disorderly passions of men whether exposing the innocent to private injury, or whether they are the arrows of divine judgment in public calamity, shall, in the end, be to the praise of God: Or, to apply it more particularly to the present state of the American Colonies, and the plague of war,—the ambition of mistaken princes, the cunning and cruelty of oppressive and corrupt ministers, and even the inhumanity of brutal soldiers, however dreadful, shall finally promote the glory of God, and in the meantime, while the storm continues, his mercy and kindness shall appear in prescribing bounds to their rage and fury.[36]

In three ways, the preacher then declares, human wrath praises God.[37] First, it "clearly points out the corruption of our nature, which is the foundation stone of the doctrine of redemption." This sermon may turn out to be political in nature, but Witherspoon obviously has not forgotten the gospel's everlasting truths.[38] Second, when human wrath praises God, "it is the instrument in his hand for bringing sinners to repentance, and for the correction and improvement of his own children." Witherspoon omits here an enumeration of any national sins, while reminding his hearers that in general "public calamities, particularly the destroying sword, is so awful that it cannot but have a powerful influence in leading men to consider the presence and the power of God." Third, God in his providence often turns the councils of wicked rulers on their head, producing outcomes that are far removed from what was intended. Examples of this truth, Witherspoon comments, can be adduced from history, where perpetrators of persecution were frustrated in their evil actions by unintentional outcomes: for instance, the sufferings and death of Jesus, or the persecutions of the Protestant Reformers, or the attacks on the English Puritans. In each of these events victory arose from apparent defeat; human wrath, in the end, praised God.

In the second half of the sermon, Witherspoon offers three ways in which human wrath praises God in the present situation.[39] The first application, delivered with some force, is familiar: Each hearer should acknowledge the truly infinite importance of the salvation of his or her own soul. The *form* of godliness will not do. Admonishes Witherspoon, "there can be no true religion, till there be a discovery of your lost state by nature and practice, and an unfeigned acceptance of Christ Jesus, as he is offered in the gospel." In the grand scheme of things, he points out, it is not of "much moment whether you and your children shall be rich or poor, at liberty or in bonds." Never forget that politics is not paramount, salvation is.

Second, we must give thanks for "the singular interposition of providence hitherto, in behalf of the American colonies." Observe how well, Witherspoon argues, we Americans have fared already: Veteran British soldiers have been "turned into confusion," very little American blood has been spilled, and Boston has had to be evacuated by the British army and navy! But there must be no boasting, no "ostentatious, vaunting expressions" of colonial superiority, no trusting in our own arm of flesh. If we brag and act tough we will be just like Goliath, and we all remember what happened to him. It is God who must get the praise; God is "the supreme disposer of all events."

With his third point, Witherspoon brightens and offers a large measure of hope and confidence to his auditors. As long as three "ifs" are obeyed, the patriots can be assured of a happy outcome: "If your cause is just,—if your principles are pure,—and if your conduct is prudent, you need not fear the multitude of opposing hosts." Each of these required trenchant comment.

It was at this critical point in the sermon that Witherspoon must have looked his congregation in the eye and told them that he was about to take the unprecedented step of injecting politics directly into a sermon! While in his own mind this may have been true, a few years later he would explain that a sermon touching on political matters was only suitable for a national day of fasting or thanksgiving, not for regular Sunday worship. Such a qualification does not detract from the fact that Witherspoon's "Dominion of Providence" message came exactly at the right time in the spring of 1776. "You are all my witnesses," he declared,

> that this is the first time of my introducing any political subject into the pulpit. At this season, however, it is not only lawful but necessary, and I willingly embrace the opportunity of declaring my opinion without any hesitation, that the cause in which America is now in arms, is the cause of justice, of liberty, and of human nature. . . . The confederacy of the colonies, has not been the effect of pride, resentment, or sedition, but of a deep and general conviction, that our civil and religious liberties, and consequently in a great measure the temporal and eternal happiness of us and our posterity depended on the issue. The knowledge of God and his truths have from the beginning of the world been chiefly, if not entirely, confined to these parts of the earth, where some degree of liberty and political justice were to be seen. . . . [In truth] there is not a single instance in history in which civil liberty was lost, and religious liberty preserved entire. If therefore we yield up our temporal property, we at the same time deliver the conscience into bondage.[40]

We should notice that the preacher is not discussing civil liberty alone. The "hinge" of the controversy with Great Britain was about religious as well as civil liberty. While Witherspoon does not reveal how religious liberty would be abandoned if civil liberty were lost, he is sure it would. For him, this is the real reason why Americans must take up arms and why their cause is just. Other reasons can be adduced, but above all, religious liberty is basic for Christian piety and, in Witherspoon's judgment, that liberty was being sorely threatened by the British. Some historical background on this point will be helpful.

The most obvious threat to religious liberty, as seen not only by Witherspoon but also by many American Congregationalists and Presbyterians, was the threat, real or imagined, of settling in America a resident bishop of the Church of England.[41] Today we have to stretch our imaginations to grasp the uproar over this issue. Those who believed this a genuine threat did not fear the possibility of bishops as religious leaders nearly as much as they feared the political power the bishops might bring with them. Colonists against bishops could point to Anglican writings on both sides of the

Atlantic urging that an American bishop be appointed, though it must be noted that the sentiment for a bishop was stronger in America than in England. In 1766, to oppose the effort of settling a bishop in America, a loose organization of Presbyterian and Congregationalist ministers was formed (which lasted until 1775). Meeting annually, its sole purpose was to guard against any Anglican encroachments on religious and civil liberties of American non-Anglicans.

Witherspoon was a member of this convention (its members sometimes called it a "Congress"), though he did not always attend. Based on the evidence available, namely, the sparse extant records of the group and the lack of any Witherspoon essay or sermon on the subject, biographer Collins concluded that Witherspoon was not active in the movement, even though his membership would point to what he perceived was a very real threat to American liberty.[42]

Next, in this 1776 sermon Witherspoon showed that he was not a violent revolutionary, explaining that he would be guilty, neither in the pulpit nor in private, of "railing at the king personally, or even his ministers and the parliament, and the people of Britain, as so many barbarous savages." Calmly and rationally, Witherspoon put himself in the position of the British and remarked that "many of their actions have probably been worse than their intentions. That they should desire unlimited dominion . . . is neither new or wonderful." After all, if they should lose the war, they would in turn lose much of value. He wondered, "Would any man who could prevent it, give up his estate, person, and family, or the disposal of his neighbor, although he had liberty to choose the wisest and best master? Surely not. This is the true and proper hinge of the controversy between Great Britain and America."[43]

In this assessment of the conflict, Witherspoon shows a great deal of restraint and perspective. He explains here and elsewhere that the great distance between the colonies and Great Britain makes it impossible for the latter to exercise a wise and prudent administration of colonial affairs. Ignorance of the state of things in America is also a factor, leading to the obvious conclusion that independence is inevitable.[44]

"If your principles are pure." Witherspoon has tried to assure his congregation that their cause is just. When he turns to principles, he advises that no one be guilty of "a seditious and turbulent spirit," "a wanton contempt of legal authority," or "a selfish rapacious

disposition." The best principle is a "concern for the interest of your country, and the safety of yourselves."[45]

"If your conduct is prudent." All Americans must maintain "a resolute adherence to your duty," in the preacher's own words. In three detailed "exhortations," he explains what that means.[46] The formula appears obvious: to fulfill these duties is to ensure the blessings of divine providence in the present crisis. The first exhortation is a plea for all to maintain zeal for the glory of God and the good of others. One of the great principles of God's moral government is that "when true religion and internal principle maintain their vigor," oppression by an enemy will fail. Therefore, the best friend to American liberty is the person who is "most sincere and active in promoting true and undefiled religion."

In the second exhortation, Witherspoon proclaims that God's blessing is sure to shine on a country whose citizens are industrious. "Industry," he urges, "is a moral duty of the greatest moment, . . . and the sure way of obtaining the blessing of God." Witherspoon's ideal of industry is the farmer who arises at the crack of dawn, plows or follows his team all day, and who "in the end is an overmatch for those effeminate and delicate soldiers [British? mercenaries?], who are nursed in the lap of self-indulgence, and whose greatest exertion is in the important preparation for, and tedious attendance on, a masquerade, or midnight ball."[47]

Frugality is the subject of the third exhortation. Here Witherspoon reverts to an essential aspect of Christian piety: self-denial. He urges moderation in meals, dress, "furniture and equipage," and then declares that "the self-denial of the gospels, should extend to your whole deportment." He also repeats an earlier theme, now tying it to providence, when he reminds his hearers that "true religion [piety] is nothing else but an inward temper and outward conduct suited to your state and circumstances in providence at any time."

The very last sentence of the address, a supplication, rephrases the vital connection he has drawn earlier in this political sermon between religious and civil liberty, the very justification for going to war. "God grant that in America true religion and civil liberty may be inseparable, and that the unjust attempts to destroy the one, may in the issue tend to the support and establishment of both."[48]

The "Dominion of Providence" sermon has received considerable attention because, according to its author, it was an openly political sermon, and because of its timing, and of what it said about the author's position on the war and how Presbyterians were to conduct themselves as the hostilities progressed. However, from the perspective of how Witherspoon continued to understand and interpret the role of providence in the affairs of people and politics, specifically Americans and the American victory over the British, the sermon that he preached on the official day of Thanksgiving, April 19, 1783, celebrating the end of the war, is just as significant as the May 1776 discourse. Based upon Psalm 3:8 ("Salvation belongeth unto the Lord"), this untitled sermon is in no sense a political commentary on current or future events; it is very much an enthusiastic thanksgiving for the dispensations of providence in granting the Americans so many and such important successes in the war.[49]

In this particular utterance, Witherspoon announces, "my proper business therefore is to engage every pious hearer to adore the providence of God in general, to offer with sincerity and gratitude the sacrifice of praise for his many mercies, and to make a wise and just improvement of the present promising situation of public affairs."[50] Almost immediately he confesses that once more he is bringing politics into the pulpit. This time he appears to be a bit uneasy about doing so, rationalizing that on a special day of national thanksgiving it is permissible, and even a minister's duty, to discuss "events of a public nature." In his own mind, however, he is clear about the fact that it has not been his practice "to intermix politics with the ordinary [Sabbath] service of the sanctuary." Thus, Witherspoon draws an important distinction for modern preachers who seek his guidance about preaching political sermons. The Witherspoon rule: Politics get into the pulpit only on special days of national fasts or thanksgiving. This was true in Scotland in 1758, in Princeton in 1776, and again in Princeton in 1783. Having explained himself, Witherspoon continued his prefatory remarks by announcing that his intention is to review the immediate past, and for the future to recommend "what remains of your duty to God, to your country, and to yourselves."

At the outset Witherspoon explains that the meaning of salvation in Psalm 3 is deliverance from an enemy, often a great and dramatic deliverance, not salvation from sin. As such, the text means that success in any attempt is in God's hands and that there shall be no excessive reliance on human cunning or means or on second causes of any sort. The text also teaches the omnipotence of providence, that nothing is impossible with God, and further, that mercy and goodness accompany this omnipotence. God *hears* the cry of the oppressed and *sends* deliverance to those who plead for help.

The long central part of this thanksgiving message is taken up with an intriguing recital of the numerous instances of divine deliverance during the war. Three headings came to Witherspoon's mind as he organized the many divine interventions on behalf of the colonists. There were the amazing successes: those victories at sea that were quite unexpected, the victory of the Americans at Princeton, the defeat of General Burgoyne at Saratoga, the assistance of the "illustrious ally" in Europe, and the success in discovering before it was too late "the black treachery of Arnold." The success above all others, however, was that providence chose George Washington, "who was so eminently qualified for the arduous task of commander in chief of the armies." Denying that it is his nature to engage in adulation or gross flattery, Witherspoon proceeds to extol the virtues of Washington with a kind of iconic reverence. The choice of Washington was nothing less than "a favor from the God of heaven," he assures his listeners. The country stood in need of "a comprehensive and penetrating mind, which understood the effect of particular measures," and that need was met in Washington. "Consider his coolness and prudence, his fortitude and perseverance, his happy talent of engaging the affection of all ranks," and one is forced to conclude that "Providence has fitted him for the charge and called him to the service."[51]

Witherspoon was not alone in his adulation of Washington. Historian Edwin Gaustad, among others, has noted how in the minds of most Americans the person of Washington was raised to "mythic status," and how those same Americans understood that divine providence had raised up Washington to lead the colonists to victory. Anglican in church membership but reticent in making known his specific beliefs, Washington himself invoked the doctrine of providence to explain what had happened in the war, calling God the "Grand Architect," "Superintending Power," and the "Great Author of every public and private good."[52]

Witherspoon had known Washington for many years, and Washington had visited Princeton several times. Perhaps the most notable visit occurred in the summer of 1783, when the Continental Congress left Philadelphia temporarily and removed to Princeton to occupy Nassau Hall and carry on its business. For several months the village of Princeton became the nation's capital. When Washington arrived, the college faculty and the village residents gathered to pay their respects to the general and listen to a brief congratulatory address, which President Witherspoon had written. Again, the devotion is obvious, as are the two references to divine providence:

> We contemplate and adore the wisdom and goodness of divine Providence . . . in the unanimous appointment of your Excellency to the command of the army. When we consider the continuance of your life and health—the discernment, prudence, fortitude and patience of your couduct [*sic*], by which you have not only sacrificed, as others have done, personal ease, and prosperity, but frequently even reputation itself, in the public cause . . . —when we consider the great and growing attachment of the army, and the cordial esteem of all ranks of men, and of every state in the Union . . . —we cannot help being of opinion, that God himself has raised you up as a fit and proper instrument for establishing and securing the liberty and happiness of those States.[53]

If the first set of divine interventions during the war was the unexpected successes, the second was the preservation from what appeared to be insurmountable difficulties. Here Witherspoon cites the avoidance of severe dissension among the colonies as well as the "perfect cordiality"(!) that marked the cooperation of the American and French armies, the success in "raising, clothing, paying and supporting an army with a depreciated currency," and the harmonious way all the states held conventions and drew up their constitutions when everyone feared anarchy and confusion once British rule was overthrown. This particular danger, Witherspoon notes, "through the divine blessing, we happily and indeed entirely escaped."

The final group of successes deals with the way the "councils of our enemies were confounded." This general heading permitted Witherspoon to range over a number of items, such as the lamentable British ignorance of people and things American, the treachery and stupidity of the Loyalists, the cruelty of the acts of Parliament in London and the behavior of the British troops in America (who were "animated with a spirit of implacable rancor"), the barbarous treatment of American prisoners, and finally, the profanation of churches, Anglican excepted, which were put to such degrading use as "hospitals, . . . storehouses, barracks, riding schools and prisons."

In Witherspoon's calculation, providence had been very busy and very powerful in insuring an American victory, so much so that he concludes boldly, "Nothing appears to me more manifest than that the separation of this country from Britain, has been of God." But this is not the end of the matter or of the sermon, for he believed that this was no time for Americans to sit back and relish a delicious victory over their foes. This deliverance from the enemy, this "salvation," demanded a response, an obedience. And Witherspoon was not slow to say what it should be:[54] There must be absolutely no crowing, no "vain-glorious boasting," that we Americans have won the war! The only proper word is the humble one of thanksgiving. Especially those of us who are fortunate enough to remain alive, Witherspoon advises, should give thanks to God twice-over: first, because God "hath spared us as monuments of his mercy." An even greater expression of thanks must acknowledge the "establishment upon a lasting foundation . . . of those liberties civil and religious for which we have been contending."

Just as urgently, Witherspoon admonishes his listeners to attend directly to matters of piety, living in the fear of God, and displaying a gospel-approved conversation. Christians must keep their values straight. Liberty may be important but piety is vital. As significant as liberty is, eternity is of even greater moment than any earthly blessing. Therefore, we must always remember that "their state is little to be envied who are free as citizens, but slaves as sinners." The practices of piety have been relaxed during the war, Witherspoon admitted, but now that hostilities have ended we must return quickly to a "conscientious strictness in every part of our practice."

Second, we must show our gratitude by upholding the "public interest of religion, and the good of others." While this obligation falls on all of us, two classes of public figures have special responsibilities in this regard: ministers and magistrates. Ministers have two serious responsibilities to help insure the stability and well-being of society: (a) "the strongest obligation to holiness and usefulness in their own lives," in other words, to set a good example; and (b) "to watch over the manners of their several members." While Witherspoon would not have clerics running up and down the streets collaring evildoers, he does want them to take some responsibility for the behavior of church members. What he has in mind would surely get a minister fired immediately today. No current minister would dare exercise the kind of "strickness in religious discipline" and "inspection of [church members'] morals" that Witherspoon proposes. But we must be aware that for him such supervision is not to empower the clergy or to purify the church; the goal is a well-behaved society. He reveals his motive when he says that people's behavior is "of the utmost moment to the stability of any civil society." Thus, the minister has important work to do in helping to create a healthy social order.

An even heavier responsibility rests on the shoulders of all who have civil authority (magistrates): lawmakers, judges, governors, rulers of any sort.[55] We have to realize that Witherspoon has an eighteenth-century conception of the magistrate in mind, informed by the section "Of the Civil Magistrate" in the seventeenth-century Confession. In his view, these public officials bear a heavy responsibility for the ordering of society and its civic health, particularly now that the country is returning to peace. Their responsibility runs in two directions: First, the electorate must choose persons running for office who are known for their "personal integrity and private virtue"; otherwise they may not be trusted. Good and able rulers are basic to a good society. "Is it reasonable to expect wisdom from the ignorant," he asks, "fidelity from the profligate, assiduity and application to public business from men of a dissipated life?" Even worse, he complains, "we have had some instances of men who have roared for liberty in taverns, and were most noisy in public meetings, who yet have turned traitors in a little time." The unalterable truth is "that civil liberty cannot long be preserved without virtue," and according to Witherspoon, there is no better place to begin to practice virtue than with elected officials who themselves ought to be upright and moral. "The people in general ought to have regard to the moral character of those whom they invest with authority, either in the legislative, executive or judicial branches, such as are so promoted may perceive what is and will be expected from them."[56] Incidentally, it is interesting to observe that even before the Constitution of the United States became the law of the land, Witherspoon was proposing a form of government with three branches, a "complex" form as he explained in his "Lectures on Moral Philosophy."[57]

The other direction that magisterial responsibility must take is the promotion of a virtuous society by all those holding public office. Today we might be satisfied, even excited, if our public officials could at least be counted on to make a good faith effort to enact and enforce intelligent laws for the good of all the people, and our courts got closer to judging cases with justice for all. Witherspoon had much more in mind for his magistrates. They were to bear a heavy burden in promoting a virtuous society. Privately, they should revere the name of God, be sober and pure in their conversation, and be punctual in their "attendance on the public and private duties of religion." Not surprisingly, they are to be nothing less than outstanding examples of piety in their own lives. "Their example is both better seen and hath greater influence than that of persons of inferior rank," Witherspoon concluded. Most modern citizens would not argue with that kind of a public person if they were given the opportunity to choose such a one. But Witherspoon mapped out duties for public officials that if carried out today would surely get them into trouble. Witherspoon would no doubt be nonplussed, for example, to hear that a current judge was in legal trouble for posting the Ten Commandments in his courtroom. Witherspoon wanted his magistrates to be "under the strongest obligation to do their utmost to promote religion, sobriety, industry, and every social virtue, among those who are committed to their care." And if they were under a mandate to promote piety, they had an equally strong obligation to prevent impiety. If their authority was to be effective, then they should "begin at the source, and reform or restrain that impiety towards God, which is the true and proper cause of every disorder."[58]

It is appropriate here to digress briefly and clarify Witherspoon's position on the magistrate. Lest we think that he was being too compulsive about the duties of public officials, we should be aware that he had even pulled back from the formulation regarding magistrates in the 1647 Confession. Then the Westminster Assembly had declared,

> The Civill Magistrate . . . hath Authoritie, and it is his duetie, to take order . . . that all Blasphemies and Heresies be suppressed, all corruptions and abuses in Worship and Discipline prevented or reformed; and all the Ordinances of God duely settled, administered, and observed.[59]

Witherspoon did not, of course, advocate what would later be called "separation of church and state," but he surely knew that the American Presbyterian Church had voted as early as 1729 to reject the theocratic understanding of church and state imbedded in that paragraph on the magistrate in the original Confession. In that year the Synod approved the Confession with the proviso that the civil magistrate did not have "a controling Power over Synods with Respect to the Exercise of their ministerial Authority; or power to persecute any for their religion."[60]

It was not possible for Witherspoon to go the distance on the issue of religious liberty; he possessed too much of the eighteenth-century mind and spirit, which permitted a certain privilege to religion, particularly the Christian religion. So while he would recognize that the civil magistrate should protect the rights of conscience and not "persecute any for their religion," Witherspoon still believed it important for the sake of a virtuous society that that same official punish impiety. In other words, he thought the state should give recognition and aid to Christianity *in general*, though not to particular churches or denominations. The government was not expected to stand aside and be quite neutral when it came to religion versus irreligion. The magistrate, he noted further in his "Lectures on Moral Philosophy," should be something "of a parent" with "a right to instruct, though not to constrain." This translated into the obligation of that official somehow to recognize and encourage the Christian religion, since Christianity was the majority religion in America, but to make full allowance for those who did not subscribe to that faith. If nothing else, such public recognition of the majority religion would surely serve to bolster the morale of everyone, churched and nonchurched alike. Here is the way he worded it in his class in moral philosophy at Princeton: "The magistrate ought to make public provision for the worship of God, in such manner as is agreeable to the great body of the society; though at the same time all who dissent from it are fully tolerated. And indeed there seems to be a good deal of reason for it, that so instruction may be provided for the bulk of common people."[61]

I am certain that Witherspoon thought he had resolved the problem of church-state relations in America, at the same time providing the means to guarantee a moral citizenry. True, he had moved a great distance beyond the established church pattern in Europe and Britain. In America, he understood no church could be established, but in order to have the ideal society undergirded by Christian piety, the state would perforce have to offer some kind of recognition to the Christian religion.[62]

In the conclusion to his 1783 sermon on providence, Witherspoon gathered up all his hearers, along with ministers and magistrates, and informed them by way of several exhortations what their responsibilities were, now that victory was assured. Notice how these pleas repeat Witherspoon's emphasis on the importance of the works of piety, with an added bit of Whig sentiment:

> (L)et us guard against using our liberty as a cloak for licentiousness. . . . Let us endeavor to bring into, and keep in credit and reputation, every thing that may serve to give vigor to an equal republican constitution. Let us cherish a love of piety, order, industry, frugality. . . . Let us in public measures put honor upon modesty, and self denial, which is the index of real merit.

His final thought was a challenge to each colony as it became a state. He promised that those states that made "piety and virtue the standard of public honor" would in the end enjoy the greatest peace, happiness, and strength.[63]

Summary

Earlier in his ministry in Scotland, Witherspoon conceived of God as "infinite, eternal, and unchangeable, in his being, wisdom, power, holiness, justice, goodness, and truth." God was "high and lifted up," far removed from ordinary needs and human affairs—with one critical exception: God's main concern, a crucial one, was to extend mercy to sinful men and women to redeem them from the terrible state into which they had cast themselves. The "real nature of God" was exposed in the person of Jesus Christ and his atoning death on the cross. Real religion was redemption.

Witherspoon's understanding of God took a remarkable turn when he began to grasp that God was Providence as well as Redeemer, that God did "uphold, direct, dispose, and govern all creatures, actions, and things, from the greatest even to the least." We have seen how Witherspoon tried to make providence very simple, substantial, and personal for the individual, "the least," but at the same time invoked the doctrine of providence to explain actions of "the greatest" kinds, those of kings and parliaments, generals and troops, and congresses.

Nowhere does Witherspoon provide a concise definition of providence. In his "Lectures on Divinity" he devotes what seems excessive attention to a discussion of "Decrees of God" (Lectures 12, 13), with only an occasional mention of providence. In the Confession, providence rates a whole chapter, as does decrees, which would lead one to think that Witherspoon might have delivered at least one short lecture on providence to his divinity students.[64] What is more apparent, and important, is that Witherspoon never confused providence with creation. He sometimes brings them close together, but in the end he adhered to the Confession and kept them separate: Creation comes first, providence second.

One has to turn to the sermons, as before, to understand what Witherspoon meant by providence. To a degree, he followed the classical Reformed understanding of the doctrine, which was to delineate three functions or operations of providence: preservation of creation, sometimes called conservation; concurrence, or God's cooperation with all things; and governance, or the direction and goal that God applies to the flow of history.[65] We have seen how he made real to his hearers that God or Providence "preserved" his creation, noting, for example, that it was legitimate for each believer "to ask of God, what is necessary [for] support and preservation in the present life." He, of course, added a cautionary note, to the effect that we should pray for and expect only what is adequate, not more, not less, for our station in life. And he was careful to define preservation further by explaining that God bestowed spiritual gifts as well as material ones.

Witherspoon did not extensively develop the concept of concurrence, God's cooperation with all creatures, a teaching that takes up the human roles of freedom and second causes. When he moved to governance, however, he saw this aspect of providence as persuasive and powerful. We have observed that both in Scotland and later in America, Witherspoon saw God's hand directing and governing all creatures, actions, and things, particularly on the national and international level. The goal of such direction was, of course, the accomplishments of the divine purpose. When Witherspoon recommended the study of history as an integral part of the "learning" of the minister, he could have made the point then that human history is the plane on which the works of providence take place. It is strange that he did not, for he surely believed that not only the experience of persons but the history of nations and rulers were subject to God. It is obvious that in the years leading to 1776, during the years of the war itself, and even after the war, Witherspoon saw God blessing and aiding the American cause. Providence, he proclaimed, did indeed dominate and overrule the passions of sinful human beings.

In modern times, Swiss theologian Karl Barth (1886–1968) reflected on the doctrine of providence at some length, including in his definition of the term the concept that God governs "in time." By providence Barth meant "the superior dealings of the Creator with His creation, the wisdom, omnipotence and goodness which He maintains and governs in time this distinct reality according to the counsel of His own will." Witherspoon would not have quibbled with that declaration, nor would he have had any qualms about Barth's notion of the aim or purpose of providence: God's providential activity is "a guiding, a leading, a ruling, and active determining of the being and activity of all the reality which is distinct from Himself. He directs it to the thing which in accordance with his good-pleasure and resolve, and on the basis of its creation, it has to do and be in the course of its history in time."[66]

Witherspoon did not discuss the work of providence in the long term. He preferred to examine recent history right up to the present in order to discern God's leading. He assumed, like Calvin and others before and after him, that providence was intelligible, at least most of the time, and that it behooved every Christian to try to discover the ways of providence to one's everlasting benefit. Every Christian, he recommended, ought to be "an observer of providence," if he or she wished to increase "holiness and comfort." Of course, the ways of providence occasionally escape us, but it was his conviction that if we would be patient we might come to a knowledge of the workings of providence, which in the end would enlarge and enrich our piety. Witherspoon's message on providence would have been even more poignant if he had employed an illustration from one of John Chrysostom's sermons on providence, and he could have done that without violating his plain preaching style. As Kathleen Norris tells it, Chrysostom drew the picture of a city dweller who knew nothing of farming, "observing a farmer collecting grain and shutting it in a barn to protect it from damp. [Later] he sees the same farmer take the same grain and cast it to the winds, spreading it on the ground, maybe even in the mud, without worrying any more about the dampness. Surely he will think the farmer has ruined the grain, and reprove the farmer." He, of course, has jumped to his conclusion too soon. If only he had waited until the end of the summer, he would have seen how the grain had ripened into a full harvest and would have understood the ways of the farmer. Chrysostom concludes with an appeal for the patience to "await the final outcome of events, remembering who it is who ploughs the earth of our souls."[67]

Witherspoon was no Pollyanna as he dealt with providence. He believed that God's ways were not always gentle and enjoyable. In the divine freedom to act, God could be a "frowning Providence" as well as a smiling and beneficial one. If a nation's morals declined or if a person suffered, God's justice might intervene in such a way as to make sure that there was spiritual improvement and that the divine will would be obeyed. The "rod of fatherly correction" was part of Witherspoon's doctrine of providence. Never to be forgotten in Witherspoon's piety is the truth that God is supreme. We must resign ourselves to his direction and governance with no hesitation or grumbling, always remembering that "every impatient complaint [of one's condition] is an act of rebellion against God." Of even greater significance is Witherspoon's unwillingness to view providence as some sterile belief unrelated to Christian life and conduct. Providence demands a clear and vigorous response.

In Witherspoon's 1783 fast day sermon we have seen how he couched certain recommendations regarding a response to God's providence in terms suitable to the military victory, but in those specific pieces of advice lie more general commands connecting providence to a person's piety. Providence should evoke thanksgiving, not only for a happy outcome on the battlefield, but for every providential mercy received. Next should be a life lived in the fear of God, and speech "such as becometh the gospel." But the more Witherspoon thought about response the more he concluded that there should be a "strictness in every part of our practice," not simply in an isolated part of our conduct, such as conversation.

We are also to respond by doing all we can to further religion in the greater society, seeking ways to do good to other persons. Thus, providence is not for private enjoyment. We recall that Witherspoon singled out ministers and magistrates for special attention, but his counsel to "be publick-spirited and useful" was directed to everyone.

It is important to set the record straight on two other matters. First, an aspect of millennialism, as understood in colonial America, was the belief in a coming ideal society. Witherspoon's doctrine of providence and his wartime experiences did not set in motion the kind of millennialism that was proclaimed by some preachers before and during the Revolution. We recall that Witherspoon said very flattering things about America and its possibilities, but he stopped short of describing it as a new Israel, calling the mission of Christian immigrants an "errand into the wilderness," denouncing Great Britain as wicked Babylon, or proposing that America would be the place for the unfolding of the kingdom of God. Nor did he ever describe the war as the decisive battle between Christ (America) and the anti-Christ (Britain).[68] For example, one will not find in Witherspoon the kind of anticipatory rhetoric that was delivered from the pulpit of the Reverend Ebenezer Baldwin in Danbury, Connecticut, who speculated that in God's providence America might become "the principal Seat of that glorious kingdom, which Christ shall erect upon Earth in the latter days." Absent also from Witherspoon's writings are the more explicit millennial interpretations of someone like the Reverend Samuel Sherwood of Fairfield, Connecticut, who, in a fiery sermon, likened Babylon's fall to the imminent collapse of Britain; identified the woman in the wilderness, that is, the bride of Christ, with the Christian Church, which would overcome tyrants and oppressors; and promised, finally, that if the Lord would but "shorten the days of tribulation," wars and tumults would cease and the kingdom would come when "the wolf and the lamb [will] lie down together."[69] As for Witherspoon, his prospects for America were at once more modest, more this-worldly, and much more contingent on the piety of its people.

A second observation is necessary: Witherspoon was no pacifist; his piety, as we have already discovered, did not require the renunciation of war. And those reprehensible and violent "passions of men," according to him, could readily be fitted into God's providential intentions. Nevertheless, there were right (just) ways of fighting and wrong (unjust) ones, according to the Princeton preacher/philosopher.[70] He did not delve into the Bible, notably the teachings of Jesus, for the principle(s) of a just war. Instead, he resorted to the "law of nature and nations," a higher law that assumed a universe ruled by moral law grounded in the being of God and known in the moral sense or conscience of all persons.

Witherspoon wrote that a war might justly be fought over a sustained violation of a perfect right (e.g., seizing property, indiscriminate killing), but it should not be started until a clear formal declaration has been issued stating the justice of the cause, and should continue only until the original injury is completely redressed and reasonable security against future attacks is assured. Clearly, a modern scorched earth tactic would be unjust.

Witherspoon's own list of what he calls generally agreed-upon cruel and inhuman acts include refusing quarter to those who surrender, killing prisoners when they can be imprisoned safely, killing women and children, employing torture, burning and destroying useful goods, using poisoned weapons (the modern equivalent of poison gas), and poisoning springs and provisions (today's germ warfare?).[71] As long as a conflict was a "just war," Witherspoon seemed to have had no trouble fitting it into a doctrine of providence and, consequently, into one's life and thought as a Christian.

At this point, I must interject an observation on Witherspoon's thought that has more to do with his general theological stance than with his piety as such, or with his particular interpretations of providence. Earlier in this study I suggested that Witherspoon's rigid, tough stance against the Moderates and what they stood for might be softening over time. We noted, for instance, that while still in Scotland he was recommending "sound learning" for a minister, stating that there was "no branch of human knowledge of which a Divine may not be the better." And when it came to the study of history, Witherspoon insisted that "a clergyman should be a man of liberal knowledge, and fit for the conversation and society of men of rank and letters."[72] The idea that sound learning needed to be joined with the everlasting truths of the gospel was later made emphatic in his "Lectures on Eloquence." His advice on liberal knowledge and polite behavior was intended not only for seminarians and young clerics but also for all the seniors graduating from the college. From 1775 to 1787, Witherspoon gave the same speech to the graduates, recommending "politeness and grace in behavior" and concluding with the hope that the advice contained in his speech would "lay the foundation for the most solid, valuable and durable politeness."[73] What a change! Is Witherspoon now preaching an "enlightened" piety? Is this the same Witherspoon who was so scornful of the polite Moderates years earlier in Scotland? Of course it is, to which the appropriate remark might be, "You've come a long way, Pastor!"

Other changes deserve notice. Francis Hutcheson, the Glasgow moral philosopher whom Witherspoon had maligned in the

"Ecclesiastical Characteristics," became one of the authorities on whom Witherspoon based his own "Lectures on Moral Philosophy," without, I might add, the attribution considered proper by today's standards. Other nonheroes criticized in the "Characteristics," such as Leibniz, Lord Shaftesbury, and Hume, became recommended authors for consideration by students of both moral philosophy and divinity.

At the beginning of the "Lectures on Moral Philosophy," Witherspoon stated that "the principles of duty and obligation must be drawn from the nature of man"—not, we might take note, from the Bible or revealed truth. As he explained, a careful study of human nature reveals that each person possesses an internal sense of beauty and moral excellence similar to the external senses that react to the physical world. This internal sense, as noted above, is the moral sense or conscience. When individuals become aware of this sense and cultivate it, they discover a feeling of obligation. Duty, thus, is not derived from some biblical command but by reason or human nature, or both. While Witherspoon offered formal obeisance to revelation, his avowed intent in his exposition of moral philosophy was to demonstrate that it was "an inquiry into the nature and grounds of moral obligation by reason, *as distinct from revelation* [italics mine]."[74] One has to admit that such an affirmation of the value of reason was not exactly new; Witherspoon, we remember, was willing in a few of his sermons to prove a point or confirm a truth by appealing to reason or experience. The difference now is a matter of emphasis. Reason can be trusted more; it plays a larger role in his thinking and in his analysis of human nature and behavior.

Simultaneously, certain parts of Witherspoon's "after walk" now receive more attention. Topics such as duty and virtue achieve a prominence not evident in his earlier sermons. Virtue, when it was presented from the Scottish pulpit, was "enlivened and animated by [Christian] piety" exclusively. It was not connected to our ultimate happiness or dispositions, nor to "benevolence of heart, and beneficence of action," nor even based on "reason and the nature of things." What is wrong with those theories, explained Witherspoon, is that they keep our obligations to God "much out of view." He concluded that the basis of virtue is in the first commandment of the law, "Thou shalt love the Lord," and the source from which all other virtues "must take their rise."[75] However, when virtue was discussed in the American classroom, "whatever God commands is virtue and duty," Witherspoon commenced, but when he continued, he shifted the impulse for virtue from God's free sovereign will to the nature of things: "Whatever he has implanted in uncorrupted nature as a principle, is to be received as his will." Similarly, the rule of duty now is not derived from God's direct command but from "conscience enlightened by reason, experience, . . . and [God's] intention in creating us such as we are."[76] Whatever its source, duty found its way into both Princeton sermon and lecture. Witherspoon preached "a resolute adherence to your duty" to the Presbyterians, and lectured at tiresome length to his students in the college on one's duty to God, to others, and to ourselves.[77] Even the most patient student must have rejoiced when the good professor finished with duty and moved to a new topic.

Anyone who has sat through high school or college baccalaureate services and commencement exercises will appreciate what President Witherspoon said in his baccalaureate sermon, "Christian Magnanimity" (text: 1 Thess. 2:12), and the accompanying address to the graduating seniors.[78] The sermon was first preached in 1775, but parts of Witherspoon's advice are timeless, and the sermon in typical plain speech illustrates in a remarkable way how he was able to strike an even balance among three sources of knowledge. Also, better than many other things he said or wrote, it illustrates his positions on reason and revelation, piety and learning, true religion and Enlightenment principle. He accomplished all this by first defining magnanimity and then throwing three different kinds of light on the subject. Once again Witherspoon was careless in his definition of a term, so the nearest we can come to his meaning of magnanimity is simply "greatness." This appears to serve his purposes well enough, though "loftiness of spirit" or "noble generosity" might be closer to our understanding and usage.

We shall let the preacher tell us what he is going to do: "I hope to be able to shew that real greatness is inseparable from sincere piety; and that any defect in the one, must necessarily be a discernible blemish in the other. With this view, I will, first, give you the principles of magnanimity in general, as a natural quality; secondly, I will shew what is necessary to give it real value, as a moral virtue; and thirdly, shew that it shines with the most perfect brightness as a Christian grace."[79] It is not necessary to delineate the several points in each of the three sections to discern Witherspoon's intent. He wants, first, the noble, second, the moral, and third, the Christian person to be able to (1) attempt great and difficult things, (2) aspire after great and valuable possessions, (3) encounter dangers with resolution, (4) struggle against difficulties with perseverance, and (5) bear sufferings with fortitude and patience.[80] While he never alludes directly to the coming war in the sermon, some of these marks of greatness could surely apply directly to someone soon to be caught up in the turmoil of war.[81] Witherspoon's genius lies, finally, in the way he takes these natural and moral virtues and transforms them into expressions of Christian piety.[82]

True piety attempts "great and difficult things" by calling every good person to remember the first and second great commandments, "to love and act for the glory of God, and the good of others." True piety "aspires after the greatest and most valuable possessions," which turn out to be nothing less than the Christian's "inheritance incorruptible and undefiled, and that fadeth not away." The Christian then looks down "with becoming indifference" on the glory of this present transitory world. "True piety encounters the greatest dangers with resolution." In the extreme, Christians bear up bravely when terrible persecution afflicts them; in more peaceful daily life, on the other hand, they will "manifest a holy resolution" if they become the objects of "reproach and derision of worldly [persons]." "True piety perseveres with constancy in opposition to continued trial." The preacher might just as well be discussing an aspect of sanctification, but he never mentions it on this occasion, reassuring the graduates and others that the person "who shall endure to the end . . . shall be saved."

"In the last place, true piety endures suffering with patience and fortitude" and, one must add, not only in the lives of the "suffering martyrs," but also in those of more ordinary saints. The following quotation from the last part of the sermon contains both a moving valedictory to the graduates and undoubtedly his best definition of magnanimity yet. For us, it can serve as the closing word to this chapter on providence:

> The believer has made an unreserved surrender of himself and his all, to the disposal of Providence. . . . For the Christian then [1] to suffer reproach, without rendering evil for evil, or railing for railing, [2] to be submissive under the loss of substance, and say with Job, Job 1:21. "Naked came I out of my mother's womb, and naked shall I return thither: the Lord gave, and the

Lord hath taken away. . . ."—[3] to yield up relations and say with David, 2 Sam. 12:23. "I shall go to him, but he shall not return to me." [4] to look forward to approaching death, and say with the apostle Paul, 2 Tim. 4:6. "I am now ready to be offered, and the time of my departure is at hand." This is magnanimity indeed; this is the most solid glory to which any child of Adam can possibly attain.[83]

Chapter Six

Practical Improvement

I proceed now to make some practical improvement of
what hath been said.

Works, 2:545.

A n entire monograph could be written on the influence of John
Witherspoon on American life and thought in the nineteenth
and twentieth centuries. His presence could be traced in the lives of
his students who became ministers, educators, public officials, and
community leaders; in the type of education he instituted at the College of New Jersey; in teaching the basic principles of a philosophy
that was to dominate American thought well into the nineteenth
century; and in the leadership he provided in forming the Presbyterian Church in America.

Our concern, however, must be more modest and restricted. Just
as Witherspoon built into every sermon a conclusion, which he
called "Practical Improvement" or "Practical Application," an
attempt to apply the text and doctrine of the discourse directly to the
lives of his hearers, we must see how his piety can "improve" the
individual and common life of Christians today. We would do well
to note that his piety has three outstanding and vital features: It is
traditional, doctrinal, and practical.

Witherspoon has history on his side as he formulates the core
tenets of piety—human sinfulness, the grace of God, redemption
through the sacrifice of Christ, and a sanctified Christian life. He
does not give credit to Augustine or to Calvin, though he might have,
for this understanding of human loss and recovery.[1] He was intelligent enough and sufficiently well-read that he could have chosen
other ways of constructing a piety, but his unfaltering conviction was
that one's holiness must be founded upon God's astounding revelation in Christ, and further, that the task of the preacher was to believe

178

this truth himself and then faithfully to proclaim this good news in so many plain words to those in the pew Sunday after Sunday.

In Witherspoon's view, religion must have content. He would remonstrate immediately with those today who would keep religion "real simple," for example, reducing it to a "Jesus saves" slogan or a "love your neighbor" goodness. He would want us to read and study our Bibles, learn our church history, understand what our worship means, and become theologically literate. Theology does matter. Genuine piety can be neither some "enthusiasm" (an extravagance based on religious devotion), nor a journey, a system of moral uprightness, therapeutic spirituality, nor some program of life improvement or affirmation. Witherspoon's piety is what current Reformed theologian Douglas Ottati has called a "theocentric piety," beginning and ending in the supremacy of God.[2] Our piety begins with God and not ourselves. To admit that we are sinners is to recognize that we have made the tragic mistake of putting someone or something else, not God, first. "God alone is God, and we should have no others," counters Ottati. Sin's corruption is never the last word; the gracious God speaks the last word of mercy and forgiveness. God never abandons sinners but instead bestows upon them a transforming grace that overcomes self-centeredness and brokenness. Such grace takes shape in the gospel, the good news that Jesus Christ redeems sinners. What Ottati calls "reforming piety" becomes "Christ-formed and even Christocentric" and makes possible a renewed, sanctified life for individuals and persons-in-community. He continues with a declaration that would surely elicit nothing less than a hearty "Amen" from eighteenth-century Witherspoon. Christians at their best, Ottati explains, "try to relate all things *appropriately* to God and to one another. . . . They witness to God's no and to God's yes. They point to sin and grace, to the cross and to glory, to judgment and mercy. They call for the dynamic ordering and reordering of all of life in faithfulness to the One on whom we depend, to whom we belong and from whom nothing can separate us."[3]

Ottati is not alone in calling for a fresh understanding of piety based on time-honored theological verities. Other contemporary theologians are urging a return to a piety based on historic Christian affirmations. For example, John Leith, professor of theology emeritus at Union Theological Seminary (Virginia), has complained that the number of particular theologies presently taught in

Reformed seminaries and in the church as a whole leave both clergy and laity lacking a sense of identity and an overall framework of theology within which they might find meaning and purpose for their lives. Professor Bruce Kuklick of the University of Pennsylvania voices a similar complaint, calling attention to what he calls "the degradation of Christian theology in America." Leith urges seminaries to return to the teaching of the "church's faith," which for him is embodied in six "foundational doctrines," his own set of everlasting truths, the center of which is "the work of God for the salvation of all people in the life and death and resurrection of Jesus Christ."[4] Theologian Shirley Guthrie of Columbia Theological Seminary concludes his *Christian Theology* with several penetrating questions to force his readers to confront their deepest spiritual needs. The answers to these needs, he submits, are contained in God's redemptive work: "God so loved the world—the *sinful* world—that God came in Jesus Christ to bring eternal life to those who believe in him. He came not to *condemn* the world but that the world—the whole world!—might be *saved* through him."[5] Similarly, theologian David Willis, as he ponders the future of Reformed theology, calls for evangelism to occupy a central place in the church's life and proclamation, the nature of the church being to proclaim and witness to the gospel.[6] Professor John McIntyre of the University of Edinburgh asks for a renewed understanding of forgiveness in the modern church and in the world. If the people in the pews are going to hear from the pulpit about the "grace of God in Jesus Christ and the forgiveness which flows therefrom," he states, "it is imperative that the preacher should build his/her presentation upon the whole foundation of salvation. . . . It is the whole Gospel which has to be preached, for it is the whole Gospel which saves."[7]

Similar calls for renewal of the church's faith come from teachers of preachers. In *A Theology of Preaching*, Professor Richard Lischer of Duke University Divinity School charges that many pastors and lay people shun theology as meaningless because so much of what has been called theology does not draw its life from the gospel. "Many church members," he remarks, "are bored or amused by the theological fads, the theologies *of*: the death of God, secularity, play, hope, story, and the like, which replace each other faster than fashion styles or football coaches." He recalls that Karl Barth once likened theological faddism to the principle of survival of the fittest, in which animals with younger teeth and horns kill off the older and weaker ones. "Only the preacher who is rooted in the church's constitutive principles, its doctrine," Lischer contends, "will be free to address the concerns of living people."[8]

It is the well-intentioned lies that are proclaimed from the pulpit that irritate Episcopal priest Robert Capon—lies such as useless programs of life improvement, the message that love is the cure of all our ills if only people will work harder at it, and the command to stop sinning and be morally upright if people want God to love them. In his lectures on preaching delivered at Seabury-Western Seminary, Capon advised future preachers to abandon these lies and straightforwardly tell their people that "God has gone and accepted every last one of them in his beloved Son and is pleased as punch with them in Jesus. If you can make up your mind," he continued, "when you go into the pulpit, to forget everything except Jesus Christ and him crucified, you'll have nothing to give them but *Good News*." For Capon this concise confession of faith is summed up in a telling homiletical motto: "A passion for the Passion."[9]

I have included these citations, from Leith to Capon, because at the dawn of the twenty-first century, it is crucial that we listen to these voices calling the church once more to a time-honored piety grounded in basic theological affirmations. Each in his own way is telling us that human beings and their needs are not *so* different today than they were in Witherspoon's time. We sin; by ourselves we cannot deal with it and we need God's mercy to rescue us; our death must be overcome by Jesus' death and resurrection; and having been rescued, we now can live out our lives as new persons, as if we had been born again.

If Witherspoon were suddenly to appear among us today, he might not find too many aggressive atheists or irascible "cultured despisers" of religion, but he no doubt would soon become aware of the several varieties of contemporary Moderates, whose Christianity is being shaped by the culture to such a degree that real religion has deteriorated into false forms. The lesson Witherspoon would have us learn is that we ought to take his everlasting truths to heart, not to repeat them verbatim like some detached formulaic mantra, but to find fresh, engaging ways to talk about sin, grace, justification, and sanctification without compromising or distorting these basic doctrines. The process will not be easy, but it is necessary.

In later centuries, the tendency of many in the church has been to write off the teachings of the Westminster Confession as too stiff, formal, propositional. We need to remember that Witherspoon himself deplored a cold formal religion, affirming in its place an evangelical piety, a lively personal experience of those vital gospel truths that were stated in classical form in the Confession. In the twentieth century, eminent theologians Karl Barth and Paul Tillich, whose own theologies hardly matched, testified to the strength and importance of the kind of Protestant orthodoxy that one finds in the Confession. While admitting that this theology cannot simply be repeated today, Barth enthusiastically praised it for its "form and substance," its "astounding richness . . . , the sterling quality, the relevant strictness, the superior style." Tillich also had high praise for this orthodoxy, calling it "a great theology" and asserting that it "was and still is the solid basis of all later developments, whether these developments . . . were directed against Orthodoxy, or were attempts at restoration of it."[10] If Barth and Tillich are correct, the basis of Witherspoon's piety in the Confession must be taken very seriously even in our time.

If Witherspoon's piety was theological—and evangelical—it was also practical. There is a prevailing pragmatic cast to his piety, and to other aspects of his thought as well. We have already noted how important it was for Witherspoon to keep faith and works bound together, and likewise, how easily at times he could appeal to reason and experience to make a point or highlight a truth. Occasionally, he could speak of "common utility" to mean usefulness, but whatever the language, practical results were what counted. It might be a garden full of vegetables alone; it might be a recommendation for a minister to study history because it will add "to a minister's knowledge of the human heart," to study Hebrew because it is "very proper and useful for a divine," and to study moral philosophy because it is a "very pleasant and improving study in itself"; or it might be Witherspoon's advice to graduating seniors that if they cultivate a "scrupulous regard to truth," it will promise them "the most assured success."[11]

At the heart of Witherspoon's contention that piety is practical lies his conviction that what one believes bears directly on what one does. Meaning in one's life does not arise from any particular moment or event in one's existence. Belief in eternal verities comes first, then to be followed by correct practice. In Witherspoon's words, "All moral action must arise from principle," which means that if one's principle is true, one's action assuredly will be moral.[12]

This is why in developing his piety, Witherspoon was so careful in defining and constructing one's inner disposition before describing a Christian's "after walk."

Repeatedly, Witherspoon told his parishioners that piety was practical, that "however concealed the inward principle may be, the practical effects must of necessity appear." He could even go so far as to employ mercantile terms in discussing the benefits of piety; computing the value of redemption was what he proposed: "Now who can compute the value of the divine favor, and all its happy effects? . . . On the one hand, deliverance from everlasting misery . . . On the other hand, what must be the value of everlasting happiness in the presence and enjoyment of God!"[13] In another sermon, he issued what he called "the very substance of practical religion." Practical religion is when the fullness of God dispels the believer's anxiety, and distressing fears, of every kind. "Does he want provision? . . . 'They that seek the Lord shall not want any good thing.' Does he want friends? God is able to make his enemies to be at peace with him. Does he want outward comfort? God is able to procure it, or make him happy without it."[14] Those are the practical results of piety. Still, he stopped short of falsifying religion by making it serve ends solely instrumental.

The idea of religion as benefit did not begin or end with Witherspoon, but his is an early voice in American religious life sounding a theme that has continued to the present—the pragmatic cast to religious life. A few decades after Witherspoon, the acute French observer of American ways, Alexis de Tocqueville, could write that American preachers were constantly preaching practical sermons, referring to earth rather than to heaven: "To touch their congregations, they always show them how favorable religious opinions are to freedom and public tranquillity; and it is often difficult to ascertain from their discourses whether the principal object of religion is to procure eternal felicity in the other world or prosperity in this."[15] One can only observe that that type of preacher is still with us. Likewise, when Paul Tillich came to America in 1933 he noticed and commented on what he called "the pragmatic-experiential approach of American theology," and complained that it was disconcerting to read a theoretical paper, even to an educated group, only to be asked, "What shall we do about it?"[16] Witherspoon was unapologetic about his own "pragmatic-experiential" approach to religion. He *knew* that piety was practical. Little did he know, however, how prescient he was in defining what was to become a prevalent element in American religious life.

Witherspoon's attention to "common utility," that which is practical, led him to think and talk about common sense. This is an aspect of his thought that, while not directly related to his piety, does serve to illustrate further the practical side of our subject. He used common sense in two ways: (1) as a means of achieving results and (2) as a way of viewing and dealing with reality. In one of his "Druid" essays, he described the person of "plain common sense" as possessing a number of admirable qualities, the most important of which was sound judgment. This, he said, was an inborn quality unachievable by formal instruction or augmented by one's environment: It was 100 percent nature, 0 percent nurture. The most likely persons to possess this quality are those of "the middle degrees of capacity," practical types who "perhaps generally, fill the most useful and important stations in human life." Witherspoon distrusted the extremes of dolt and genius: The former needs pity and the latter, who is "often accompanied with certain irregularities," merits our criticism and correction. "A very great genius, is often like a very fine flower, to be wondered at, but of little service either for food or medicine." His last piece of advice to those who would be eminent was, in effect, to cultivate some of those features of the pious person, to be noted for "sobriety, prudence and patient industry, which are the genuine dictates of *plain common sense.*"[17]

The other meaning of common sense was more significant and lasted longer. As articulated in parts of the "Lectures on Moral Philosophy," it was a way of apprehending and acting upon the world about us. Witherspoon peremptorily dismissed the philosophy of idealism (he called it "immaterialism") in vogue at the College of New Jersey when he arrived, and replaced it with an early form of common sense realism. His dismissal was not gentle: "The immaterial system is a wild and ridiculous attempt to unsettle the principles of common sense by metaphysical reasoning, which can hardly produce any thing but contempt in the generality of persons who hear it." His counterproposal: "That our senses are to be trusted in the information they give us, seems to me a first principle, because they are the foundation of all our reasonings." Later Witherspoon cited with approval what certain Scottish moral philosophers had done to refute the skeptics and idealists: "Some late writers have advanced with great apparent reason, that there are certain first principles or dictates of common sense, which are either simple perceptions, or seen with intuitive evidence. They can no more be proved than you can prove an axiom in mathematical science." With these words to his students, Witherspoon was inaugurating the long American career of Scottish common sense philosophy, which was to be so influential in the American collegiate classroom and Protestant pulpit for nearly a century.[18]

Although he may have upheld the value of plain common sense and taught the college seniors the first principles of common sense thought, at the point of their graduation President Witherspoon reinforced the preeminence of piety. Each graduating class from 1775 onward heard the same advice:

> Do not think it enough to be prudent, cautious, or decent in your conduct, or to attain a character formed upon worldly principles, and governed by worldly motives. . . . But alas! the evil lies deeper. "Except a man be born again, he cannot enter the Kingdom of God." True religion must arise from a clear and deep conviction of your lost state by nature and practice, and an unfeigned reliance on the pardoning mercy and sanctifying grace of God.[19]

Another way Witherspoon made piety practical, for his people and for us today, is in his solid conviction that politics had to rest on the bedrock of virtue, and virtue, in turn, upon religion. Put simply, free and honorable government must be built on a solid moral base. Of course, others in the eighteenth century besides Witherspoon held this truth to be inviolable. No less a personage than George Washington affirmed the connection between politics of integrity and vital religion. In his famous Farewell Address (1796), he stated, "Of all the dispositions and habits which lead to political prosperity, Religion and morality are essential supports. . . . And let us with caution indulge the supposition, that morality can be maintained without religion."[20] Even such a skeptic as Benjamin Franklin had decided that a high level of public morality was derived from organized religion, so he went to church now and then, not because he was a believer but because it was, as he said, "decent and proper."[21] Piety produced virtuous people and pious persons would in turn guarantee a free republican government.

This truth is part of the larger "God-Caesar" question, as Pittsburgh Theological Seminary professor Ronald Stone calls it, found in scripture and permeating much of western history.[22] Since the time of Calvin, Reformed Christians have been especially sensitive to the problem of being both religious and political. In raising this particular issue at the time of the American Revolution, Witherspoon was showing his true colors as a Reformed thinker. His own participation in politics provides considerable insight into his answer to the God-Caesar question. While he never advocated that every Christian hold public office, he did want piety to serve the public good, proclaiming from the pulpit, "In a public view, every good [person] is called to live and act for the glory of God, and the good of others. . . . Nor am I able to conceive any character more truly great than that of one, whatever be his station or profession, who is devoted to the public good under the immediate order of Providence."[23] What caused disruption and would eventually tear apart the moral fabric of a society was the blatant immorality and irresponsibility of the citizen who did not care one whit about the public good and with jaw set and hands on hips shouted something like, "What I do is my own business and nobody else's!" Witherspoon will have none of that attitude, in his day or ours: "It is common to say of a dissolute liver, that he does harm to none but himself; than which I think there is not a greater falsehood that ever obtained credit in a deceived world. Drunkards, swearers, profane and lascivious jesters, and the whole tribe of those who do harm to none but themselves, are the pests of society, [and] the corrupters of the youth."[24] Earlier, in 1776, in a longer and more eloquent statement, he had stated his principle of the importance of morality to the health of society:

> Nothing is more certain than that a general philosophy and corruption of manners makes a people ripe for destruction. A good form of government may hold the rotten materials together for a time, but beyond a certain pitch even the best constitution will be ineffectual, and slavery must ensue. On the other hand, when the manners of a nation are pure, when true religion and internal principles maintain their vigor, the attempts of the most powerful enemies to oppress them are commonly baffled and disappointed.[25]

By the time Tocqueville toured America, the majority of Americans had made Witherspoon's principle their own. Tocqueville observed that in general Americans considered religion to be indispensable to the mainstream of the republic. Later, as he continued his reflections on American life, he remarked how religion was considered useful to each citizen as well as to the whole state: "Americans show by their practice that they feel the high necessity of imparting morality to democratic communities by means of religion."[26]

Throughout the nineteenth and early twentieth centuries, Americans of the Reformed faith confirmed Tocqueville's observation and reflected Witherspoon's thesis that some kind of public recognition and support ought to be extended to the Christian religion, especially in its Protestant form. More recently, argues David Little in his perceptive overview of the Reformed faith and religious liberty, some if not many Reformed church members have moved away from the earlier position of Christian piety supporting public order to one of a radical separation of church and state, more in line with the thinking of James Madison.[27] Little sees a persistent tension in the Reformed understanding of the relation of religion to the civil order, for alongside those who argue for the sharp separation of church and state, there are still many voices proclaiming that America is a religious, if not Christian, nation, and must constantly refer to its religious heritage if it is to remain strong and virtuous. Witherspoon's position cannot be ours today, but his several statements on the need for a virtuous nation ought to push modern readers to reflect more carefully than they might about the connection between personal virtue and social-political well-being. There is some evidence that contemporary Americans are beginning to realize again that a healthy society requires virtue of its citizens. The National Commission on Civic Renewal, co-chaired by former Secretary of Education William Bennett and former Senator Sam Nunn, has much to say about the importance of trust and virtue in American national life. In its final report, the commission stated, "From the origin of our republic, we have been a strongly religious nation, and the Founders were near-unanimous in viewing religion as an aid and friend to the constitutional order. . . . Today, because we remain a strongly religious nation, faithful citizens and faith-based institutions are pivotal to any American movement for civic renewal."[28]

There are three other ways Witherspoon's piety can improve or enhance the life of Christians today. First, we have seen how the doctrine of providence demanded so much of his attention as he got closer to Princeton and became caught up in the cause of independence. To reflect on his discussion of providence, for the individual and for the nation, is to make us face the question squarely: What significance does the doctrine of providence have for the believer today? No doubt we are on smooth and familiar terrain when we affirm Witherspoon's teaching that God truly cares for us and showers each one of us with his mercies, temporal and spiritual. However, even setting aside for the moment the nagging problem of so-called natural evil—floods, famine, and the like (and that is no slight exception)—can Christians today declare wholeheartedly, especially after the Holocaust and the ongoing barbarisms since 1945, that God has absolute "dominion over the passions of men"? That God rules over the machinations of politicians in Washington and other world capitals? That God will work out a divine purpose in the attacks of terrorists, let alone in the violence and crime of our inner cities? Evil seems so virulent and pervasive in our time. No wonder Reformed theologian G. C. Berkouwer can pose the present contradiction for believers: "the comfort of the old confession of God's Providence versus the dread that rises from the events of the [twentieth] century."[29] It is understandable that many today hold firmly to what I call a "reductionist" doctrine of providence: Providence provides direction, healing, and comfort for our lives and those we love, but has little to do with presidents and parliaments, ethnic butchery, and evil run amok. Anecdotal evidence taken from Sunday pastoral prayers would lead one to conclude that God no longer "governs all things," as the Confession instructs, only *some* things and only those that are closest to home. Shirley Guthrie proposes that too many contemporary church members and ministers have reduced providence to a discussion of "God the provider," nice peaceful talk for "quiet peaceful sanctuaries with stained glass windows [people] can't see through to see what life in the world is really like."[30] Witherspoon would surely call us back to a full appreciation of the work of providence, if not to a complete understanding of how the doctrine plays out in modern times. We must, he would tell us, completely trust God's ultimate goodness, wisdom, and power, and above all, trust the God who secured a victory over all evil in Christ. At the same time, we must forfeit the attempt to understand and explain every last thing that God does or does not do in our troubled world.

Next, the reader must have noticed in several parts of this study Witherspoon's particular concern for proper speech. Sometimes he excoriated those who swore or blasphemed. The obvious reason for this condemnation of profanity and blasphemy was that such usage defamed God, a grievous sin. At other times, Witherspoon recommended "the government of the tongue" and "purity and sincerity of your outward conversation." Two contemporary writers, Kathleen Norris and Barbara Brown Taylor, would surely find themselves concurring with Witherspoon's advice. Norris complains of modern "word bombardment" from the pulpit, while asking us to think of language as "the human venture that begins with the ear and tongue and reaches for the stars." Taylor puts the matter even more forcefully: "In our lifetimes language has taken a terrible hit. . . . [There are] so many frontal assaults on language, on the reliability of the word that it is difficult to list them all." Witherspoon never did get around to proposing his theory of language, but in his own mind there was no doubt that there was a direct link between thought and word, inward disposition and outward practice. Pure thought brings forth pure language, which, we have discovered, is a mark of the pious individual. "The world must know whether your conversation is pure and inoffensive at all times, and profitable, as opportunities present themselves," the practical Witherspoon added.[31]

In our day, philosopher Susanne Langer, discussing the interrelatedness of thought and word, claims that for humans, conception, "the process of *envisaging* facts, values, hopes and fears underlies our whole behavior pattern; and this process is reflected in the evolution of an extraordinary phenomenon . . . [,] the phenomenon of language. . . . The power it bestows is almost inestimable, for without it anything properly called 'thought' is impossible."[32] Witherspoon could not have made the point better.

Preacher Witherspoon has spoken; now we are asked to listen to what eloquence professor Witherspoon has to say. When we speak, we should prove our pure conversation by using good or correct English, he instructs. He gets down to basics, forbidding the following: "double epithets," couplets such as "happiness and felicity," "pain and anguish," or "truth and sincerity"; grammatical errors such as "between you and I" or "it lays for it lies"; vulgarisms such as the contradictions "I can't, I shan't" and "this here, that there"; and redundancies such as "fellow countrymen."[33] He would have nodded in agreement if he could have read some of the pleas of contemporary writers for proper English, particularly the essay by arts critic John Simon, "Why Good English Is Good for You." Simon's spirited quarrel is with basic linguistic sloppiness or ignorance or defiance of proper English, prompting him to observe that "there is a close connection between the ability to think and the ability to use English correctly." His disdain for bad English is palpable. He grumbles, "The person who does not respect words and their proper relationship cannot have much respect for ideas—very possibly cannot have ideas at all."[34] For his part, Witherspoon the educator explained why he was so insistent on proper English usage. Care must be taken, he warned, "to form the scholars to taste, propriety and accuracy, in that language which they must speak and write all their life afterwards."[35]

Consistent with his devotion to good English were his complaints about the shortcuts to learning that he was observing. His remarks are so pertinent that they could have been written only yesterday:

> For every thing is now more compendiously taught, and more superficially understood, than formerly. . . . In the very mechanic arts, laborious diligence gives way to elegance and ease; as the lumpish, strong, old Gothic buildings, to more genteel, though slighter, modern ones. There have been schemes published for teaching children to read by way of diversion. Every year gives us a shorter method of learning some branch of knowledge. In short, in these last days the quintessence of every thing has been extracted, and is presented us, as it were, in little phials; so that we may come to all learning by one act of intuition.[36]

Finally, Witherspoon bequeaths himself! He gives us himself as an example of piety. Admittedly, we would not want to become like him in every respect, but some of the important qualities of his life are worth emulating. On the other hand, he never set himself up as an example. He was too modest for that, and such a suggestion would have compromised his belief that *all* honor ought to go to God. Self-denial did not allow for any breast-beating. So, though Witherspoon would never have pushed himself forward as an example of piety, he did emphasize the need for everyone to set an example in the life of piety. We recall how he wanted his people to be "shining examples of piety" because, he intoned, "a blameless life, such as becometh the gospel, is a more effectual reprimand to vice, and a more inviting argument to the practice of religion, than the best of reasoning."[37] Ministers were to be examples, as were magistrates, teachers, parents, and finally, everyone. Undoubtedly, he hoped his own example would be heeded, and one very good reason to receive him as exemplar is that he is, literally, as good as his word! He is genuine. He did not just talk or preach about piety. He was pious.

Two friends who knew him well testified to his own practice of piety. Both Ashbel Green and John Rodgers explained that in addition to daily prayers, Witherspoon annually set aside December 31 for "fasting, humiliation and prayer" as well as other times when required.[38] Not only was he preaching piety and undertaking the exercises of piety, he was telling his people, "Be publick-spirited and useful." And in the 1770s, John Witherspoon, minister and patriot, set out from Princeton to prove that he was public-spirited and useful. We must take very seriously a person whose practice is consistent with what he or she preaches. With a person like Witherspoon, we are not restricted to his utterances from the pulpit. We can profit by his example.

Reformed Christians have always affirmed that justification must be followed by good works, that is, a responsible energetic sanctification. According to Alan Geyer, a Methodist ethicist, "Presbyterian leaders have almost always had a sensitive nose for moral evils," not sitting down once they had identified and damned the evils. "They have just as regularly insisted that we must *do something* about those evils."[39] Witherspoon advised against being conformed to the world, but he countered with the charge that "it is an error, on the other hand, to place religion in voluntary poverty, in monkish austerity, or uncommanded maceration of the body. This is not doing, but deserting our duty; it is not crucifying the world, but going out of it; it is not overcoming the world, but flying from it."[40]

Witherspoon's counsel and example are telling us that real piety is not of this world, but is *for* this world. Pious people know that in the world they are free, free from all forms of enslavement, even the worst one of all; free to do one's duty, to work for a more virtuous society, and to be overtly political when they must. Free, too, to take history seriously and try to see their place in it. Knowledge of history, promised Witherspoon, will give us "such a view of the place of Providence, as may excite us to the exercise of the duties of adoration, thankfulness, trust, and submission to the supreme Disposer of all events."[41]

The surprising truth of Witherspoon is that we do not have to sit and listen to his word from a distant pulpit. We can actually observe the ways in which he embodied his own advice. In times of peace, he said, as well as in those of difficulty and trial, "it is in the [person] of piety and inward principle that we may expect to find the uncorrupted patriot, the useful citizen, and the invincible soldier."[42] There is no better way to describe John Witherspoon!

Appendix A

The Titles of John Witherspoon's Sermons Included in
Practical Discourses on the Leading Truths of the Gospel
(Edinburgh, 1768)

    I. All Mankind by nature under sin (Rom. 3:23)

   II. The Sinner Without Excuse Before God (Ps. 130:3)

  III. Hope of Forgiveness with God (Ps. 130:4)

  IV. The Nature of Faith (1 John 3:23)

   V. Christ's Death a Proper Atonement for Sin (1 John 2:2)

  VI. The Love of Christ in Redemption (Rev. 1:5)

 VII. Redemption the Subject of Admiration to the Angels
(1 Pet. 1:12)

VIII. Glorying in the Cross (Gal. 6:14)

  IX. The World Crucified by the Cross of Christ (Gal. 6:14)

   X. The World Crucified by the Cross of Christ (Gal. 6:14)

  XI. Fervency and Importunity in Prayer (Gen. 32:26)

 XII. Fervency and Importunity in Prayer (Gen. 32:26)

XIII. Obedience and Sacrifice Compared (1 Sam. 15:22)

Appendix B

A List of Books of Character
as Collected by Dr. Witherspoon
~1773~
Transcribed at Nassau-Hall by
William Beekman, Jun[r]

List of Books of Character in different Branches of Science to direct Students, especially in Divinity, either in the Course of their Reading or furnishing their Libraries.

Theology

Systems
Calvini Institutiones
Limborchi Theologia
Theses Ludovici le Blanc
Pictate Theologie Chretienne
Pearson on the Creed
Burnet on the 39 Articles
Wittenbachii Theologia
Doddridge's Lectures
Witsii OEconomia Foederum
Cameronis Opera
Episcopii Opera
Forbesii Instructiones historico-theologiae

Commentators
and Criticks
Poli Synopsis Criticorum
Ainsworth on the Pentateuch
Patrick's Commentary, w[t] Lowth's Continuation
Vitringa in Isaiam
Vitringa de Synagoga vetere
Calvin's Commentaries
Saurin Discours de la Bible

Commentators	Doddridge's Paraphrase
and Criticks	Gain's Paraphrase
	Calvin's Harmony
	Lightfoot's Works
	Whitby on the New Testament
	Benson's History of the Acts of The Apostles
	Abbadie sur L'overture de sept Seaux
	Lowman on the Revelations
	Sherlock on Prophecy
	Newton on Prophecy
	Stillingfleet's Origines sacrae
	Blackwall's Sacred Classics
	Gausonius de Verbo Dei

Controversy

On The Roman Catholic Side

Popish	Bellarmine's Works
	Arnauld's [Prejuges] legitimes contre les Calvinistes

On the Protestant Side

Claude's Defence de la Reformation
Funeral of the Mass, by Rhodon [Derodon]
Chillingworth's Safe Way
Tillotson's Rule of Faith, & Sermons
Barrow on The Pope's Supremacy
    and all The Systems when treating on
        the Church, & on the Sacraments

Arian &	The Systems in general &
Socinian	Clark's Scripture Doctrine of the Trinity
	Waterland's Sermons
	Calamy on the Trinity
	Taylor on the Romans
	Taylor on Original Sin
	Watt's Ruin & Recovery of Mankind
	Edwards on Original Sin
	Westley's on D° [D° = ditto, i.e., John Wesley
	on Original Sin]
	Dr. Erskine's Dissertations

Deistical	Grotius de Veritate Christianae Religionis
	Abbadie de la Verite de la Religion Chretienne
	The English Deistical Writers may be all summed
	up in *Leland's View*. The chief of them were:
	Lord Herbert of Cherbury
	Tindal
	Morgan
	Collins
	Chubb
	Shaftsbury
	Hume

On the Contrary Side not only the Particular
Answers to each of them, but

Deistical	Ditton on The Resurrection
	West on The Resurrection
	Lardner's Credibility of Y^e Gospel History
	Macknight's Credibility [Truth] of Y^e Gospel History
	Adams against David Hume on Miracles
	Dr Campbel on Miracles
	Beatty on Truth
Arminian	This may be found in all the Systems.
	See likewise,
	Placette de la Foi divine, & his Treatise on
	Repentance, & on Justification
	Baxter on the Imputation of Christ's
	Righteousness.

N.B. The Controversy with the proper Arminians is not Modern, there being few, if any, in the Present Age, who (like Dr Whitby) are strenuous Advocates for the Divinity of Christ, & the Satisfaction, and yet believe with the Arminians on the Subject of the Decrees, the Sovereignty of divine grace, &c. The Controversy at present is much more with Socinian & Pelagian Principles.

Church	King's State of the Primitive Church
Government	The Principles of the Cyprianic Age
	Parker's Ecclesiastic Polity
	Marvel's Rehearsal transprosed [sic]
	Alsop's melius Inquirendum

Mr White & the Dissenting Gentlemen in
several Tracts against each other; which is the
most modern Controversy on this Subject in
Britain — In America, the same Controversy
has been carried on by Dr Chandler of
Elizabeth Town & Dr Chauncy of N. England
& others.
Particularly Dr Chauncy's Account of the
Ancient Fathers

Practical   Tillotson
Writers in   Barrow
English   Hopkins
                     Sherlock
                     Scott
                     Seed
                     Baxter
                     Doddridge
                     Watts
                     Evans
                     Bennet's Christian Oratory
                     Walker's Sermons

Practical   Essais de Portroyal. And
Writers in   The Works of Claude
French   _____ Dubose
                     _____ Daille
                     _____ Werenfels
                     _____ Du Moulin (Father & Son)
                     _____ Drelincourt
                     _____ Placette
                     _____ Massillon
                     _____ Bourdalouse

Moral Philosophy

Principles   Of The Ancients
of
Morals   Plato
                     The Remains of Socrates, as cited by different
                        Authors, & particularly collected by
                     Xenophon in his Memorabilia.

Plutarch's Morals
Cicero in his Books, de Officiis, de Legibus, & de
   Natura Deorum

Of The Moderns
Cudworth's Intellectual System (particularly
   valuable for containing almost everything which
   deserves Notice in the Writings of the Heathen
   Philosophers) —
Malbranch
Leibnitz's Theodicae & his Letters
Shaftsbury
Hutchison [sic] of Glasgow
Butler's Analogy
Balfeur's [sic] Delineation of Morality
Smith's Theory of Moral Sentiment
Clarke's Demonstration of the Being & Attributes
   of God
Mandeville's Fable of The Bees
Reid's Inquiry
Oswald on Common Sense
Baxter (Andrew) on The Immateriality of the Soul
D° on human Liberty
Campbell's Inquiry

The Same	Grotius
as applied	Selden
to	Cumberland
Government	Puffendorf
& Civil	Barbyrac
Society	Burlamaque [sic]

History

History &	Shuckford's Connection
Antiquities	Prideaux's Connection
in General	The Universal History
	Montesquieu's Spirit of Laws
	Goguet's Rise & Progress of Arts & Sciences
	Dupin's Ecclesiastical History
	Bingham's Christian Antiquities
	Wallace on The Numbers of Mankind

Ferguson's History of Civil Society
Kennet's Roman Antiquities
Potter's Greek Antiquities
Montague's Rise & Fall of The Ancient Republics

Particular	Heroditus
Historians	Thucidides
	Plutarch
Ancient	Livy
	Herodian
	Arrian's Life of Alexander
	Suetonius
	Tacitus

French	The Modern Universal History
	Du Halde's History of China
	Temple's Observations on The Netherlands
	Thuanus
	Davilu
	Vertot
	Voltaire

English	Rapin
	Hume
	Smollet
	Robertson
	Anson's Voyages

Belles Lettres & Criticism

Taste	Aristotle
&	Cicero
Criticism	Quintilian
	Rollin
	Rapin
	Fenelon, Archbishop of Cambray
	Addison's Works
	Bourke [Burke] on the Sublime
	Ld Kaim's Elements of Criticism
	Hogarth's Analysis of Beauty
	Theory of agreeable Sensations,—
	- (transcribed lated from the French)
	Lawson's Lectures on Oratory

Young on Original Sin
Gerrard's Essay on Taste
Traite de Beau by Mr Crousar
   -(in French)

Poetry	Homer
Ancient	Virgil
	Horace

English	Shakespeare
	Spenser
	Dryden
	Waller
	Milton
	Addison
	Pope
	Swift
	Young
	Gay
	Glover
	Gray

French	Corneille
	Racine
	Moliere
	Boileau

Wit and	Lucian's Dialogues of the Dead
Humour	Fontanelle's Dialogues of the Dead
	Moliere's Plays
	Pascal's Provincial Letters
	Cervantes's Don Quixote
	Butler's Hudibras
	Marvel's Rehearsal Transposed
	Alsop's Melius Inquirendum
	Swift
	Gay
	Shakespeare &c.

1773

William Beekman Junr

Notes

Preface

1. *Institutes*, 1.2.1.41. On this topic, see especially Serene Jones, *Calvin and the Rhetoric of Piety* (Louisville, Ky.: Westminster John Knox Press, 1995).
2. Charles E. Hambrick-Stowe, "Piety," in *Encyclopedia of the Reformed Faith*, ed. Donald K. McKim (Louisville, Ky.: Westminster/John Knox Press, 1992).
3. Historian Edwin Gaustad has noted how important the Bible was and how widespread its influence, stating that it acquired in American life "an imposing cultural centrality" and became "a kind of national shrine to be honored by everyone and defamed by none." See Edwin S. Gaustad, *Faith of Our Fathers: Religion and the New Nation* (San Francisco: Harper & Row, 1987), 129.
4. John Murrin, "Religion and Politics in America from the First Settlements to the Civil War" in Mark A. Noll, ed., *Religion and American Politics: From the Colonial Period to the 1980s* (New York: Oxford University Press, 1990), 26–27.
5. Mark A. Noll, Nathan O. Hatch, George M. Marsden, *The Search for Christian America* (Westchester, Ill.: Crossway Books, 1983), 72–76.
6. Ashbel Green, *The Life of the Revd John Witherspoon, D.D., LL.D.*, ed. Henry Lyttleton Savage (Princeton, N.J.: Princeton University Press, 1973), 161. See also Varnum Lansing Collins, *President Witherspoon: A Biography* (Princeton, N.J.: Princeton University Press, 1925; reprinted, New York: Arno Press and the New York Times, 1969), 2:195.
7. "The Faithful Servant Rewarded . . ." (Witherspoon's funeral sermon preached by John Rodgers), *Works*, 1:34.
8. Noll et al. *Search for Christian America*, 88–95; Mark A. Noll, *Christians in the American Revolution* (Washington, D.C.: Christian University Press, 1977), 65–68. For a general review of the role of religion in the period of the American Revolution, see Martin E. Marty, *Pilgrims in Their Own Land: 500 Years of Religion in America* (Boston: Little, Brown & Co., 1984), 131–66, and the excellent brief bibliography for the period, pp. 482–83. For a recent account of the role of American Presbyterians in the Revolution, see James H. Smylie, *A Brief History of the Presbyterians* (Louisville, Ky.: Geneva Press, 1996), 57–67.
9. "Lectures on Eloquence," *Works*, 3:394.
10. There were two Scottish editions based on the second American edition, 1804–1805 and 1815. I have used the first American edition. A careful comparison will disclose that the second edition is virtually the same as the first. Green has explained that the changes were only those of corrections in spelling and

punctuation, and a different, more logical ordering of Witherspoon's writings. See his "Advertisement to the Second American Edition," preceding the table of contents in vol. 1.

11.   Martha Lou Lemmon Stohlman, *John Witherspoon: Parson, Politician, Patriot* (Philadelphia: Westminster Press, 1976), 126; Green, *Life of the Revd John Witherspoon*, 19, 127; Green, "Advertisement to the Second American Edition," in *Works* ; Collins, *President Witherspoon*, 2:235–37.

12.   Jack Scott, ed., *An Annotated Edition of Lectures on Moral Philosophy by John Witherspoon* (Newark, Del.: University of Delaware Press, 1982). See also Thomas Miller, ed., *The Selected Writings of John Witherspoon* (Carbondale, Ill.: Southern Illinois University Press, 1990). Miller has written his introduction and has chosen selections from Witherspoon's *Works* to make the case for the "strong traditional relationship between rhetoric and the ethical and political concerns of moral philosophy." He has included among other writings the text of two sermons by Witherspoon and the full text of his "Lectures on Moral Philosophy" and "Lectures on Eloquence." A brief bibliography is placed at the end of the introduction, but regrettably this edition contains neither critical notes nor an index. One other item from the Witherspoon corpus published recently, lacking an introduction and critical notes, is his May 17, 1776 sermon, "The Dominion of Providence over the Passions of Men," as an example of a Revolutionary War "political sermon." See Ellis Sandoz, ed., *Political Sermons of the American Founding Era, 1730–1805* (Indianapolis: Liberty Fund, 1991), 533–58. Sandoz has collected an impressive number of sermons in his volume of 1596 pages. See also *Works,* 2:407–36.

13.   Thomas Crichton, "Memoir of the Life and Writings of John Witherspoon," *Edinburgh Christian Instructor* 28 (October 1829): 673–94. David D. Bartley has printed the entire Crichton "Memoir" in his unpublished dissertation, "John Witherspoon and the Right of Resistance" (Ph.D. diss., Ball State University, 1989).

14.   Green, *Life of the Revd John Witherspoon*. See earlier note for full citation.

15.   See earlier note for full citation.

16.   See earlier note for full citation.

17.   The one exception is the unpublished dissertation by Wayne Witte, who does not systematically analyze Witherspoon's theology but all too quickly draws a connection between certain doctrines and Witherspoon's accomplishments, especially in American politics. Witte's facile references to Witherspon's "Calvinism" are undeveloped and occasionally unjustified. Witherspoon's theology should not be characterized and discussed as "Calvinism geared for liberty," as Witte has done in chapter 3. See Wayne W. Witte, "John Witherspoon: An Exposition and Interpretation of His Theological Views as the Motivation of His Ecclesiastical, Educational, and Political Career in Scotland and America" (Th.D. diss., Princeton Theological Seminary, 1953). Lyman Atwater wrote a brief article on Witherspoon's theology in 1863, which is virtually useless for present purposes. The impulse for the article was a charge that Witherspoon was a trustworthy spokesperson for New School theology in the 1837–1838 Old School/New School division in the American Presbyterian Church. Atwater set out to refute the claim, stating emphatically that Wither-

spoon was very much "Old School." See Lyman Atwater, "Witherspoon's Theology," *Biblical Repertory and Princeton Review* 35, no. 4 (October 1863): 596–610. For a succinct account of the Old School/New School split, see Smylie, *Brief History of the Presbyterians*, 78–80.

18. *Practical Discourses on the Leading Truths of the Gospel.* (Edinburgh: Kincaid & Bell & Gray, 1768). Two years later, W. & T. Bradford published an American edition in Philadelphia. The second British edition (London, 1792) included an "Advertisement" that Witherspoon had written in 1768, explaining that the sermons formed "a little system of the truths of the gospel, to point out their relation to one another, and their influence on practice . . . an attempt to illustrate the scripture-doctrine by experience and observation on human life." See Collins, *President Witherspoon*, 2:246.

19. William D. Maxwell, *A History of Worship in the Church of Scotland* (London: Oxford University Press, 1955), 5.

Introduction

1. Martin E. Marty, *Pilgrims in Their Own Land: 500 Years of Religion in America* (Boston: Little, Brown & Co., 1984), viii. See also Jacques Maritain, *Reflections on America* (New York: Charles Scribner's Sons, 1958), 93.

2. "An Address to the Students of the Senior Class," *Works*, 2:620; "The Success of the Gospel Entirely of God," *Works*, 2:547.

3. There is no documentary evidence for the date of Witherspoon's birth, although parish records state that John was baptized on February 10, 1723. Since it was customary to baptize infants within two weeks of birth, there is no reason to dispute the traditional birthdate.

4. See Varnum Lansing Collins, *President Witherspoon: A Biography* (Princeton, N.J.: Princeton University Press, 1973), 1:8–10.

5. *New Statistical Account of Scotland* (Edinburgh, 1845), 2:158–59.

6. Ashbel Green, *The Life of the Revd John Witherspoon, D.D, LL.D.*, ed. Henry Lyttleton Savage (Princeton, N.J.: Princeton University Press, 1973), 29.

7. Collins, *President Witherspoon*, 1:7; William Oliver Brackett, "John Witherspoon: His Scottish Ministry" (Ph.D. diss., University of Edinburgh, 1935), 26.

8. Brackett, "John Witherspoon," 25, and the appendix; Green, *Life of the Revd John Witherspoon*, 26, 275; Collins, *President Witherspoon*, 1:5, 6. These and others have made a careful study of this claim with inconclusive results.

9. The grammar school curriculum at Haddington would not have deviated significantly from the six-year plan in force in Glasgow or the similar five-year *Ordo Scholae Grammaticae Ediensis* described by Thomas Ruddiman. For the Glasgow scheme, see Henry Grey Graham, *The Social Life of Scotland in the Eighteenth Century* (London: Adam & Charles Black, 1950), 443–44; for the Edinburgh subjects and authors studied, see George Chalmers, *The Life of Thomas Ruddiman* (London, 1794), 88–90.

10. James Miller, *The Lamp of Lothian: Or, the History of Haddington* (Haddington: William Sinclair, 1900), 196.

11. Graham, *Social Life of Scotland*, 439–40.

12. "A Serious Inquiry into the Nature and Effects of the Stage," *Works*, 3:50–52; "A Letter Respecting Play Actors," *Works*, 3:100.

13. By today's standards, eighteenth-century students enrolled in universities at an uncommonly early age. Hugh Blair, Scottish minister and rhetorician, also entered at thirteen. Philosopher David Hume and William Robertson, minister, historian, and principal of Edinburgh University, were only eleven.

14. Carlyle, later the minister at Inveresk (now Musselburgh), was a student at the University during Witherspoon's time. See Alexander Carlyle, *Autobiography of the Rev. Alexander Carlyle* (Edinburgh: William Blackwood & Sons, 1860), 30. Carlyle's recollections are not altogether reliable as a factual record of persons and events, especially in his early years. He began writing his memoirs at the age of 79, and his biases sometimes are apparent.

15. Collins, *President Witherspoon*, 1:12–13. Proficiency in Latin was the sine qua non of an educated person, and Latin was taught extensively in Scottish grammar schools (see Graham, *Social Life of Scotland*, 453). Witherspoon's ability in French was more unusual. Since his father read French authors, Witherspoon may have learned French at home. In 1780, Marquis de Chastellux, who met Witherspoon in Princeton, opined that he spoke French as one who had learned the language from "reading rather than conversation." See Green, *Life of the Revd John Witherspoon*, 131.

16. Carlyle, *Autobiography*, 31–32, 42–43, 46–50. Carlyle not only lists the subjects he studied but offers an evaluation of his professors.

17. Alexander Bower, *The History of the University of Edinburgh* (Edinburgh: printed by Alex Smellie, 1817–1830), 2:269–81; Alexander Grant, *The Story of the University of Edinburgh during Its First Three Hundred Years* (London: Longmans, Green & Co., 1884), 1:273; 2:328–30.

18. Roger Jerome Fechner, "The Moral Philosophy of John Witherspoon and the Scottish-American Enlightenment" (Ph.D. diss., University of Iowa, 1974), 68. Fechner, relying on Bower and Grant, provides an excellent analysis of the professors and courses at the University of Edinburgh during Witherspoon's time.

19. Bower, *History of the University of Edinburgh*, 2:274–75.

20. Carlyle, *Autobiography*, 42–43. See Hugh Blair, *Lectures on Rhetoric and Belles Lettres*, 2 vols. (London, 1783). Robertson's testimony can be found in Grant, *Story of the University of Edinburgh*, 2:329–30. See also John Erskine, *Discourses Preached on Several Occasions*, 2d ed. (Edinburgh: For Wm. Creech and Arch. Constable, 1801), 1:266; and Thomas Somerville, *My Own Life and Times, 1741–1814* (Edinburgh: Edmonston & Douglas, 1861), 13–14.

21. Robert Schmitz misquotes Collins in his endeavor to extract a positive word for Stevenson from Witherspoon. See Robert Schmitz, *Hugh Blair* (New York: King's Crown Press, 1948), 11.

22. See Richard M. Gummere, "A Scottish Classicist in Colonial America," *Publications of the Colonial Society of Massachusetts* 35 (1944): 146–61.

23. "Lectures on Eloquence," *Works*, 3:375–495; "The Druid" [Essays], 4:168–97. Ashbel Green noticed a "striking similarity" between the lectures on eloquence by Hugh Blair and those by Witherspoon, concluding that since the two had not exchanged ideas on the topic of eloquence, the similarity must be attributed to the fact that both had studied under Stevenson. See Green, *Life of the Revd John Witherspoon*, 128–29.

24. For the English translation, see appendix I in George E. Rich, "John Wither-spoon: His Scottish Intellectual Background" (D.S.S. diss., Syracuse University, 1964).

25. Fechner, "Moral Philosophy of John Witherspoon," 77–83; Rich, "John With-erspoon," 52–57.

26. Fechner, "Moral Philosophy of John Witherspoon," 82; Rich, "John Wither-spoon," 168.

27. William Dawson taught Hebrew using Leusden's Hebrew grammar; Patrick Cumming delivered his lectures on Jean Alphonse Turretin's *Compendium His-toriae Ecclesiasticae*. See Graham, *Social Life of Scotland*, 466–68; and Grant, *Story of the University of Edinburgh*, 1:334–36.

28. Bower, *History of the University of Edinburgh*, 2:283–85 (Benedictus Pictetus, *Theologia Christiana ex puris SS. Literarum fontibus hausta* [Geneva, 1696]). Pictet was professor of theology at the University of Geneva from 1687 to 1724.

29. Carlyle, *Autobiography*, 56–57. In spite of what Carlyle thought, Pictet had con-siderable staying power at Edinburgh throughout the eighteenth century. Gowdie's successor, Robert Hamilton (professor, 1754–1779), used Pictet, as did his successor, Andrew Hamilton (1779–1809). See Somerville, *My Own Life and Times*, 17–18; and Hugo Arnot, *The History of Edinburgh, From the Earliest Account to the Year 1780* (Edinburgh: Thomas Turnbull, 1816), 304. Arnot's work appeared in earlier editions, 1779 and 1788.

30. Witherspoon thought enough of Pictet that he owned a French edition of the *Theologia*. He twice paid Pictet an indirect compliment in his essay "Ecclesias-tical Characteristics," *Works*, 3:162, 192. See below for the full citation of the "Characteristics." Pictet was also on a list of recommended works for American ministerial candidates. See Witherspoon's "A List of Books of Character" in appendix B. Pictet was also translated into English (London, 1834; Philadel-phia: Presbyterian Board of Publication, 1845). I have used the 1845 edition when quoting Pictet. I wish to thank Professor John Leith for informing me that James Henley Thornwell (1812–1862), prominent Southern Presbyterian theologian, considered Pictet to be an important member of the Swiss Reformed pantheon. See B. M. Palmer, *The Life and Letters of James Henley Thornwell* (Richmond, 1875), 458, and John B. Adger, ed., *The Collected Writings of James Henley Thornwell* (Richmond, 1871), 1:304; 3:332.

31. A brief discussion of Pictet's theological position can be found in Martin I. Klauber, "Reformed Orthodoxy in Transition: Bénédict Pictet (1655–1724) and Enlightened Orthodoxy in Post-Reformation Geneva," in *Later Calvinism: International Perspectives*, ed. W. Fred Graham (Kirksville, Mo.: Sixteenth Cen-tury Journal Publishers, 1994), 93–113. See also Robert D. Lindner, "Pictet, Benedict (1655–1724)," in McKim, ed., *Encyclopedia of the Reformed Faith*; James I. Good, *History of the Swiss Reformed Church since the Reformation* (Philadelphia: Publication and Sunday School Board of the Reformed Church in the United States, 1913), 176–78, 282.

32. In 1736, the trials consisted of eight requirements: a catechetical examination; a homily; an exegesis; an exercise and addition on a biblical text; a lecture; a pop-ular sermon; an examination in church history, especially the history of the

Church of Scotland; and examinations in biblical Hebrew and Greek. See Archibald Main, "The Church and Education in the Eighteenth Century," *Records of the Scottish Church History Society* 3 (1929): 192–93.

33. Stewart Mechie points to one reason why there would seem to be an unnecessary delay between Witherspoon's licensure and ordination. The General Assembly had passed an act in 1711 that decreed that six years had to elapse between the end of a candidate's undergraduate course and his trials for license. In Witherspoon's case, he may have felt that there would have to be the requisite six years between his undergraduate degree (1739) and his ordination (1745). See Stewart Mechie, "Education for the Ministry in Scotland since the Reformation," *Records of the Scottish Church History Society* 14 (1963): 124. See also Brackett, "John Witherspoon," 52–55.

34. William D. Maxwell, *A History of Worship in the Church of Scotland* (London: Oxford University Press, 1955), 139–40; Graham, *Social Life of Scotland*, 293–95; John Watson, *The Scot of the Eighteenth Century* (London: Hodder & Stoughton, 1907), 108–10; G. D. Henderson, *Religious Life in Seventeenth-Century Scotland* (Cambridge: Cambridge University Press, 1937), 7–8, 10.

35. Brackett, "John Witherspoon," 62.

36. J. H. S. Burleigh, *A Church History of Scotland* (London: Oxford University Press, 1960), 268–69; Graham, *Social Life of Scotland*, 314–34.

37. Brackett, "John Witherspoon," 63–64. For example, a local laird (landed proprietor) accused by a young woman of being the father of her child was prosecuted as quickly as if he had been a person of lower social standing, and there are several cases of men punished for encroaching on the "poor lands."

38. Ibid., 65.

39. Until recently most of the scholarly work on these parties had been done on the Moderates, for example, Andrew L. Drummond and James Bulloch, *The Scottish Church, 1688–1843: The Age of the Moderates* (Edinburgh: Saint Andrew Press, 1973); Ian D. L. Clark, "From Protest to Reaction: The Moderate Regime in the Church of Scotland, 1752–1805," in *Scotland in the Age of Improvement*, ed. N. T. Phillipson and Rosalind Mitchison (Edinburgh: Edinburgh University Press, 1970); and an excellent and more recent study, Richard B. Sher, *Church and University in the Scottish Enlightenment: The Moderate Literati of Edinburgh* (Princeton, N.J.: Princeton University Press, 1985). Two writers have now helped fill the void in Popular party studies. Ned C. Landsman has published essays in *Scotland and America in the Age of the Enlightenment*, ed. Richard B. Sher and Jeffrey R. Smitten (Princeton, N.J.: Princeton University Press, 1990), 29–132. See also his essay, "Presbyterians and Provincial Society: The Evangelical Enlightenment in the West of Scotland, 1740–1755," in *Sociability and Society in Eighteenth-Century Scotland*, ed. John Dwyer and Richard B. Sher, published in the journal *Eighteenth-Century Life* 15 (February/May 1991):194–209. An exhaustive study of the Popular party has been completed by John R. McIntosh, "The Popular Party in the Church of Scotland, 1740–1800" (Ph.D. diss., University of Glasgow, 1989), published in 1998 as *Church and Theology in Enlightenment Scotland: The Popular Party, 1740–1800* (East Linton, East Lothian, Scotland: Tuckwell Press). Sher and Clark claim that the term *Moderate* should be restricted to a group of Scottish clergy and

laity that emerged shortly after 1750 under the leadership of William Robertson and his friends (it excludes certain older ministers known for their learning and moderation such as Francis Hutcheson).

40. See Sher, *Church and University*, 121, and McIntosh, "Popular Party," 41–45. It is difficult to determine the exact numbers in each party.

41. K. R. Ross, "Patron, Patronage, Patronage Acts," in *Dictionary of Scottish Church History and Theology*, ed. David F. Wright, David C. Lachman, and Donald E. Mack (Edinburgh: T. & T. Clark, 1993); Burleigh, *Church History of Scotland*, 277–85; and Sher, *Church and University*, 47–57.

42. Church historian A. C. Cheyne has noted several instances during the 1760s and 1770s when Moderates demonstrated either their criticism or neglect of strict subscription to the Confession. A. C. Cheyne, "The Place of the Confession through Three Centuries" in Alasdair I. C. Heron, ed., *The Westminster Confession in the Church Today* (Edinburgh: Saint Andrew Press, 1982), 20.

43. Burleigh, *Church History of Scotland*, 302–5; Sher, *Church and University*, 35, 57–59, 63; McIntosh, "Popular Party," 46, 52–54, 458–66, 469.

44. See Peter Gay, *The Enlightenment: An Interpretation* (New York: Alfred A. Knopf, 1960), and his further works on the Enlightenment; Paul Hazard, *The European Mind, 1680–1715* (New Haven, Conn.: Yale University Press, 1953); James M. Byrne, *Religion and the Enlightenment: From Descartes to Kant* (Louisville, Ky.: Westminster John Knox Press, 1996). For the Enlightenment in America, see Henry F. May, *The Enlightenment in America* (New York: Oxford University Press, 1976), and Donald H. Meyer, *The Democratic Enlightenment* (New York: G. P. Putnam's Sons, 1976).

45. Recent studies of the Enlightenment in Scotland, in addition to Sher, *Church and University* (see especially 3–19, 151–65), include R. H. Campbell and Andrew S. Skinner, eds., *The Origin and Nature of the Scottish Enlightenment* (Edinburgh: John Donald Publishers, 1982); Sher and Smitten, *Scotland and America* ; Dwyer and Sher, *Sociability and Society;* David Daiches, Peter Jones, and Jean Jones, eds., *A Hotbed of Genius: The Scottish Enlightenment, 1730–90* (Edinburgh: Edinburgh University Press, 1986); D. W. Bebbington, "Enlightenment," in Wright et al., eds., *Dictionary of Scottish Church History and Theology*.

46. Throughout "Ecclesiastical Characteristics," *Works*, 3:101–63, Witherspoon uses the term "the Orthodox" to refer to his own party. See pp. 111 and 121 in the same volume for acknowledgment of the term "high-flying."

47. D. W. Bebbington, writing from a British perspective, has reduced the features of evangelicalism to four, "a quadrilateral of priorities," he calls them: "conversionism, the belief that lives need to be changed; activism, the expression of the gospel in effort; biblicism, a particular regard for the Bible; and what may be called crucicentrism, a stress on the sacrifice of Christ on the cross." See D. W. Bebbington, *Evangelicalism in Modern Britain: A History from the 1730s to the 1980s* (London: Unwin Hyman, 1989), 2–3. Three of those four would go far in characterizing Witherspoon's evangelical piety; however, his devotion to and use of the Bible would hardly be called "biblicism" unless that term were very carefully defined. See the discussion of his understanding of "Sermon and Scripture." See also the "salient themes" of evangelicalism drawn up by Donald

G. Bloesch in Donald W. Masser and Joseph L. Price, eds., *A New Handbook of Christian Theology* (Nashville: Abingdon Press, 1992), 172.

48. McIntosh has shown that there was no uniform theology within the Popular party. For example, he has identified three "directions" that Popular party piety followed: First, some regarded piety as embodied in those holy dispositions that lead to a life of holiness. A second group, to which Witherspoon belonged, placed holiness or piety in the balance between dispositions and actions. The third group simply stressed the example of Christ and expected Christians to adopt it. See McIntosh, *Church and Theology*, 54–57.

49. Brief accounts of Moderate and Popular party disputes can be found in Drummond and Bulloch, *Scottish Church, 1688–1843*, and Sher, *Church and University*, 45–64, 120–47.

50. Carlyle, *Autobiography*, 65, and Brackett, "John Witherspoon," 131–32.

51. These quotations are from "Ecclesiastical Characteristics," included in *Works*, 3:101–63 (see especially 3:113). See also "The Absolute Necessity of Salvation through Christ," *Works*, 1:260; "The Trial of Religious Truth by Its Moral Influence," *Works*, 1:308.

52. The third earl of Shaftesbury was Anthony Ashley Cooper. Witherspoon borrowed part of the title of his *Characteristics of Men, Manners, Opinions, and Times* (1711) for his own essay. See "A Serious Apology for the Ecclesiastical Characteristics," *Works*, 3:187.

53. Ibid., 135–36.

54. The entire *Douglas* affair is described in fascinating detail in Sher, *Church and University*, 74–92. The 1757 General Assembly ultimately voted a mild measure that presbyteries "take care that none of the ministers of this church . . . attend the theatre." It had little effect. The Edinburgh theater prospered, and by 1784 the General Assembly was carefully scheduling its sessions so that the commissioners could conveniently attend the theater and enjoy the performances of the famous Sarah Siddons.

55. This essay appears in *Works*, 3:25–93. The reasons that Witherspoon supplies for opposing the theater will be considered in a later chapter, since they bear directly on his exposition of Christian piety, both for the layperson and the minister.

56. The Laigh Kirk, or Low Church, was the second congregation of the Church of Scotland in Paisley. His salary, one hundred pounds per year, was the same as that earned by the minister of the High Kirk.

57. "Absolute Necessity of Salvation," *Works*, 1:259–87; "Prayer for National Prosperity," 1:357–81. Both sermons were published in 1758, the former in Edinburgh, the latter in London. A jeremiad is generally understood to be a prolonged lamentation on the sin(s) of a nation or society, with the prescription of a return to God's ways for public redemption or restoration.

58. The title of the ordination sermon, based on Acts 11:6, was "The Charge of Sedition and Faction against Good Men, Especially Faithful Ministers, Considered and Accounted For" (Glasgow, 1758). The synod sermon, based on Matthew 7:20, bore the title, "The Trial of Religious Truth by Its Moral Influence" (Glasgow, 1759). See *Works*, 1:319–55 and 289–317.

59. The complete titles are as follows: (1) "Essay on the Connection between the

Doctrine of Justification by the Imputed Righteousness of Christ, and Holiness of Life: With Some Reflections upon the Reception Which That Doctrine Hath Generally Met with in the World" (Glasgow, 1756), hereafter, "Justification"; (2) "A Practical Treatise on Regeneration" (London, 1764), hereafter, "Regeneration."

60. One such volume, previously noted, was *Practical Discourses on the Leading Truths of the Gospel.* See appendix A for titles and texts.

61. The College of New Jersey was founded in 1746 in Elizabeth, New Jersey, and moved to Princeton in 1756. From 1756 to 1766, the college suffered from a rapid turnover in leadership, each president dying while still in office. See Thomas Jefferson Wertenbacker, *Princeton, 1746–1896* (Princeton, N.J.: Princeton University Press, 1946), for an account of the founding and early days of Princeton. Wertenbacker correctly traces the creation of the college back to the Great Awakening and to William Tennent's Log College.

62. James H. Smylie, *A Brief History of the Presbyterians* (Louisville, Ky.: Geneva Press, 1996), 48–49, 54. The Presbyterian Church had split in 1741, chiefly over the issue of revivalism, especially the emotional outcroppings, versus ordered, traditional Presbyterian standards and procedures. The reunion of the two parties occurred in 1758. See also Leonard J. Trinterud, *The Forming of an American Tradition: A Re-examination of Colonial Presbyterianism* (Philadelphia: Westminster Press, 1949; reprinted, New York: Books for Library Press, 1970), 109–65.

63. Wertenbacker, *Princeton*, 48–51. The account of Witherspoon's refusal of the invitation is narrated in L. H. Butterfield, ed., *John Witherspoon Comes to America* (Princeton, N.J.: Princeton University Press, 1953). See also the chapter, "The Wooing of a President," in Martha Lou Lemmon Stohlman, *John Witherspoon: Parson, Politician, Patriot* (Philadelphia: Westminster Press, 1976), 48–68. Many of the letters in the Butterfield volume are exchanges between Witherspoon and Rush, a medical student in Edinburgh, 1766–1768. Rush eventually became a leading American physician and a signer of the Declaration of Independence.

64. Green, *Life of the Revd John Witherspoon*, 31, 32, 120. Of the five children who came to America, Anne married Samuel Stanhope Smith, who succeeded Witherspoon as president of the college; James served in the Continental Army during the Revolution and was killed in the Battle of Germantown, 1777; John became a physician and was lost at sea in 1795; Frances, a favorite of her father, married medical doctor David Ramsay and lived until her death in 1784 in Charleston, South Carolina; David, who graduated from the college in the class of 1774, studied and practiced law in North Carolina and served for a time in the North Carolina legislature.

65. Ibid., 120.

66. Paul Tillich, *On the Boundary: An Autobiographical Sketch* (New York: Charles Scribner's Sons, 1966). For a "boundary" interpretation of Witherspoon, see L. Gordon Tait, "John Witherspoon, American Intellectual Leader," *Journal of Religious Studies* (Ohio) 12 (1986): 1–13.

67. "Address to the Natives of Scotland Residing in America," *Works*, 2:437. For similar expressions of love for his native land, see such essays as "Letter Sent to

Scotland for the Scots Magazine," "Ignorance of the British with Respect to America," and "On the Contest between Great Britain and America," *Works*, 4:287–302.

68. Collins, *President Witherspoon*, 2:119–20, 161, 219.
69. Green, *Life of the Revd John Witherspoon*, 125. In a 1772 pamphlet, Witherspoon proposed the following curriculum: Year One, Latin, Greek, Roman and Greek antiquities, rhetoric; Year Two, more Latin and Greek, geography, introductory philosophy, and mathematics; Year Three, chiefly mathematics and science; Year Four, higher classics, mathematics, science, and moral philosophy. In addition to these subjects, Witherspoon delivered two sets of lectures to juniors and seniors on (1) chronology and history and (2) composition and literary criticism. See "Address to the Inhabitants of Jamaica, and Other West-India Islands, in behalf of the College of New Jersey," *Works*, 4:349.
70. Howard C. Rice, *The Rittenhouse Orrery: Princeton's Eighteenth-Century Planetarium, 1767–1954* (Princeton, N.J.: Princeton University Library, 1954).
71. In addition to sources mentioned earlier, see the many references to Witherspoon's political thought and activity in "Presbyterians and the American Revolution: A Documentary Account," *Journal of Presbyterian History* 52 (winter 1974), and "Presbyterians and the American Revolution: An Interpretative Account," *Journal of Presbyterian History* 54 (spring 1976).
72. Jack Scott, ed., *An Annotated Edition of Lectures on Moral Philosophy by John Witherspoon* (Newark, Del.: University of Delaware Press, 1982), 12–16.
73. "On Conducting the American Controversy," *Works* 4:210–11.
74. John Rodgers, "Faithful Servant Rewarded," *Works*, 1:32.
75. "Ignorance of the British," *Works*, 4:296–97.
76. Lecture 12, "Of Civil Society," in Scott, ed., *Lectures on Moral Philosophy*, 145. See also David D. Bartley, "John Witherspoon and the Right of Resistance" (Ph.D. diss., Ball State University, 1989).
77. Committees of Correspondence were created in the colonies, usually on the county and provincial levels, initially to provide a means of communication among the colonies on political matters, but later to urge opposition to British measures and to express support for the Continental Congress. Larry Gerlach has described the work of these committees in New Jersey in his *Prologue to Independence: New Jersey in the Coming of the American Revolution* (New Brunswick, N.J.: Rutgers University Press, 1976), 208–23. See also "Thoughts on American Liberty," *Works*, 4:213–16.
78. Lyman H. Butterfield et al., eds., *The Diary and Autobiography of John Adams* (Cambridge, Mass.: Harvard University Press, 1961), 2:112.
79. The term *Whig* has had several meanings, including simply one favoring a limitation on royal authority while increasing parliamentary power, but at the time of the American Revolution it referred to anyone who favored independence from Britain and who propounded natural rights, the social contract, and right of resistance, ideas that Witherspoon was regularly teaching his students at Princeton. See "Lectures on Moral Philosophy," *Works*, 3:269–374; and Scott, *Lectures on Moral Philosophy*, 65–188. See also Daniel Walker Howe, *The Political Culture of the American Whigs* (Chicago: University of Chicago Press, 1979).
80. Green, *Life of the Revd John Witherspoon*, 160. The elderly Green is the only

source for this remark, but whether the comment is historical or not, it reflects Witherspoon's position at the time.

81. "Memorial and Manifesto of the United States of North America," *Works*, 4:217–25; Collins, *President Witherspoon*, 2:55–58, 195.

82. See Mark A. Noll, *Princeton and the Republic, 1768–1822: The Search for a Christian Enlightenment in the Era of Samuel Stanhope Smith* (Princeton, N.J.: Princeton University Press, 1989) for a superb study of the life and work of Smith, who, in addition to being vice-president, taught moral philosophy and divinity. He succeeded Witherspoon as president in 1795 and served the college in that office until 1812.

83. Collins, *President Witherspoon*, 2:164–68.

84. Green, *Life of the Revd John Witherspoon*, 161; Rodgers, "Faithful Servant Rewarded," *Works*, 1:34.

85. For example, his brief "Almanac" records that in the autumn of 1768 he preached in six locales: New York City; Boston (four times in three days); New Haven; Weston, Massachusetts; and New Brunswick, New Jersey (*Almanac and Memorandum Book of Dr. John Witherspoon, 1768*, Firestone Library, Princeton University, General Manuscripts, AM18653).

86. Of the eighty-eight meetings held during Witherspoon's years of membership, he was present only thirty-six times. See Collins, *President Witherspoon*, 2:159.

87. "A Pastoral Letter from the Synod of New York and Philadelphia," *Works*, 3:599–605.

88. "Dominion of Providence," *Works*, 2:407–436.

89. Ibid., 426–27.

90. "[Sermon] Delivered at a Public Thanksgiving after Peace," *Works*, 2:474–75.

91. See Trinterud, *American Tradition*, chapter 16, especially p. 297. Trinterud is quoting from the preface to the new Plan of Government as found in the *Records of the Presbyterian Church in the U.S.A.*, William H. Roberts, ed., Philadelphia, 1904.

92. Smylie, *Brief History of the Presbyterians*, 62–64. It is correct to say that a copy of this sermon as preached at the first General Assembly has not been preserved, but incorrect to state that the sermon itself has not been preserved. In all likelihood it is identical to the sermon that Witherspoon preached when he first arrived in Princeton in 1768, "The Success of the Gospel Entirely of God" (*Works*, 2:531–48). Green claims that it *is* the same sermon. See Green, *Life of the Revd John Witherspoon*, 148. Witherspoon was not above repeating sermons, especially as he got older. The theme of the sermon was an appropriate one for the new General Assembly: human weakness and humility contrasted with God's power and providence. Witherspoon also presided over the election of the first official moderator, who was none other than his friend John Rodgers.

93. Collins, *President Witherspoon*, 2:223. At the 1791 General Assembly, Witherspoon boasted to Green that at that Assembly "a decided majority of all ministerial members have not only been sons of our college, but my own pupils." Of the 36 ministers present, 28 were Princeton graduates, 16 of them Witherspoon's students. See Green, *Life of the Revd John Witherspoon*, 130.

94. Green, *Life of the Revd John Witherspoon*, 242.

95. John Ramsay Witherspoon, a student at the college and a cousin of President

Witherspoon, was his unofficial secretary from 1792 until his death. Every third Saturday evening he would read to Witherspoon one of his old sermons, which was sufficient preparation for the delivery of the sermon the following morning. See Green, *Life of the Revd John Witherspoon*, 252.

96. James Downey, *The Eighteenth Century Pulpit: A Study of the Sermons of Butler, Berkeley, Seeker, Sterne, Whitefield, and Wesley* (Oxford: Clarendon Press, 1969), 1, 9–10; Elwyn Allen Smith, *The Presbyterian Ministry in American Culture: A Study in Changing Concepts, 1700–1900* (Philadelphia: Westminster Press, 1962), 95.

97. See John F. Wilson, *Pulpit in Parliament: Puritanism during the English Civil Wars, 1640–1648* (Princeton, N.J.: Princeton University Press, 1969); Emory Elliott, *Power and the Pulpit in Puritan New England* (Princeton, N.J.: Princeton University Press, 1975); Harry S. Stout, *The New England Soul: Preaching and Religious Culture in Colonial New England* (New York: Oxford University Press, 1986), especially pp. 3–10; and, of course, the writings of Perry Miller.

98. Henderson, *Religious Life in Seventeenth-Century Scotland*, 190.

99. *Institutes*, 4.1.9.1023.

100. Quoted in Henderson, *Religious Life in Seventeenth-Century Scotland*, 190.

101. "Trust in God," *Works*, 2:322.

102. Among other analyses of the plain style, see Wilson, *Pulpit in Parliament*, 139–46; Charles E. Hambrick-Stowe, *The Practice of Piety: Puritan Devotional Disciplines in Seventeenth-Century New England* (Chapel Hill, N.C.: University of North Carolina Press, 1982), 118–19; and H. Richard Niebuhr and Daniel D. Williams, eds., *The Ministry in Historical Perspective* (New York: Harper & Brothers, 1956), 187–89.

103. G. D. Henderson, *The Claims of the Church of Scotland* (London: Hodder & Stoughton, 1951), 186.

104. For example, in his sermon, "The Absolute Necessity of Salvation through Christ," he included forty-seven biblical references or quotations in a sermon twenty-seven pages in its printed form. See *Works*, 1:259–87.

105. Occasionally, notably in some of the "Action" or Communion sermons, sections one and two were conflated so that there were just two divisions to the sermon, doctrines/reasons and application. Occasionally Witherspoon might expand the three-point message to four points. See *Works*, 1:585–602; 2:45–70.

106. In his sermon, "Trust in God," Witherspoon warned against grabbing a verse from the Bible "as an immediate message from God" that would profit ourselves. Rather, he counsels, one must apply certain tests to see if a verse is "from the spirit of God." See *Works*, 2:339.

107. "The Security of Those Who Trust in God," *Works*, 2:57.

108. See Witherspoon's interpretations of Isaiah 40:9–11; 41:10–13; 53:4–8; and Psalm 72:17–19 (*Works*, 1:235, 276, 472–73, 483, 536). This typology was a widespread "way of reading" not confined to preachers and theologians. It informs the poetry of the sixteenth and seventeenth centuries, for instance.

109. See the opening chapter of the Confession, 6.001–6.010.

110. "Sedition and Faction," *Works*, 1:331; "The Love of Christ in Redemption," *Works*, 1:490; "Glorying in the Cross," *Works*, 1:533, 535; "On the Religious Education of Children," *Works*, 2:394–95, 401.

111. Henderson, *Religious Life in Seventeenth-Century Scotland*, 68.

112. "Sedition and Faction," *Works*, 1:337; "Religious Education," *Works*, 2:397. Other references to Baxter can be found in "Sedition and Faction," *Works*, 1:326; "A Serious Apology for the Ecclesiastical Characteristics," *Works*, 3:177; "Lectures on Eloquence," *Works*, 3:442.

113. Richard Baxter, *The Reformed Pastor*, ed. William Brown (Edinburgh: Banner of Truth Trust, 1974), 137, 243, 254.

114. "The Charge [to Mr. Archibald Davidson] attached to the sermon, 'Sedition and Faction,'" *Works*, 1:347–48.

115. Baxter, *Reformed Pastor*, 115.

116. "The Charge [to Mr. Archibald Davidson]," 347–48.

117. Green, *Life of the Revd John Witherspoon*, 271.

118. Whitefield's effect on Franklin and Garrick is reported in Catherine L. Albanese, *America: Religion and Religions*, 2d ed., (Belmont, Calif.: Wadsworth Publishing Co., 1992), 396. Witherspoon did admit that under certain circumstances one might preach like Whitefield. See "Ecclesiastical Characteristics," *Works*, 3:128.

119. Butterfield et al., *Diary of John Adams*, 2:113.

120. Green, *Life of the Revd John Witherspoon*, 266–67.

121. Quoted in Collins, *President Witherspoon*, 1:84.

122. Ibid., 2:201. Manasseh Cutler, another critic, asserted that Witherspoon's sermons contained "good sense and clear reasoning," but that he was "a bad speaker" (Ibid., 2:161).

123. Rodgers, "Faithful Servant Rewarded," *Works*, 1:27.

124. "Preface" to vol. 1., *Works*; "Justification," *Works*, 1:57, 75; "Obedience and Sacrifice Compared," *Works*, 2:34, 38; "Seeking a Competency in the Wisdom of Providence," *Works*, 2:368; "Religious Education," *Works*, 2:402. Once Witherspoon was so sure of the role of reason that he omitted scripture. He was preaching on the text, "By their fruits ye shall know them," and was so certain of the rational principle that every belief should be validated by its results that he pronounced, "Reason is the best guide and director of human life!" See "Trial of Religious Truth," *Works*, 1:298.

125. Douglas Sloan, *The Scottish Enlightenment and the American College Ideal* (New York: Teachers College Press, 1971), 128.

126. "The World Crucified by the Cross of Christ," *Works*, 1:575; on sin and sinners, "All Mankind by Nature under Sin," *Works*, 1:407, 411–12; "The Sinner without Excuse before God," *Works*, 1:425; "The Deceitfulness of Sin," *Works*, 2:118, and "Man in His Natural State," *Works*, 2:301, 304–5, 308.

127. Lecture 1, Scott, *Lectures on Moral Philosophy*, 64.

128. "The Yoke of Christ," *Works*, 2:556. At other times, Witherspoon appealed to the reasonableness of scripture itself, declaring that there was an innate reasonableness in God's requiring a fervency, wrestling, and importunity in prayer. See "Fervency and Importunity in Prayer," *Works*, 2:8.

Chapter 1—Holy Dispositions

1. William D. Maxwell, *A History of Worship in the Church of Scotland* (London: Oxford University Press, 1955), 139–40.

2. Among recent studies of the Westminster Assembly, see George S. Hendry, *The Westminster Confession for Today: A Contemporary Interpretation* (Richmond: John Knox Press, 1960); Alasdair I. C. Heron, ed., *The Westminster Confession in the Church Today* (Edinburgh: Saint Andrew Press, 1982); John H. Leith, *Assembly at Westminster: Reformed Theology in the Making* (Richmond: John Knox Press, 1973); Robert S. Paul, *The Assembly of the Lord: Politics and Religion in the Westminster Assembly and the "Grand Debate"* (Edinburgh: T. & T. Clark, 1985); Jack B. Rogers, *Scripture in the Westminster Confession: A Problem of Historical Interpretation for American Presbyterianism* (Grand Rapids: Wm. B. Eerdmans Publishing Co., 1967); and S. B. Ferguson, "Westminster Assembly and Documents," in Wright et al., eds., *Dictionary of Scottish Church History and Theology*.

3. These other documents include *The Directory for Public Worship* (1645), *The Form of Church Government* (1645), *The Larger Catechism* (1647), and *The Shorter Catechism* (1648).

4. Thomas F. Torrance, *Scottish Theology: From John Knox to John McLeod Campbell* (Edinburgh: T. & T. Clark, 1996), 125. Torrance has equally high praise for the Westminster Shorter Catechism. When approved in 1648, he states, "it became at once the most popular and widely used Catechism in Scotland as in England, and has been more influential than any other document in shaping religious thought and temperament in Scotland ever since." See Thomas F. Torrance, ed., *The School of Faith: The Catechisms of the Reformed Church* (New York: Harper & Brothers, 1959), 261.

5. John Leith has listed and described four key features of the Confession in his *Assembly at Westminster: Reformed Theology in the Making* (Atlanta: John Knox Press, 1973)

6. Confession, 6.005.

7. William C. Placher, *The Domestication of Transcendence: How Modern Thinking about God Went Wrong* (Louisville, Ky.: Westminster John Knox Press, 1996), 53.

8. The term is derived from the Latin *foedus*, meaning "covenant."

9. The Palatinate is an area in Southwest Germany, west of the Rhine River. David Weir's research has revealed two stages in the development of the covenant of works: the first, a proposal by Zacharias Ursinus (1534–1583), the second by several Reformed theologians between 1584 and 1590. See David A. Weir, *The Origins of the Federal Theology in Sixteenth-Century Reformation Thought* (Oxford: Clarendon Press, 1990). See also Charles S. McCoy and J. Wayne Baker, *Fountainhead of Federalism: Heinrich Bullinger and the Covenantal Tradition* (Louisville, Ky.: Westminster/John Knox Press, 1991), especially chapter 2, "The Development of the Federal Theological Tradition."

10. As early as the late 1640s the General Assembly of the Church of Scotland had expressed approval of the Westminster Confession, but it was not until 1690 that that body voted to require all ministers and ministerial candidates to subscribe to the Confession. See Heron, *Westminster Confession in the Church Today*, 18.

11. Pictet treats the two covenants at some length, preferring to call the first "The Covenant of Nature," though he occasionally designates it "The Covenant of Works" or "Old Covenant." See Pictet, 139–43, 280–84.

12.   On the covenant of works, see "The Nature of Faith," *Works*, 1:466; "Yoke of Christ," 2:550; and "Justification," 1:59. On Jesus as central to the covenant of grace, see "Regeneration," 1:231; "The Nature of Faith," 1:458, 462; "The Glory of Christ in His Humiliation," 2:100; and "Love of Christ," 1:489.

13.   "Christ's Death a Proper Atonement for Sin," *Works*, 1:485; "Fervency in Prayer," 1:591; "Love of Christ," 1:485; and "The Believer Going to God as His Exceeding Joy," 2:167.

14.   See, for example, "The Charge," appended to the ordination sermon, "Sedition and Faction," *Works*, 1:347; "All Mankind under Sin," 1:417; "Ministerial Character and Duty," 2:287; and "Success of the Gospel," 2:537.

15.   "The Object of a Christian's Desire in Worship," *Works*, 2:71.

16.   "Justification," *Works*, 1:62–67, especially 66.

17.   "The Shorter Catechism," *The Book of Confessions*, Presbyterian Church (U.S.A.), (Louisville, Ky.: 1996), 7.001; "Regeneration," *Works*, 1:142, 149. See also "Yoke of Christ," *Works*, 2:556.

18.   "Shorter Catechism," 7.004.

19.   "Regeneration," *Works*, 1:139; "Sinner without Excuse," *Works*, 1:424–26; "Glorying in the Cross," *Works*, 1:542; "Fervency in Prayer," *Works*, 1:591.

20.   "Object of a Christian's Desire," *Works*, 2:73–74. Witherspoon was joined in his understanding of the importance of the divine attributes by other Popular party preachers such as Alexander Webster and Robert Dick. See John R. McIntosh, *Church and Theology in Enlightenment Scotland: The Popular Party, 1740–1800* (East Linton, East Lothian, Scotland: Tuckwell Press, 1998). 40–41.

21.   The Westminster Divines did just this. At Parliament's request, proof texts from scripture were submitted for virtually every part of the Confession.

22.   See, for example, "The Glory of the Redeemer in the Perpetuity of His Work," *Works*, 2:570–71.

23.   Confession, 6.001; Pictet, 74. The Scottish divine John MacLaurin also discovered God's perfections. See John MacLaurin, "On Christian Piety," *Works of the Rev. John MacLaurin* (Glasgow: William Collins, 1830), 105, 114, 123, 134. He connects the "incomparable display of the perfections of God" with God's mercy shown to sinners.

24.   These quotations are from several sermons found in *Works*, 1:139, 426, 591; 2:47.

25.   Placher, *Domestication of Transcendence*, 83–86.

26.   "Security of Those," *Works*, 2:49.

27.   "A View of the Glory of God Humbling to the Soul," *Works*, 2:211.

28.   The love of God theme runs through a number of sermons and much of the "Practical Treatise on Regeneration" (*Works*, 1:106, 139–41, 164, 203, 207, and 239).

29.   Among other selections, see "Yoke of Christ," *Works*, 2:558; "The Nature and Extent of Visible Religion," 1:397; and "All Mankind under Sin," 1:418.

30.   "Object of a Christian's Desire," *Works*, 2:71–84; "Believer Going to God," 2:157; "The Christian's Disposition under a Sense of Mercies Received," 2:181.

31.   "Object of a Christian's Desire," *Works*, 2:74; "Devotedness to God," 2:509; "Yoke of Christ," 2:558.

32.   "Trial of Religious Truth," *Works*, 1:299.

33. "Justification," *Works*, 1:84; "Sinner without Excuse," 1:428, 432; "Nature of Faith," 1:463; "Love of Christ," 1:506; "Christ in His Humiliation," 2:99; "Ministerial Fidelity in Declaring the Whole Counsel of God," 2:244.

34. These "grand and leading truths of the gospel," as he calls them, "are clearly contained in the Confession of Faith, which every minister in Scotland has subscribed." See "The Charge" appended to the ordination sermon, "Sedition and Faction," *Works*, 1:347.

35. "Trial of Religious Truth," *Works*, 1:308. Of the many references to and statements of these doctrines, in addition to those already cited, see the following: "Justification," 1:42–43, 82; "Absolute Necessity of Salvation," 1:260; "Sinner without Excuse," 1:428, 432; "Nature of Faith," 1:455–60; "Love of Christ," 1:506; "Christ in His Humiliation," 2:99; "Ministerial Fidelity," 2:444–45. Once he combined the second and third to reduce the count to three doctrines; another time he expanded the list to bring the number to six: the lost state of humanity, salvation through Christ, the suffering of the Savior in the sinner's place, free forgiveness through the blood of the atonement, regeneration, and sanctification. See "Absolute Necessity of Salvation," 1:260; "Ministerial Fidelity," 2:245.

36. "Serious Apology," *Works*, 3:196.

37. "Ministerial Fidelity," *Works*, 2:245.

38. See the action sermon, "Nature of Faith," *Works*, 1:453–68, in which the four truths, which comprise the "object of faith," are developed at some length with appropriate scriptural support.

39. John Erskine, "The Qualifications Necessary for Teachers of Christianity," in *Discourses Preached on Several Occasions*, 2d ed. (Edinburgh: For Wm. Creech and Arch. Constable, 1801), 1:13–14; MacLaurin, "On Christian Piety," 106–8. J. R. McIntosh has shown that two more Popular party preachers of the time shared Witherspoon's orientation to piety, Patrick Bannerman and Alexander Webster. See McIntosh, *Church and Theology*, 56.

40. See appendix A.

41. "All Mankind under Sin" (Rom. 3:23) and "Sinner without Excuse" (Ps. 130:3), *Works*, 1:405–36. The same approach, appealing to scripture and history, is used in the short sermon, "Man in His Natural State," 2:299–308.

42. "All Mankind under Sin," *Works*, 1:419.

43. "Seasonable Advice to Young Persons," *Works*, 2:483; "All Mankind under Sin," 1:408.

44. *Institutes*, 2.1.8–10.250–54. Confession, 6.033: " . . . the same death in sin and corrupted nature [of our first parents was] conveyed to all their posterity." See sermons, "All Mankind under Sin," *Works*, 1:414, 418–19; "Sinner without Excuse," 1:425, 428; "Deceitfulness of Sin," 2:142 ("polluted nature"), 144; "Seasonable Advice to Young Persons," 2:486.

45. "Deceitfulness of Sin," *Works*, 2:107, 129; "All Mankind under Sin," 1:417; "Sinner without Excuse," 1:429; "Obedience and Sacrifice Compared," 2:28; "Nature and Effects of the Stage," 3:43.

46. "Deceitfulness of Sin," *Works*, 2:112–20; "All Mankind under Sin," 1:421.

47. James Smylie, "Madison and Witherspoon: Theological Roots of American Political Thought," *Princeton University Library Chronicle* 22 (spring 1961): 118–32.

48. Chrysostom is quoted in Kathleen Norris, *The Cloister Walk* (New York: River-head Books, 1996), 275; Reinhold Niebuhr, "Sin," in *A Handbook of Christian Theology*, ed. Marvin Halverson and Arthur A. Cohen (Cleveland and New York: World Publishing Company, 1958), 350. Witherspoon roundly denounced the sin of pride, or vanity, in many of his sermons. See especially "Justification," *Works*, 1:66; "Regeneration," 1:146; "On the Purity of the Heart," 2:354. It is worth noting that Witherspoon found the much quoted formal definition of sin in the Shorter Catechism to be closely related to rebellion against God: "Sin is any want of conformity unto our [sic] transgression of the law of God." Witherspoon has thus misquoted the Catechism. See "All Mankind under Sin," 1:417.

49. "The Petitions of the Insincere Unavailing," *Works*, 2:595. Other such lists can be found in *Works*, 1:141, 144–46, 521; 2:474.

50. "All Mankind under Sin," *Works*, 1:420–21; "Sinner without Excuse," 1:429–34; "Purity of the Heart," 2:351, 356.

51. "Regeneration," *Works*, 1:111, 131; "All Mankind under Sin," 1:420.

52. Jack Scott, ed., *An Annotated Edition of Lectures on Moral Philosophy by John Witherspoon* (Newark, Del.: University of Delaware Press, 1982), 126.

53. State Archives, New Jersey State Library, Trenton.

54. Scott, *Lectures on Moral Philosophy*, 45, 125; Varnum Lansing Collins, *President Witherspoon: A Biography* (Princeton, N.J.: Princeton University Press, 1925), 2:167–68. During Witherspoon's tenure as president of the college, there was what we would call a token integration of minorities. From 1774 to 1776, two free blacks, John Quamine and Bristol Yamma, studied privately with the president. The Revolutionary War abruptly ended their education. In 1793, John Chavis, a black Revolutionary War veteran, probably studied at the college for a short time. A total of four Delaware Native Americans came to Princeton: Two attended the grammar school connected to the college for a brief period. The other two, Bartholomew Scott Calvin, also known as Shawuskukhkung or Wilted Grass, and George Morgan White Eyes, were enrolled in the college, classes of 1776 and 1789 respectively, though they never graduated. Witherspoon eventually decided that attempts to educate Native Americans on the college level were unproductive. "Seldom or never did they prove either good or useful," he explained. These efforts at minority education are reported by John Murrin in his "Introduction" to Ruth L. Woodward and Wesley Frank Craven, eds., *Princetonians, 1784–1790: A Biographical Dictionary* (Princeton, N.J.: Princeton University Press, 1991), i–iiii.

55. "Deceitfulness of Sin," *Works*, 2:133, 141. See also "Justification," 1:131; "Dominion of Providence," 2:433; "All Mankind under Sin," 1:420; and "Sinner without Excuse," 1:430, which contains, predictably, a long quotation on the tongue found in James 3:2–8.

56. The following quotations are to be found in "Nature and Effects of the Stage," *Works*, 3:25–93.

57. "Deceitfulness of Sin," *Works*, 2:123–31.

58. Ibid., 131. Witherspoon cited Isaiah 6:10; John 12:39, 40; Romans 1:28; and 2 Thessalonians 2:11, 12, as scriptural support for the fact that gross sinners have brought this judgment upon themselves.

59. Ibid., 132–33.

60. See Confession, 6.037–6.042, and Pictet, 281. Pictet describes the covenant of grace as "a free and gratuitous agreement between an offended God and offending man, in which God promises to man pardon and salvation through the merits and satisfaction of Christ, and man on his part promises faith and obedience." Pertinent passages in the *Institutes* include 1.6.1; 2.6.3–4; 2.8.21; 2.10.1–5, 7, 8; 2.11.4, 7, 11; 3.17.15; 3.21.5–7; 4.13.6. See also "Fervency in Prayer," *Works*, 1:591; "Christ's Death," 1:485; and "Love of Christ," 1:489.

61. He makes this claim several times: "Justification," *Works*, 1:73; "Hope of Forgiveness," 1:437. See also George W. Stroup, "Grace," in McKim, ed., *Encyclopedia of the Reformed Faith*. Stroup writes, "In most forms of Reformed theology, God's grace is understood as the foundation for all things."

62. "Justification," *Works*, 1:60.

63. "Hope of Forgiveness," *Works*, 1:437–51.

64. Ibid., 437, 444–45, 449–51.

65. Ibid., 445; "Love of Christ," *Works*, 1:496. For other references to God's sovereign will in electing which persons are to receive grace and be saved and to the helplessness of humans, see "Love of Christ," 502; "Believer Going to God," 2:168; "Trust in God," 2:330–31; "The Righteous Scarcely Saved, and the Wicked Certainly Destroyed," 2:521.

66. "Christ's Death," *Works*, 1:480. For a similar analysis, see "Love of Christ," 1:503: "If you reject the counsel of God against yourselves, your blood shall be upon your own heads."

67. One might even get the impression that he was merely paying lip service to the Confession. See "Necessity of Salvation," *Works*, 1:279; "Hope of Forgiveness," 1:444–45; "Christ in His Humiliation," 2:85. The term "the elect" was occasionally used simply as a synonym for believers. See "Regeneration," 1:245; "Christ in his Humiliation," 2:97.

68. "Love of Christ," *Works*, 1:491, 496; "Righteous Scarcely Saved," 2:522.

69. "Regeneration," *Works*, 1:85–257.

70. Donald G. Bloesch, "Sanctification," in McKim, ed., *Encyclopedia of the Reformed Faith*; William Stacy Johnson and John H. Leith, eds., *Reformed Reader: A Sourcebook in Christian Theology*, (Louisville, Ky.: Westminster/John Knox Press, 1993), 1:249–52.

71. "Regeneration," *Works*, 1:92–94, 149, 186–87.

72. Ibid., 129, 132, 197.

73. Ibid., 134.

74. Apparently, two student revivals occurred at Princeton early in Witherspoon's presidency without his sponsorship or leadership. It is unclear whether or not he approved of them. In 1770, the Reverend Jedidiah Chapman of Newark, invited by the students, spent a week at the college preaching and meeting inquirers in small groups ("praying societies"). In 1772, the Reverend Elihu Spencer of Trenton, responding to a student invitation, visited the campus and preached, it was said, with "a great deal of warmth and zeal." See Collins, *President Witherspoon*, 1:135.

75. See Lewis R. Rambo, *Understanding Religious Conversion* (New Haven, Conn., and London: Yale University Press, 1993), 5–19, for a recognition and classifi-

cation of types of conversion. See also John M. Mulder, "Conversion," in McKim, ed., *Encyclopedia of the Reformed Faith*.

76. Henri J. M. Nouwen, *Making All Things New* (San Francisco: Harper & Row, 1981), 57–58; Peter J. Gomes, *The Good Book: Reading the Bible with Mind and Heart* (New York: William Morrow & Co., 1996), 187–88.

77. "Regeneration," *Works*, 1:96–97, 181–83, 216–17.

78. "Christ's Death," *Works*, 1:480.

79. Ibid., 479–81.

80. "Necessity of Salvation," *Works*, 1:284; "Love of Christ," 1:507.

81. "Believer Going to God," *Works*, 2:168; "Success of the Gospel," 2:548; "Christ's Death," 1:480.

82. "Regeneration," *Works*, 1:94, 133; "Love of Christ," 1:504.

83. "Christ in His Humiliation," *Works*, 2:101–2.

84. The full title reads *Essay on the Connection between the Doctrine of Justification by the Imputed Righteousness of Christ, and Holiness of Life: With Some Reflections upon the Reception Which That Doctrine Hath Generally Met with in the World.*

85. Witherspoon uses the two terms, *justification* and *atonement*, interchangeably. In "Justification" with its numerous statements on the doctrine of justification, Witherspoon comments that "God would not forgive sin without an atonement," and further, that God's children "rest on the perfect atonement made by their Saviour and substitute." See *Works*, 1:48, 71. For other references to the atonement, see "Necessity of Salvation," 1:270, and the entire sermon, "Christ's Death," 1:469–86.

86. "Justification," *Works*, 1:37–84. See also "Necessity of Salvation," 1:259–87; "Christ's Death," 1:469–86; "Love of Christ," 1:487–507; "Glorying in the Cross," 1:525–43; "Christ in His Humiliation," 2:85–104. Witherspoon relied mainly on Romans for scriptural support for his treatment of justification, usually Romans 3:22–28 and 5:17–19, but occasionally 2 Corinthians 5:19, 21. He rarely quoted Romans 4:5–8. Cf. Confession, 6.068–6.073 and Pictet, 310–20. Pictet's definition of justification is "a judicial act on the part of God, as the supreme and merciful Governor, whereby he forgives the sins of those who repent, and gives them a title to eternal life, on account of the satisfaction and obedience of Jesus Christ imputed to them, and apprehended by faith" (311). Even earlier Calvin had taught justification by the imputed righteousness of Christ. See *Institutes*, 3.11.1–2, 23. See also Dennis E. Tamburello, *Union with Christ: John Calvin and the Mysticism of St. Bernard*, Columbia Series in Reformed Theology (Louisville, Ky.: Westminster John Knox Press, 1994), 50–63.

87. "Justification," *Works*, 1:60, 63, 73; "Necessity of Salvation," 1:278–79; "Hope of Forgiveness," 1:442 ("transaction"); "Christ's Death," 1:480; "Christ in His Humiliation," 2:97–98; "Believer Going to God," 2:155 ("divine contrivance"); "Trust in God," 2:331. This is one instance in which Witherspoon differs from the Confession, for the latter does not employ the several terms that Witherspoon uses.

88. "Love of Christ," *Works*, 1:490.

89. "Regeneration," *Works*, 1:183,185.

90. "Justification," *Works*, 1:63; "Regeneration," 1:238; Torrance, *Scottish Theology*, 250.

91. "Justification," *Works*, 1:44; "Hope of Forgiveness," 1:442, 447; "Nature of Faith," 1:457; "Christ's Death," 1:475, 480; "Christ in His Humiliation," 2:93. It is worth noting that in several sermons, Witherspoon quotes verses from Isaiah 53:5–10 and other suffering servant passages in Isaiah, applying these to Christ and his sacrificial death. Also, several passages in the Confession speak of satisfaction: 6.047, 6.068, 6.070, 6.083. There is no evidence that Witherspoon had Anselm (1033–1109) in mind when he described the atonement as satisfaction. Anselm, of course, had given classic expression to the satisfaction theory. Pictet has a separate, substantial chapter on satisfaction (Pictet, 219–25). For an excellent modern treatment of the biblical images of the atonement, including the satisfaction theory, see Shirley C. Guthrie, *Christian Doctrine*, rev. ed. (Louisville, Ky.: Westminster John Knox Press, 1994), 250–69.

92. Selected citations of these terms include: "Justification," *Works*, 1:51, 56, 63; "Regeneration," 1:243; "Necessity of Salvation," 1:260, 270–71, 279; "Christ's Death," 1:471–76.

93. "Nature of Faith," *Works*, 1:457. See also "Justification," 1:63.

94. To support his theory of satisfaction, and satisfaction with substitution, Witherspoon could have cited the *Institutes*, 2.12.2–3 and 2.15.6; the Confession, 6.047, 6.070; or Pictet, 222, 257; but he makes use of none of these.

95. "Christ's Death," *Works*, 1:472. In this sermon Witherspoon did not take up the challenge of Faustus Socinus (1539–1604) to the idea of Christ's satisfaction for sin, but he did consider it important for ministers to know the Socinian position and how to cope with it. See Lecture 16 in "Lectures on Divinity," *Works*, 4:103–9.

96. "Nature of Faith," *Works*, 1:458. See also *Institutes*, 2.12–14; Confession, "Of Christ the Mediator," 6.043–6.050; Pictet, 219, 268–70. It was not by chance that the theme of the "Confession of 1967" in the Presbyterian *Book of Confessions* was reconciliation.

97. "Christ's Death," *Works*, 1:480; "Christ in His Humiliation," 2:98. Witherspoon did not think the person of Christ needed to be explained to his congregation; all would know that Christ was fully God and fully human. For a reference to the incarnation as a "wonderful union indeed," see "Redemption the Subject of Admiration to the Angels," 1:511–12.

98. Other references to Christ as mediator include "Regeneration," *Works*, 1:231; "Christ's Death," 1:470; "Redemption the Subject of Admiration," 1:518; "An Inducement to Come to Christ," 2:315. Witherspoon also states that as mediator, Christ is our "intercessor and advocate." See "Justification," 1:57.

99. The Shorter Catechism, *The Book of Confessions*, 7.023–7.026. For Calvin's exposition of the *munus triplex*, the threefold office of prophet, priest, and king, see *Institutes*, 2.15.1–6. Briefly, Calvin stated that Christ as prophet taught "the perfect doctrine"; as priest, he is "a pure and stainless Mediator" who sacrifices himself for our salvation; and as king, he exercises a spiritual kingship, and "will provide for our needs until, our warfare ended, we are called to triumph." See also Pictet, 271–80, and George W. Stroup, "Munus triplex," in McKim, ed., *Encyclopedia of the Reformed Faith*.

100. "Christ's Death," *Works*, 1:483.

101. Confession, 6.046. The Shorter Catechism spells out Christ's humiliation and

exaltation in a way that the Confession does not. His humiliation consists of his humble birth, experiencing "the miseries of this life," God's wrath, the crucifixion, and being put under the power of death for a time. His exaltation consists of his resurrection, ascension to heaven, being placed at the right hand of the Father, and his second coming to judge the world. See "The Shorter Catechism," *The Book of Confessions*, 7.027–7.028.

102. "Christ's Death," *Works*, 1:482; "Love of Christ," 1:502; "Redemption the Subject of Admiration," 1:524; "Believer Going to God," 2:163. The humiliation and exaltation of Christ are tied together in "Glory of the Redeemer," 2:564.

103. "Justification," *Works*, 1:50; "Love of Christ," 1:498.

104. The following account of Christ's humiliation is taken from Witherspoon's sermon, "Christ in His Humiliation," *Works*, 2:85–104.

105. Scriptural support for these statements comes from Isaiah 53:3, 52:14; Psalm 22:14, 15; Job 16:8. Witherspoon gives no clue why he thinks Jesus was of a "tender frame."

106. In addition to the sermon "Christ in His Humiliation" and others that in part describe the crucifixion, three address the crucifixion directly, all based on the same text, Galatians 6:14 ("But God forbid that I should glory, save in the cross of our Lord Jesus Christ"): "Glorying in the Cross," *Works*, 1:525–43; and a series of two bearing the title "The World Crucified by the Cross of Christ," 1:545–584.

107. "Necessity of Salvation," *Works*, 1:260. Witherspoon does have a brief account of the unusual conditions surrounding the birth of Jesus. See "Redemption the Subject of Admiration," 1:513. Once, in discussing the content of revelation, he remarked that Jesus gave us "his laws as a teacher." See "Ministerial Fidelity," 2:242. This is the only reference to Jesus as teacher that I could find.

108. "The Confession of 1967," *The Book of Confessions*, Presbyterian Church (U.S.A.) (Louisville, 1996), 9.08. Calvin's portrayal of Jesus was not so grim as Witherspoon's. Calvin regarded Jesus' whole life as one of obedience, and as soon as he appeared in human form he began as a servant to pay the price of liberation for human redemption. See *Institutes*, 2.16.5; see also Torrance, *Scottish Theology*, 138.

109. "Justification," *Works*, 1:44–62.

110. Witherspoon stressed the element of gratitude a number of times. See "Regeneration," *Works*, 1:237; "Hope of Forgiveness," 1:444; "Love of Christ," 1:500, 505; "Devotedness to God," 2:513.

111. "Justification," *Works*, 1:65.

112. There is no indication that Witherspoon was aware of how Calvin described the act of reconciliation. Brian Gerrish has written that in Calvin's theology, God was not only likened to a just judge but "a kindly-disposed father as well." The purpose of the work of Christ, then, is to provide access to this gracious God. Calvin used both forensic and familial imagery in discussing the atonement. See Brian Gerrish, *Grace and Gratitude: The Eucharistic Theology of John Calvin* (Minneapolis: Fortress Press, 1993), 60.

113. "Nature of Faith," based on 1 John 3:23, *Works*, 1:453–68, and two sermons with the title, "Trust in God," based on Isaiah 50:10 (2:319–43). These latter two sermons have more to do with Christians living a life that demonstrates

trust in God than they are an analysis of faith. Witherspoon defines trust as a "reliance or confidence in God" to supply us with all "that is within the reach of divine power and wisdom." These discourses, especially the second, contain an extensive treatment of two kinds of God's promises, absolute and conditional.

114.   Shirley C. Guthrie, in his discussion of justification by grace, describes faith as trust. It is not mere intellectual assent to doctrines, but rather a full commitment of ourselves to the God who has already loved us long before we even thought of loving God. See Guthrie, *Christian Doctrine*, 322–23. See also Daniel L. Migliore, "Faith," in McKim, ed., *Encyclopedia of the Reformed Faith*.

115.   By the time Witherspoon describes faith as an assent to what is revealed of Christ and the consent of the heart, he has come close to Calvin's definition of faith: "A firm and certain knowledge of God's benevolence toward us, founded upon the truth of the freely given promise in Christ, both revealed to our minds and sealed upon our hearts through the Holy Spirit" (*Institutes*, 3.2.7). See also Tamburello, *Union with Christ*, 52. On many occasions Witherspoon drew the distinction between a cold formal intellectual assent to the truth of Christianity and a "lively exercise of faith," which he described as "a real and personal conviction of it upon the heart." This is nothing more than an exercise of the will in testifying to the *truth* of Christianity. See " Nature of Faith," *Works*, 1:461; "Love of Christ," 1:492; "Security of Those," 2:53–54; "Object of a Christian's Desire," 2:72.

116.   "Nature of Faith," *Works*, 1:464. This is not what the Confession says about faith. Justification is to be received by faith, which is "the gift of God," or it is the "work of the Spirit of Christ" in the hearts of the elect. See the Confession, 6.068, 6.078. Some other appeals to individuals to acquire faith can be found in "Regeneration," 1:216–17, 248–57; "Love of Christ," 1:507; "Christ in His Humiliation," 2:101–2; "Inducement to Come to Christ," 2:309–17; "Righteous Scarcely Saved," 2:521–22.

117.   Cf. the verbs used here with those in the chapter on "Saving Faith" in the Confession: *accepting, receiving,* and *resting* (6.079).

118.   "Justification," *Works*, 1:70–72.

119.   It is worth remembering that in the New Testament, the church as the people of God is called "a holy nation" (1 Pet. 2:9), and Christians are called "saints," or holy ones (Rom. 1:7).

120.   See "John Calvin: The Reformed Relationship between Justification and Sanctification" in Johnson and Leith, *Reformed Reader,* 249–52. For his part, Calvin wrote that "actual holiness of life, so to speak, is not separated from free imputation of righteousness." See *Institutes*, 3.3.1; see also the Confession, 6.075–6.077.

121.   John H. Leith, *An Introduction to the Reformed Tradition*, rev. ed. (Atlanta: John Knox Press, 1981), 79–80. Shirley Guthrie presents a fine statement on the relation between justification and sanctification, what he terms Christian faith (justification) and Christian action (sanctification), in his *Christian Doctrine*, 330–37. Pictet devotes a short chapter to "Sanctification and its connexion with justification," defining sanctification as a divine operation whereby the justified sinner "is, by the ministry of the word and the power of the Spirit, more and more

separated from the world, delivered from his natural corruption, and made conformable to the image of God." See Pictet, 327. Witherspoon does not come close to such a formal definition of sanctification.

122. "Regeneration," *Works*, 1:234.
123. For the powerful and effectual aid driven by the Holy Spirit, see "Justification," *Works*, 1:70–74.
124. "Regeneration," *Works*, 1:150–63.
125. See also the sermon "Christian's Disposition," 1:169–93. Although this sermon is about divine providence, it does describe sanctification.
126. Confession, 6.075–6.077; Pictet, 329.
127. "Regeneration," *Works*, 1:164; "Yoke of Christ," 2:554; "Nature and Effects of the Stage," 3:45.
128. "Christ in His Humiliation," *Works*, 2:103; "Trust in God," 2:324. Pictet sagely notes "the *imperfection* [italics in original] of this sanctification," and adds that God "does not sanctify his people perfectly." God may "will us to be perfectly holy, but not in this life." See Pictet, 329–30.
129. "Regeneration," *Works*, 1:171.
130. Ibid., 172; "Righteous Scarcely Saved," *Works*, 2:524–25. See also "Yoke of Christ," 2:554, and "Petitions of the Insincere," 2:597, where he counsels that special vigilance and effort are needed to guard against besetting sins. He issues a veritable call to arms: "If you cannot wholly destroy them, I beseech you, wound and weaken them."
131. "Regeneration," *Works*, 1:217–18. See also "Object of a Christian's Desire," 2:82, and "Petitions of the Insincere," 2:595, for further admonitions encouraging self-examination.
132. "Deceitfulness of Sin," *Works*, 2:132–33. See also "Trust in God," 2:332.
133. "Regeneration," *Works*, 1:175–77.
134. William J. Bouwsma, "The Spirituality of John Calvin," in *Christian Spirituality: High Middle Ages and Reformation*, ed. Jill Raitt (New York: Crossroad, 1987), 332.
135. Ibid., 178.
136. "Object of a Christian's Desire," *Works*, 2:79–80; "Sedition and Faction," 1:342; "Righteous Scarcely Saved," 2:525 (over all adversities "the believer must obtain the victory, and shall obtain it in his Redeemer's strength"). Witherspoon was but echoing what the Confession states in the chapters, "Of the Perseverance of the Saints," and "Of the Assurance of Grace and Salvation" (6.094–6.100). See also Pictet, "Of the Perseverance of Faith," 305–7.

Chapter 2—Pious and Useful Actions

1. "Regeneration," *Works*, 1:230, 236.
2. "Preface," *Works*, 1:3.
3. "Visible Religion," *Works*, 1:403. It is worth noting that Pictet makes a close connection between good works and sanctification: "Sanctification is displayed and promoted by *good works* [italics in original]." See Pictet, 330–34.
4. This and the following quotations are from "Trial of Religious Truth," *Works*, 1:289–317.
5. "Visible Religion," *Works*, 1:383–404.

6. "Necessity of Salvation," *Works*, 1:282.
7. "Regeneration," *Works*, 1:154; "Sinner without Excuse," 1:434; "View of the Glory of God," 2:217; "Purity of the Heart," 2:354; "Seeking a Competency," 2:368.
8. "Hope of Forgiveness," *Works*, 1:451.
9. "Sinner without Excuse," *Works*, 1:426; "Nature and Effects of the Stage," 3:47–48.
10. "Justification," *Works*, 1:73.
11. "Regeneration," *Works*, 1:218–19.
12. "World Crucified," *Works*, 1:557, 560; "Sedition and Faction," 1:342; "Seasonable Advice to Young Persons," 2:487; "Nature and Effects of the Stage," 3:43; "Address to the Senior Class," 2:624. See also "Trial of Religious Truth," 1:307; "World Crucified," 1:582; "Religious Education," 2:399, 403; "Seasonable Advice to Young Persons," 2:502. Witherspoon was especially concerned that young children be taught the several qualities of pious behavior including self-control.
13. "Address to the Senior Class," *Works*, 2:625; "Lectures on Eloquence," 3:394–97.
14. *Lectures on Rhetoric and Belles Lettres*, 1783. Blair taught at the University of Edinburgh (1760–1784), and was minister of Edinburgh's High Kirk (St. Giles' Cathedral) from 1758 to 1800.
15. Witherspoon has numerous references, on the one hand, to profaning the name of God (*Works*, 1:205, 397, 515–16), and on the other, holding sacred God's name (1:387–88; 2:432, 473).
16. "Visible Religion," *Works*, 1:389.
17. Ibid., 400–402; "Nature of Faith," 1:466; "Fervency in Prayer," 2:21; "Obedience and Sacrifice Compared," 2:34; "Dominion of Providence," 2:434; "Public Thanksgiving," 2:468; "Address to the Senior Class," 2:626.
18. "Visible Religion," *Works*, 1:388.
19. "Address to the Senior Class," *Works*, 2:617; "Trust in God," 2:335.
20. As quoted in an article, which originally appeared in the *New York Times Magazine*, authored by Jim Wooten, Carter's biographer, and reproduced in Robert Fulghum, *Words I Wish I Wrote: A Collection of Writing That Inspired My Ideas* (New York: HarperCollins, 1997), 86.
21. "Security of Those," *Works*, 2:60–63.
22. "The Danger of Adversity," *Works*, 2:386; "Public Thanksgiving," 2:475.
23. Charles I's complaint is reported in Peter J. Gomes, *The Good Book: Reading the Bible with Mind and Heart* (New York: William Morrow & Co., 1996), 233.
24. "Obedience and Sacrifice Compared," *Works*, 2:23–44, especially p. 44; "Security of Those," 2:70; "Christian Magnanimity," 2:610.
25. "Purity of the Heart," *Works*, 2:358–59; "Danger of Adversity," 2:387; "Address to the Senior Class," 2:632.
26. "Regeneration," *Works*, 1:239–41. In two other places he cites the second great commandment: "Visible Religion," 1:396, and "Yoke of Christ," 2:556. In the first instance, loving others means trying to convert them from sin to salvation; in the second, Witherspoon is merely proving how reasonable it is to love both God and neighbor.

27. "Regeneration," *Works*, 1:240. In "Visible Religion," Witherspoon states that loving one's enemies is a "rare virtue," and quotes Matthew 5:44 ("Love your enemies"), 1:386.

28. "Sinner without Excuse," *Works*, 1:428. See also "Trial of Religious Truth," *Works*, 1:301; 1:428; "Hope of Forgiveness," 1:549; "World Crucified," 1:581; "Obedience and Sacrifice Compared," 2:41; "Dominion of Providence," 2:436.

29. "Visible Religion," *Works*, 1:387. The two sermons are found in *Works*, 1:545–84, and subsequent quotations, unless otherwise identified, are taken from these sermons. See also "Dominion of Providence," 2:435.

30. "World Crucified," *Works*, 1:549. Witherspoon said the same thing in his critique of the theater, "Nature and Effects of the Stage," 3:49. He was reflecting the rejection by Calvin and Luther of the medieval "double standard" of a higher and lower vocation in the world. They abolished the distinction between sacred and secular callings and wanted *all* Christians to stay in the world to live out their vocation. See Robert McAfee Brown, *The Spirit of Protestantism* (New York: Oxford University Press, 1961), 108–9.

31. "World Crucified," *Works*, 1:550–51, 559; "Seasonable Advice to Young Persons," 2:504.

32. A further reason to back away from the world lies in the fact that so many persons *think* they are shunning the world but have no awareness that worldliness itself is "the inward principle" that gives impetus to all their other sins. See "Purity of the Heart," *Works*, 2:350–52; "World Crucified," 1:554–59. For more on Witherspoon's response to the question of the amount of wealth a Christian should possess, see chapter 5, especially the survey of his sermon, "Seeking a Competency in the Wisdom of Providence."

33. "World Crucified," *Works*, 1:560–61.

34. Robert Wuthnow, *After Heaven: Spirituality in America since the 1950s* (Berkeley and Los Angeles: University of California Press, 1998), 196. See especially his chapter, "The Practice of Spirituality," and the last part of that chapter, "The Value of Spiritual Practice."

35. "Inducement to Come to Christ," 2:316–17; "Fervency in Prayer," 1:598. In this matter Witherspoon was following the pattern of the Confession, which restricts the ordinances to (1) the preaching of the Word, and presumably those elements of worship surrounding the sermon, and (2) the administration of the sacraments of Baptism and the Lord's Supper. See the Confession, 6.042. Chapter 21 (6.112–6.119) is given over to religious worship and the Sabbath.

36. William D. Maxwell, *A History of Worship in the Church of Scotland* (London: Oxford University Press, 1955), 102–5. See Charles E. Hambrick-Stowe, *The Practice of Piety: Puritan Devotional Disciplines in Seventeenth-Century New England* (Chapel Hill, N.C.: University of North Carolina Press, 1982), 93–135, for a fine treatment of all the New England Puritan ordinances of public worship.

37. "Devotedness to God," *Works*, 2:516; "Public Thanksgiving," 2:470, 474.

38. "The Happiness of the Saints in Heaven," *Works*, 2:236; "Regeneration," 1:222.

39. "Letters on Education," *Works*, 3:526; "Ministerial Fidelity," 2:280.

40. Confession, 6.140–6.145. "Regeneration," *Works*, 1:245; "Religious Education," 2:393.

41. "Glory of the Redeemer," *Works*, 2:575; "Fervency in Prayer," 1:601.

42. "Trust in God," *Works*, 2:322, 512; "Serious Apology," 3:169. Stating that the church was both clergy and laity was probably only a slightly veiled criticism of lay patronage.

43. "Happiness of the Saints," *Works*, 2:232; "Trust in God," 2:322.

44. "Object of a Christian's Desire," *Works*, 2:81; "Happiness of the Saints," 2:234. Each of the four acts is explained at some length (pp. 222–29).

45. "Regeneration," *Works*, 1:203, 222; "Sinner without Excuse," 1:432; "Fervency in Prayer," 2:18, 19; "Object of a Christian's Desire," 2:81, 84; "Happiness of the Saints," 2:236.

46. "Obedience and Sacrifice Compared," *Works*, 2:39. The text for the sermon was 1 Samuel 15:32. Witherspoon has equally harsh words for those who are "habitual despisers" of public worship. Any virtues they may exhibit are weak and feeble because they are not enlivened "by piety towards God." See "Happiness of the Saints," 2:235.

47. "Sinner without Excuse," *Works*, 1:432.

48. "Love of Christ," *Works*, 1:432. The Shorter Catechism defines a sacrament this way: "A sacrament is a holy ordinance instituted by Christ, wherein by sensible signs, Christ and the benefits of the new covenant are represented, sealed, and applied to believers" (7.092). Calvin, of course, noted that sacraments were seals, comparing them to the official seals attached to government documents. Sacraments are seals, he further explained, by which God's promises are confirmed in our lives. See *Institutes*, 4.14.5. See also Gerrish, *Grace and Gratitude*, 102–3. Pictet concludes his *Christian Theology* with a long chapter on the sacraments, also calling them "seals, which confirm to us God's promises." See Pictet, 399–434. See also George S. Hendry, *The Westminster Confession for Today: A Contemporary Interpretation* (Richmond: John Knox Press, 1960), 222.

49. "Love of Christ," *Works*, 1:498; "Glorying in the Cross," 1:540; "Religious Education," 2:393; "Devotedness to God," 2:512. The Confession declares that "the infants of one or both believing parents are to be baptized" (6.157). With apparent approval, Witherspoon repeated the tradition that Ignatius, bishop of Antioch, had been baptized by Christ as an infant. He said he saw no reason to deny the report, reasoning that Ignatius would have been between 70 and 80 years of age when he was martyred in A.D. 108. See "Religious Education," 2:394.

50. "Ministerial Fidelity," *Works*, 2:265–66.

51. The seven sermons so labeled are "Nature of Faith," "Christ's Death," "Love of Christ," "Redemption the Subject of Admiration," "Glorying in the Cross," "Devotedness to God," and "Glory of the Redeemer" (*Works*, 1:453–543; 2:507–16, 563–79). The two unidentified Communion sermons are "Christ in His Humiliation" (2:85–104) and "Believer Going to God" (2:149–68). In addition, two other sermons bearing the title "Fervency and Importunity in Prayer," judging by their content, must have been preached in the Communion season, perhaps as a conclusion to the celebration of the Lord's Supper.

52. "Redemption the Subject of Admiration," *Works*, 1:523–24. These themes are mentioned in other action sermons. See especially "Christ's Death," 1:474; "Love of Christ," 1:498; "Glorying in the Cross," 1:525, 542; "Christ in His Humiliation," 2:104.

53. Maxwell, *History of Worship*, 141–75; Henry Grey Graham, *The Social Life of*

Scotland in the Eighteenth Century (London: Adam & Charles Black, 1950), 302–14. Note the "Sacramental Directory," "Sacramental Meditations," "Sacramental Advices," and even "A Sacramental Catechism" in *The Practical Works of the Rev. John Willison* (Glasgow: Blackie & Son, 1844).

54. *Works*, 2:149–68.

55. Ibid., 152. Other passages that speak of commemoration include "Believer Going to God," 2:150; "Redemption the Subject of Admiration," 1:524; "Glorying in the Cross," 1:525, 542.

56. "Believer Going to God," *Works*, 2:158. For another powerful passage that recounts Christ's victory in the sacrament, see "Glory of the Redeemer," 2:575: "Hell itself may rage, and the princes of this world may combine to shake his glorious throne, but he that sits in heaven shall laugh."

57. "Believer Going to God," *Works*, 2:158–64.

58. "Love of Christ," *Works*, 1:498–99; "Regeneration," 1:157–58. See also the reference cited in note 50, "Glorying in the Cross," 1:525, 542, where Witherspoon alludes to Christ's suffering, to his broken body and blood poured out.

59. "Christ in His Humiliation," *Works*, 2:104; "Believer Going to God," 2:150, 157; "Devotedness to God," 2:512–13.

60. "Devotedness to God," *Works*, 2:514–15.

61. "Glory of the Redeemer," *Works*, 2:578–79. See also Thomas F. Torrance, *Scottish Theology: From John Knox to John McLeod Campbell* (Edinburgh: T. & T. Clark, 1996), 233.

62. Rodgers, "Faithful Servant Rewarded," *Works*, 1:35. Witherspoon instructed his divinity students to "remember the importance of the exercises of piety and the duties of the closet." See "Lectures on Divinity," *Works*, 4:14.

63. "Happiness of the Saints," *Works*, 2:236; "View of the Glory of God," 2:217. More criticism of omitting family worship can be found in "Letters on Education," 3:526, and "Ecclesiastical Characteristics," 3:191.

64. "Religious Education," *Works*, 2:401.

65. Graham, *Social Life of Scotland*, 337; John Watson, *The Scot of the Eighteenth Century* (London: Hodder & Stoughton, 1907), 269. See also "Justification," *Works*, 1:39.

66. "Inducement to Come to Christ," *Works*, 2:316; "Regeneration," 1:235.

67. "Love of Christ," *Works*, 1:498; "Inducement to Come to Christ," 2:317.

68. Henri J. M. Nouwen, *Making All Things New* (San Francisco: Harper & Row, 1981), 69–78. See also his *Out of Solitude: Three Meditations on the Christian Life* (Notre Dame, Ind.: Ave Maria Press, 1974). Kathleen Norris, *The Cloister Walk* (New York: Riverhead Books, 1996), 31, 144, 267.

69. "Security of Those," *Works*, 2:59; "Purity of the Heart," 2:345. The two sermons bear the same title and text, "Fervency and Importunity in Prayer" (text: Gen. 32:26), 1:585–602; 2:7–22.

70. "Christian's Disposition," *Works*, 2:192.

71. Witherspoon's use of the word "lawful" is reminiscent of the Confession, 6.115: "Prayer is to be made for things lawful." In his sermon, "On the Purity of the Heart," he observes that it is, in fact, easier to pray for material blessings than spiritual ones. So it is incumbent upon us to pay more attention to "what we ask for our souls than for our bodies" (*Works*, 2:357).

72. "Trust in God," *Works*, 2:336–37.
73. "Fervency in Prayer," *Works*, 1:587–97.
74. Ibid., 597–601; "Object of a Christian's Desire," *Works*, 2:83–84.
75. Elie Wiesel, *All Rivers Run to the Sea: Memoirs* (New York: Alfred A. Knopf, 1995), 84.
76. "Fervency in Prayer," *Works*, 2:12–17.
77. Ibid. Witherspoon cites a number of Bible passages to undergird God's faithfulness in answering prayer: Proverbs 2:3–5; Luke 18:1–7; Matthew 17:19–21; James 5:16. Specific examples of answered prayer are to be found in Genesis 18 (Abraham's intercessory prayer for Sodom); James 5:17–18 (Elijah's prayer for and against rain); Daniel 2:17–19 (Daniel's prayer to God to reveal his secret); and Matthew 15:21–28 (the woman of Canaan who pled for her daughter to be healed). In another sermon, "The Security of Those Who Trust in God," he supplies additional references to "the promises of a gracious answer to our prayers": Matthew 7:7 and 21:22; John 14:13; Psalm 34:6, 17. See *Works*, 2:59.
78. "Fervency in Prayer," *Works*, 2:21–22. Witherspoon sets out two other ways to improve one's prayer life: (1) Develop a clear conscience by "habitual watchfulness" to keep from sinning. He also recommends habitual watchfulness in his sermon, "Purity of the Heart," 2:358. (2) Remember the blessing of divine providence, which will keep one's prayers concrete and focused.
79. This advice, quoted earlier, is now being "frequently repeated" by the present author!
80. A few of these "nonessential" doctrines, such as creation, inspiration of scripture, and adoption, Witherspoon chose to ignore either as being peripheral to piety or not necessary to explain since he and his parishioners were of the same mind and understanding. Brief references to the resurrection can be found in "Regeneration," *Works*, 1:149; "Love of Christ," 1:502; "Happiness of the Saints," 2:230; "Glory of the Redeemer," 2:564. A number of references to the final judgment are contained in "Regeneration," 1:246; "Sedition and Faction," 1:344; "Sinner without Excuse," 1:435; "Nature of Faith," 1:468; "Christ in His Humiliation," 2:100; "Danger of Adversity," 2:383; "Righteous Scarcely Saved," 2:517, 519, 527. Many of these passages include Witherspoon's rhetorical pleas to sinners to accept God's grace and Jesus as their Savior before death and the last judgment. His doctrine of last things, his eschatology, also stated that Jesus would return to earth at the culmination of human history. See "Christ's Death," 1:482; "Redemption the Subject of Admiration," 1:524; "Believer Going to God," 2:160–64. The Confession has a separate chapter on the perseverance of the saints; Witherspoon subsumed this belief under sanctification. He discussed the decrees and the Trinity in his "Lectures on Divinity." Lastly, the doctrine of providence merits special attention in the present volume in a later chapter since it is a central doctrine in the transformation of Witherspoon's piety in America.
81. "Nature of Faith," *Works*, 1:455. Thomas F. Torrance makes the same point as he studies several catechisms of the Reformed tradition in *The School of Faith: The Catechisms of the Reformed Church* (New York: Harper & Brothers, 1959), xx–xxi.
82. On one occasion he went so far as to promise that piety would bring wonderful

material blessings, stating that "true religion is the way to health, peace, opulence [*sic*] and public esteem." See "Seasonable Advice to Young Persons," *Works*, 2:499.

83. "Sedition and Faction," *Works*, 1:342.
84. Brian Gerrish, "Tradition in the Modern World: The Reformed Habit of Mind" in David Willis and Michael Welker, eds., *Toward the Future of Reformed Theology: Tasks, Topics, Traditions* (Grand Rapids: Wm. B. Eerdmans Publishing Co., 1999), 17, 18; *Institutes*, 1.14.4. Chrysostom is quoted in Richard H. Bell, *Sensing the Spirit* (Philadelphia: Westminster Press, 1984), 100. Bell himself emphasizes that part of the discovery of loving God is to maintain a balance between "contemplation and action."
85. "Danger of Adversity," *Works*, 2:388–89.

Chapter 3—Real Religion for a Minister

1. The titles of the sermons are respectively, "Ministerial Character and Duty" (text: 2 Cor. 4:13), *Works*, 2:285–99, "The Charge of Sedition and Faction against Good Men, Especially Faithful Ministers, Considered and Accounted For" (text: Acts 17:6), 1:319–55. Bound with the latter sermon is Witherspoon's "Charge" to the new minister and the "Exhortation to the People," that is, the Paisley Abbey Church congregation.
2. "Ministerial Character," *Works*, 2:286–88.
3. "The Charge" appended to "Sedition and Faction," *Works*, 1:345–46.
4. Ibid., 347.
5. "Ministerial Character," *Works*, 2:291–92.
6. "Seasonable Advice to Young Persons," *Works*, 2:483–505; Martha Lou Lemmon Stohlman, *John Witherspoon: Parson, Politician, Patriot* (Philadelphia: Westminster Press, 1976), 38–40; Ashbel Green, *The Life of the Revd John Witherspoon, D.D., LL.D.*, ed. Henry Lyttleton Savage (Princeton, N.J.: Princeton University Press, 1973), 82–91; Thomas Crichton, "Memoir of the Life and Writings of John Witherspoon," *Edinburgh Christian Instructor* 28 (October 1829): 673–94.
7. "Ministerial Character," *Works*, 2:289–90.
8. Ibid., 292–93.
9. Ibid., 294–95.
10. "The Charge," appended to "Sedition and Faction," *Works*, 1:351.
11. "Ecclesiastical Characteristics," *Works*, 3:101–63.
12. Witherspoon adds a sarcastic conclusion to this maxim by noting, "I might have spared myself the trouble of inserting this maxim, the present rising generation being of themselves sufficiently disposed to observe it." See "Ecclesiastical Characteristics," 131.
13. Lord Shaftesbury (1671–1713), Gottfried W. Leibniz (1646–1716), Anthony Collins (1676–1729), Francis Hutcheson (1694–1746), and David Hume (1711–1776).
14. "Ministerial Fidelity," *Works*, 2:239–84.
15. Ibid., 262.
16. Ibid., 263.
17. Ibid., 269. Witherspoon continues by noting several temptations that ministers

of integrity will resist when facing opposition: They may be tempted to soften their message in order to avoid criticism and contempt, or to maintain a "sinful silence" to avoid censure, or to lose courage in the discharge of their duties, or to commit a sin by imprudence or passion when facing the opposition of wicked persons (269–71).

18. "Success of the Gospel," *Works*, 2:531–48.
19. Ibid., 536.
20. Ibid., 537–38.
21. Ibid., 538–39.
22. Ibid., 540–41, 543.
23. Ibid., 545.
24. Ibid., 547–48.
25. Rodgers, "Faithful Servant Rewarded," *Works*, 1:30.
26. "Address in behalf of the College," *Works*, 4:344.
27. "Lectures on Moral Philosophy," *Works*, 3:373. One could also speculate that he had "constant intercourse" with Moderate William Leechman (1706–1785), former minister at Beith who became professor of divinity at Glasgow in 1744, or even William Wight, Carlyle's cousin and intimate friend, who was professor of ecclesiastical history beginning in 1762.
28. See the next chapter for more on this development.
29. "Ministerial Fidelity," *Works*, 2:279. Several years later, when he came to address the seniors at Princeton, Witherspoon was wishing for them the "most solid, valuable and durable politeness" and proposing that they have "intercourse with the best company." See "Address to the Senior Class," *Works*, 1:630–31.
30. "Ministerial Character," *Works*, 2:289. Another piece of evidence that Witherspoon's intellectual—and theological—outlook was not circumscribed is found in an article he wrote for *The Scots Magazine* in 1753, in which he attacks a Moderate, Lord Kames, for his ideas on the human will. See John Witherspoon, "Remarks on an Essay on Human Liberty," *The Scots Magazine* 15 (April 1753): 165–70. In this essay he defends the faithfulness of our senses, declaring "that the ideas we receive by our senses, and the persuasions we derive immediately from them, are exactly according to truth, or real truth." While this is not the stuff of sermons, it does support Witherspoon's later claim that he had proposed common sense realism at an early date. Incidentally, this piece was sent later by the Reverend John Erskine to the American Joseph Bellamy, a friend of Jonathan Edwards. See Varnum Lansing Collins, *President Witherspoon: A Biography* (Princeton, N.J.: Princeton University Press, 1925), 1:41; Mark Noll, *Princeton and the Republic, 1768–1822* (Princeton, N.J.: Princeton University Press, 1989), 25.
31. "Ministerial Character," *Works*, 2:287.

Chapter 4—Piety and Learning / From Proof to Promise

1. "Lectures on Divinity," *Works*, 4:10.
2. The first national Presbyterian seminary was established in Princeton in 1812, although the present Pittsburgh Theological Seminary traces its beginnings to 1794.

3. The outstanding Presbyterian example of this kind of theological training is the "Log College" established by the Reverend William Tennent (1673–1746) in Neshaminy, Pennsylvania. Between 1727 and 1746 he trained nineteen young men for the ministry. See Randall Balmer and John R. Fitzmier, *The Presbyterians* (Westport, Conn.: Greenwood Press, 1993), 27–31, 229–31; see also "Theological Education in Manse, Academy, and College," in Elwyn Allen Smith, *The Presbyterian Ministry in American Culture: A Study in Changing Concepts, 1700–1900* (Philadelphia: Westminster Press, 1962), 68–79. The work of New England pastor-professors such as Jonathan Edwards, Joseph Bellamy, Nathanael Emmons, and Samuel Hopkins, as well as graduate study in divinity at the colleges, is recounted in Mary L. Gambrell, *Ministerial Training in Eighteenth-Century New England* (New York: Columbia University Press, 1937).

4. H. Richard Niebuhr and Daniel D. Williams, eds., *The Ministry in Historical Perspective* (New York: Harper & Brothers, 1956), 231–33, and Leonard J. Trinterud, *The Forming of an American Tradition: A Re-examination of Colonial Presbyterianism* (Philadelphia: Westminster Press, 1949), 300.

5. Thomas Jefferson Wertenbaker, *Princeton 1746–1896* (Princeton, N.J.: Princeton University Press, 1946), 24–45; James McLachlan, ed., *Princetonians 1748–1768: A Biographical Dictionary* (Princeton, N.J.: Princeton University Press, 1976), xviii, xxi, xxii. See especially Bryan F. Le Beau, *Jonathan Dickinson and the Formative Years of American Presbyterianism* (Lexington, Ky.: University Press of Kentucky, 1997), 184.

6. Richard A. Harrison, ed. *Princetonians, 1769–1775: A Biographical Dictionary* (Princeton, N.J.: Princeton University Press, 1980), 42, 161. In the class of 1773 no less than four of the thirty-one members of the class studied theology with Witherspoon after graduation: James F. Armstrong, Ebenezer Bradford, Lewis F. Wilson, and William Beekman, the last of whom provided a recommended reading list for divinity students studying with President Witherspoon (see below) (263–66, 269–71, 272–76, 352–54). Witherspoon was proud of his record in educating Presbyterian ministers. We have already observed how pleased he was of the number of his students who had become ministers.

7. "Lectures on Divinity," *Works*, 4:10.

8. Ibid.

9. Ibid., 11.

10. Ibid., 12.

11. Although Witherspoon cites Hebrews 6:2, he must surely mean v. 11, "And we desire that every one of you do shew the same diligence to the full assurance of hope unto the end."

12. "Lectures on Divinity," *Works*, 4:13.

13. Ibid., 13–14.

14. Ibid.

15. Ibid., 15.

16. "Lectures on Eloquence," *Works*, 3:470–71.

17. "Lectures on Divinity," *Works*, 4:20–22.

18. He has specific authors in mind who will be identified later.

19. "Lectures on Eloquence," *Works*, 3:464–71.

20. "Lectures on Divinity," *Works*, 4:22. Witherspoon was not the only eighteenth-

century intellectual who compiled a "list of books." For some examples, see Cotton Mather, *Manuductio ad Ministerium: Direction for a Candidate of the Ministry* (Boston, 1726), who also advocated for the young minister piety first and then learning; "Advice to a Young Student at the University by a Divine of the Church of England," probably by Daniel Waterland, in *The Present State of the Republick of Letters* 4 (December, 1729); and more generally, beyond divinity, Charles B. Sanford, *Thomas Jefferson and His Library* (Hamden, Conn.: Archon Books, 1977). In Jefferson's list of books there were some 175 on religion and ecclesiastical history. Finally, see Samuel Johnson (1696–1772), *An Introduction to the Study of Philosophy Exhibiting a General View of All the Arts and Sciences, for the Use of Pupils. With a Catalogue of some of the most valuable Authors necessary to be read in order to instruct them in a thorough Knowledge of each of them.* (New London, Conn., 1743). See Norman S. Fiering, "President Samuel Johnson and the Circle of Knowledge," *William and Mary Quarterly*, Third Series 28 (April 1971): 199–236.

21.   Johannes Wollebius, *Compendium theologiae Christianae* (Basel, 1626); François Turretin, *Institutio theologiae elencticae* (Geneva, 1679–1685).

22.   John Leland, *A View of the Principal Deistical Writers That Have Appeared in England in the Last and Present Centuries*, 2 vols. (1754–1756).

23.   Jean Baptiste Molière, *The Would-Be Gentleman*, act 2, scene 4; Blaise Pascal, *Provincial Letters*, no. 16. In his "A Serious Apology for the Ecclesiastical Characteristics," Witherspoon refers to Molière's *Le Tartuffe* with some approval, and quotes from Pascal's *Lettres Provinciales* with even more admiration. See "Serious Apology," *Works*, 3:178–79, 183.

24.   Rodgers, "Faithful Servant Rewarded," *Works*, 1:30; Ashbel Green, *The Life of the Revd John Witherspoon, D.D., LL.D.*, ed. Henry Lyttleton Savage (Princeton, N.J.: Princeton University Press, 1973), 274; Lyman H. Butterfield et al., eds., *The Diary and Autobiography of John Adams* (Cambridge, Mass.: Harvard University Press, 1961), 2:112. Merchant Jaques Voorhees of Somerset County, New Jersey, sold the wine to Witherspoon on August 27, 1793, at fifteen shillings per gallon. See Ralph Voorhees, "The Raritan and Its Early Holland Settlers," *Our Home* 1 (1873), 470.

25.   See Sir Henry Raeburn, "The Reverend Robert Walker Skating on Duddingston Loch," oil on canvas, National Gallery of Scotland, Edinburgh. A copy of the painting graces the cover of *In Britain* 7 (December 1997); Varnum Lansing Collins, *President Witherspoon: A Biography* (Princeton, N.J.: Princeton University Press), 1:24, 2:185. Both incidents illustrating Witherspoon's love of curling are recorded in the Paisley Central Library, Paisley, Scotland, in the Cairn of Lochwinyoch Mss., XXX(II), 91–92. See also Andrew Hook's brief report on the incidents in his "Witherspoon on Ice," *Princeton University Library Chronicle* 41 (autumn 1979): 50–53. In one incident, a woman of Witherspoon's congregation chided him for staying so late (11 P.M.) on a Saturday night at Strand's Inn with his curling friends, when, she told him, he should have been at home preparing for the Lord's Day.

26.   Witherspoon did not devote much time or energy in any of his writings to infidels such as Hume or Voltaire. He was, he said, more concerned to answer the objections of Christianity than to religion in general. See "Lectures on Divin-

ity," *Works*, 4:23–24. He identified the two enemies as "atheists and theists." This is surely a misprint, for he goes on to discuss the deists, not theists.

27. "Lectures on Divinity," *Works*, 4:46.
28. Ibid., 22–62. His lengthy defense of revelation in these pages is organized under three kinds of evidence: direct, presumptive, and consequential.
29. Ibid., 24–25.
30. Ibid., 47.
31. Ibid., 28–41.
32. Ibid., 42, 43.
33. Ibid., 43–49.
34. Ibid., 49–55.
35. Ibid., 54.
36. Before turning to the exposition of the several doctrines of the Confession for the benefit of his theological students (beginning with Divinity Lecture 9), Witherspoon lists four objections against the Christian religion. Two of these he had already discussed—the sufficiency of reason, not revelation; and the impossibility of miracles. He introduces and refutes two more: Christianity's lack of universality and the responsibility Christianity must bear for introducing persecution into the world. The answer to the first is that it is in God's hands, not ours, as to "the time of the publication" of the good news and "the extent of the progress of the gospel light, or even the numbers that are benefited by it." The answer to the second is that instead of persecuting non-Christians, it is the Christians, those "meek believers in Christ," who were persecuted by Jews and non-Christians for the first three hundred years and have been persecuted by "the spirit of the world" in every age (Ibid., 60–62).
37. Ibid., 65.
38. John Milton, *Paradise Lost*, 2.557–61:

> Others apart sat on a hill retired,
> In thoughts more elevate, and reasoned high
> Of providence, foreknowledge, will and fate,
> Fixed fate, free will, foreknowledge absolute,
> And found no end, in wandering mazes lost.

39. "Lectures on Divinity," *Works*, 4:87–88.
40. Ibid., 67.
41. Douglas Sloan, *The Scottish Enlightenment and the American College Ideal* (New York: Teachers College Press, 1971), 122.
42. "Lectures on Divinity," *Works*, 4:92–93.
43. Ibid., 96, 99–100. The best definition of sin, Witherspoon declares, can be found in the Shorter Catechism: "A want of conformity unto, or transgression of the law of God." He is merely repeating what he preached in one of his sermons on sin. See "All Mankind under Sin," *Works*, 1:417. Here he instructs his students in the several ways sins can be categorized: voluntary/involuntary; of total/partial ignorance; those of thought/word/deed; and occasional/reigning.
44. Lecture 16, "Of the Covenant of Grace," "Lectures on Divinity," *Works*, 4:103–23.

45. Ibid., 112–13. When Witherspoon speaks of eternal life, he is clearly intending life beyond the grave, "the promise of a glorious immortality," not, as he might have said, the resurrection of the body.

Chapter 5—Providence

1. "The Confession of 1967" has included the truth that even the scriptures themselves are "conditioned by the language, thought forms, and literary fashions of the places and times at which they were written." See "The Confession of 1967," *The Book of Confessions*, 9.29. If this is true of the Bible, it is no less true of any expression of Christian piety.

2. Previously, no one except Wayne Witte in his Princeton Seminary dissertation has noticed Witherspoon's considerable attention to the doctrine of providence before and especially after his transfer to America. Unfortunately, Witte did not develop Witherspoon's understanding of the doctrine sufficiently. See Wayne W. Witte, "John Witherspoon: An Exposition and Interpretation of His Theological Views as the Motivation of His Ecclesiastical, Educational, and Political Career in Scotland and America" (Th.D. diss., Princeton Theological Seminary, 1953)," 209–21. Other changes or different emphases in Witherspoon's thought that appeared when he took up his teaching at Princeton have been noticed by several historians, who have offered their own explanations. See Mark A. Noll, "The Irony of the Enlightenment for Presbyterians in the Early Republic," *Journal of the Early Republic* 5 (1985): 149–75; Richard B. Sher, *Church and University in the Scottish Enlightenment: The Moderate Literati of Edinburgh* (Princeton, N.J.: Princeton University Press, 1985), 160–61; Henry F. May, *The Enlightenment in America* (New York: Oxford University Press, 1976), 62–65, 346–47; Ned C. Landsman, "Witherspoon and the Problem of Provincial Identity in Scottish Evangelical Culture," in *Scotland and America in the Age of the Enlightenment*, ed. Richard B. Sher and Jeffrey R. Smitten (Princeton, N.J.: Princeton University Press, 1990), 29–45. See also William Ferguson, *Scotland: 1689 to the Present* (Edinburgh: Oliver & Boyd, 1968), 228. Both Ferguson and Sher have noted that in Scotland the Popular party itself was changing, following, according to Sher, a "pattern of accommodation to the cultural and intellectual values of Moderation during the second half of the eighteenth century." Landsman argues persuasively that Witherspoon remained faithful to Popular party and orthodox Presbyterian positions, but that it was "orthodoxy itself that changed during the eighteenth century." Likewise, John McIntosh has noted that the Popular party did not remain doctrinally static in the eighteenth century, for many in the party felt challenged by the Enlightenment and modified established positions accordingly. See John R. McIntosh, *Church and Theology in Enlightenment Scotland: The Popular Party, 1740–1800* (East Linton, East Lothian, Scotland: Tuckwell Press, 1998), 236–39. Jack Scott has also commented on the "erosion" of some of Witherspoon's beliefs, and concluded that "rationalism had entered the house of Calvinism." See his edited volume, *An Annotated Edition of Lectures on Moral Philosophy by John Witherspoon* (Newark, Del.: University of Delaware Press, 1982), 39–40. Finally, Douglas Sloan has argued that Witherspoon had absorbed much of the Moderate outlook by the time he left for America and that this influence is visible in his lectures in divin-

ity and moral philosophy. See Douglas Sloan, *The Scottish Enlightenment and the American College Ideal* (New York: Teachers College Press, 1971), 119–31.

3. "Deceitfulness of Sin," *Works*, 2:120; "World Crucified," 2:548; "Believer Going to God," 2:158.

4. A few examples of Witherspoon's use of "Providence" in place of "God": "Instead of finding fault with Providence . . . ," in "All Mankind under Sin," *Works*, 1:420; " . . . learned of the wisdom or goodness of Providence, from reading or conversation," in "Security of Those," 2:58; " . . . by giving proper views of the wisdom and sovereignty of Providence," in "Ministerial Fidelity," 2:257; " . . . a confident dependence on the power and wisdom of Providence," in "Trust in God," 2:336.

5. This phrase can be found in "Regeneration," 1:81, 86, and "Man in His Natural State," 2:301–3, for example.

6. The sermon is found in *Works*, 2:361–69.

7. William J. Bouwsma, *John Calvin: A Sixteenth Century Portrait* (New York: Oxford University Press, 1988), 196. Calvin did, however, speculate that there was a greater likelihood of the poor being among the elect than the wealthy, who tend to "choke on their riches."

8. The author of the hymn is Cecil Frances Alexander (1823–1895), and the absent verse can be found in Robert McAfee Brown, *The Spirit of Protestantism* (New York: Oxford University Press, 1961), 111. Accompanying any discussion of Witherspoon's views on poverty and wealth must be the recognition of his insistence upon the inviolability of private property. See Scott, ed., *Lectures on Moral Philosophy*, 126–28.

9. "Nature and Effects of the Stage," *Works*, 3:46. See also McIntosh, *Church and Theology*, 80–81.

10. "Seeking a Competency," *Works*, 2:367. This passage demonstrates that Witherspoon was no more suspicious of the wealthy, as McIntosh claims, than critical of the poor who complain about their condition. McIntosh's conclusion is based solely on Witherspoon's assessment that rich theatergoers tend to be "enemies to pure and undefiled religion." See McIntosh, *Church and Theology*, 81; and "Nature and Effects of the Stage," *Works*, 3:58.

11. "Christian's Disposition," *Works*, 2:169–93.

12. Ibid., 178–79.

13. Ibid., 184.

14. Ibid., 191. Another example of how Witherspoon brought the doctrine of providence into the lives of his hearers is found in a section of the sermon, "The Security of Those Who Trust in God" (text: Prov. 18:10). Much of what he expounds here is pointed more toward God as "a most powerful protector" than one who "governs and directs all visible things." In the face of an enemy, extreme danger, or simply the ordinary evils of life, the believer "will renounce all dependence on created help, as such, and place his ultimate hope only on the power and sovereignty of Divine Providence." See *Works*, 2:50–63, especially p. 62.

15. Confession, 6.024.

16. "Believer Going to God," *Works*, 2:160; "Christian's Disposition," 2:176–77, 186. Witherspoon was not afraid to tackle troubling biblical references to God's

destructive providential acts. In preaching on 1 Samuel 15, Witherspoon confronted God's "awful command" to Saul to slay "both man and woman, infant and suckling" of the Amalekites (1 Sam. 15:3). Witherspoon had, in fact, two explanations. First, a righteous God will take all our lives when he so decides, and infants are dying daily with "the foreknowledge and Providence of God." Second, those Amalekites really were bad people, and their children would have been raised "to murder and rapine, and all sorts of wickedness." Is it not better to cut off these children in infancy before they grow up and commit terrible and tragic sins? See "Obedience and Sacrifice Compared," *Works*, 2:26–27. For his part, Calvin never used the term "frowning Providence," but he was quick to point out that God sometimes uses adversity to further his ends, and explained that for the faithful, suffering could bring about "a spiritual improvement" (to use Witherspoon's phrase). See Bouwsma, *John Calvin*, 170–71.

17. "Prayer for National Prosperity," *Works*, 1:357–81.

18. Ibid., 358–59. See also p. 376, where Witherspoon bemoans the fact that the public fast has become nothing more than "an unmeaning and lifeless form."

19. Ibid., 369.

20. What is called in Britain the Seven Years' War is known in American history books as the French and Indian War. See also *Works*, 1:283–84.

21. "Prayer for National Prosperity," *Works*, 1:374–77. Although Witherspoon could have done so, he stopped short in this sermon of posing his views on national growth and decline that he briefly described in his "Nature and Effects of the Stage," *Works*, 3:90: States move inexorably from poverty to industry and wealth, then to luxury and vice, and finally they decline into poverty and subjection again.

22. Ibid., 361.

23. Ibid., 379. Witherspoon also saw God's hand in the forming and signing of the National Covenant in 1638, and the Revolution Settlement of 1690 (Ibid., 380). See also J. H. S. Burleigh, *A Church History of Scotland* (London: Oxford University Press, 1960), 217–18, 253–55, 420.

24. "Prayer for National Prosperity," *Works*, 1:380–81.

25. "Ministerial Fidelity," *Works*, 2:239–40, 277, 283.

26. When he inserted the words, "though contrary to all human probability," was he thinking of his wife's reluctance to move to America, or possibly the offer of considerable wealth from a Scottish admirer if he would remain in Scotland? John Rodgers noted in his eulogy at Witherspoon's funeral that an elderly rich "bachelor, and a relation of the family, promised to make him [Witherspoon] his heir, if he would not go to America." See "Faithful Servant Rewarded," *Works*, 1:25. In the face of Witherspoon's insistence that it was providence that sent him to America, it is wrong to suggest that a national decline in morals prompted his emigration. See McIntosh, *Church and Theology*, 81.

27. L. H. Butterfield, ed., *John Witherspoon Comes to America: A Documentary Account Based Largely on New Materials* (Princeton, N.J.: Princeton University Library, 1953), 29, 38, 52.

28. "Success of the Gospel," *Works*, 2:531, 548. See also "Letter Sent to Scotland," 4:294, where Witherspoon explains that "Providence has sent me to this part of the world."

29. See p. 27 of "Manuscript Sermons of Dr. Witherspoon, Mr. Gowary, Mr. West and Mr. Bacon. Presented by Rev. Edward F. Fish of Illinois," MS W771 Se 67(1) in the Presbyterian Historical Society Library, Philadelphia. The twenty-two Witherspoon sermons here recorded were preached in 1774–1775, and the notes on the sermons were undoubtedly taken by Peter Fish, class of 1774, the College of New Jersey, and handed down in his family (J. B. Fish reports that he discovered these notes in 1836). Peter Fish remained at Princeton until 1776, studying theology with Witherspoon. He was ordained a Presbyterian minister on March 25, 1789. See Harrison, ed., *Princetonians 1769–1775*, 375–76. Fish's notes reveal that Witherspoon preached other sermons, whole or in part, on providence. See "Manuscript Sermons," 3, 9, 10, 18, 25, 27–28. The notes also disclose that Witherspoon preached several sermons that included exhortations to carry out one's Christian duty, which may have included the advice, only thinly disguised, to perform one's duty in public affairs as well as in one's station in society or occupation.

30. "Sedition and Faction," *Works*, 1:342.

31. "A Pastoral Letter from the Synod of New York and Philadelphia," *Works*, 3:599–605. An original copy of the letter is held in the John Carter Brown Library, Providence, Rhode Island. The "advices" are as follows: Presbyterians should (1) maintain respect for the king, (2) support the Continental Congress, (3) lead moral lives, (4) pay their debts, (5) be as humane and merciful as possible (for those who fight), and, finally, (6) observe fasts and pray frequently.

32. Ibid., 602.

33. Leonard J. Trinterud, *The Forming of an American Tradition: A Re-examination of Colonial Presbyterianism* (Philadelphia: Westminster Press, 1949), 249.

34. The sermon can be found in *Works*, 2:407–36.

35. See Richard B. Sher, "Witherspoon's *Dominion of Providence* and the Scottish Jeremiad Tradition," in Sher and Smitten, *Scotland and America*, 46–64. Sher argues that there is a legitimate Scottish Presbyterian jeremiad tradition and that Witherspoon's sermon is a fine example of it. He does admit that the sermon "vacillated on the thorny issue of the role of sin in bringing about the present crisis" (57).

36. "Dominion of Providence," *Works*, 2:408–10. Calvin, too, could see God making use of what to humans were dangers and adversities. They could be "God's weapons," he said, and if it pleased God, he might even "incite enemies" against the faithful. See Bouwsma, *John Calvin*, 170.

37. Ibid., 410–21.

38. This sermon is unique in that it is one of the few that contain explanatory footnotes, no doubt added by Witherspoon before the sermon was first published later in 1776 in Philadelphia. The longest note is a vociferous complaint against Paine's *Common Sense*, which contains a critique of the doctrine of original sin. After quoting the offending passage, Witherspoon accuses Paine of representing, "without the shadow of reasoning," the doctrine of original sin, "as an object of contempt or abhorrence." Witherspoon continues by noting that Paine was immodest, imprudent, and unjust in denouncing this doctrine in such a public manner (Ibid., 413–14).

39. Ibid., 421–26.
40. Ibid., 426–27.
41. The issue has been treated at length by Carl Bridenbaugh, *Mitre and Sceptre: Transatlantic Faiths, Ideas, Personalities, and Politics, 1689–1775* (New York: Oxford University Press, 1962), and Frederick V. Mills, *Bishops by Ballot: An Eighteenth Century Ecclesiastical Revolution* (New York: Oxford University Press, 1978).
42. See Patricia U. Bonomi, *Under the Cope of Heaven: Religion, Society, and Politics in Colonial America* (New York: Oxford University Press, 1986), 199–216, especially 206–7. Bonomi has more recently argued that "the single most important fact about colonial religion is that a majority of Americans were Dissenters." She further points out that "by the time of the Revolution three-quarters or more of Americans did not conform to the Church of England." She interprets this numerical preponderance of Dissenters as helping to "shape a worldview that was in significant ways at odds with English values, not only religious values but political ones as well." See Patricia U. Bonomi, "Religious Dissent and the Case for American Exceptionalism," in *Religion in a Revolutionary Age*, ed. Ronald Hoffman and Peter J. Albert (Charlottesville, Va.: University Press of Virginia, 1994), 33–34, 50–51. Varnum Lansing Collins has recorded Witherspoon's participation, or lack of it, in this Presbyterian/Congregational convention in *President Witherspoon: A Biography* (Princeton, N.J.: Princeton University Press, 1925), 1:139–40.
43. "Dominion of Providence," *Works*, 2:426–27.
44. Ibid., 427–28; "Letter Sent to Scotland"; "Ignorance of the British"; and "On the Contest," *Works*, 4:287–302. See also "Address to the Natives," 3:438.
45. "Dominion of Providence," *Works*, 2:428–29.
46. Ibid., 430–36.
47. Ibid., 434–35.
48. Ibid., 436. Two years later, Witherspoon was even more explicit in declaring that the war was a providential action. In a September 1778 letter sent to Scotland, in which Witherspoon tried to explain to his Scottish correspondent why America had gone to war, he stated, "I look upon the separation of America from Britain to be the visible intention of Providence." He further wrote that this was the intention of Providence "for many reasons," though he does not list them. See "On the Contest," *Works*, 4:300.
49. "[Sermon] Delivered at a Public Thanksgiving after Peace," *Works*, 2:451–75. Collins provides an interesting account of the day's events, based upon the report in the April 23, 1783, issue of the *New Jersey Gazette*. See Collins, *President Witherspoon*, 2:125.
50. "Public Thanksgiving," *Works*, 2:451–52.
51. Ibid., 458–59.
52. Gaustad has nicely summarized the great outpouring of devotion to Washington in his *Faith of Our Fathers: Religion and the New Nation* (San Francisco: Harper & Row, 1987), 71–84. James Smylie has described how clergy of all denominations reverted to biblical archetypes to praise Washington, likening him to Joshua, David, even Hezekiah and Josiah, but especially to Moses. See James H. Smylie, "America's Political Covenants, the Bible, and Calvinists," *Journal of Presbyterian History* 75 (fall 1997): 160–61.

53. "Address to General Washington," *Works*, 4:285–86. For a description of Washington's visits to Princeton, see Collins, *President Witherspoon*, 2:131, 162, 165.
54. "Public Thanksgiving," *Works*, 2:469–75.
55. Ibid., 472–73.
56. Ibid.
57. Ibid., 473. See Scott, ed., *Lectures on Moral Philosophy*, 144. In his "Lectures on Moral Philosophy," Witherspoon did not mention the three branches as such, rather calling for a mixed form of government in which there would be "a balance of different bodies" connected by a *nexus imperii*, an interlacing of the power of control. He rejected all "simple" forms of government—monarchy, oligarchy, and pure democracy. American Whigs looked with approval on Witherspoon's concept of "complex government." See Daniel Walker Howe, *The Political Culture of the American Whigs* (Chicago: University of Chicago Press, 1979), 76.
58. "Public Thanksgiving," *Works*, 2:473–74. For additional thoughts that Witherspoon had on the duty of magistrates, see Scott, ed., *Lectures on Moral Philosophy*, 159–61.
59. Confession, 6.127–6.130.
60. Guy S. Klett, ed., *Minutes of the Presbyterian Church in America, 1706–1788* (Philadelphia: Presbyterian Historical Society, 1976), 104; James H. Nichols, "John Witherspoon on Church and State," in George L. Hunt, ed., *Calvinism and the Political Order* (Philadelphia: Westminster Press, 1965), 135. Church historian Nichols has correctly observed that since the 1647 version of the Confession had declared both powers emphatically, this 1729 clarification, required for the American situation, "constituted radical surgery."
61. Scott, ed., *Lectures on Moral Philosophy*, 160–61. We have already noted in chapter 1 that Witherspoon was responsible for the statement on religious liberty in the preface to the new Form of Government for the national church in 1788: "Therefore, [we] reassert the rights of private judgement in matters of religion, repudiate all ties to the civil government, and call for full freedom of religion for all." See Trinterud, *American Tradition*, 297. See also David Little, "Reformed Faith and Religious Liberty," *Church and Society* (May/June 1986): 22.
62. James Madison, Witherspoon's former student and later president of the United States, was willing to go further than his former professor in guaranteeing the right of conscience. In his famous 1785 "Memorial and Remonstrance," he declared that religion should be a completely voluntary act and no church or no religion should receive any aid or recognition from the government. He did not want chaplains in the armed forces supported by the government, nor were presidents to call for national days of prayer, no matter what the occasion. A summary of Madison's position and the text of his "Memorial and Remonstrance" can be found in Gaustad, *Faith of Our Fathers*, 36–58, 141–49. James Smylie has shown that Madison was no atheist or religious illiterate, though he was remarkably silent about his own beliefs. See Smylie, "Madison and Witherspoon: Theological Roots of American Political Thought," *Princeton University Library Chronicle* 22 (spring 1961): 118–32.
63. "Public Thanksgiving," *Works*, 2:474–75.

64. See "Lectures on Divinity," *Works*, 4:75–91, for Witherspoon's discussion of the decrees of God. Very few modern Reformed theologians have spoken of the divine decrees. One who has, linking the divine decree(s) with Christology, is Karl Barth. See his *Church Dogmatics*, ed. G. W. Bromiley and T. F. Torrance (Edinburgh: T. & T. Clark, 1957), II/1:519–22; II/2:94–101, 128–45, 179–84, 325–26.

65. A helpful survey of the Reformed doctrine of providence is to be found in Benjamin Wirt Farley, *The Providence of God* (Grand Rapids: Baker Book House, 1988), 15–46. Chapter 11 of this work has been reprinted as "The Providence of God in Reformed Perspective," in *Major Themes in the Reformed Tradition*, ed. Donald K. McKim (Grand Rapids: Wm. B. Eerdmans Publishing Co., 1992), 87–93.

66. Barth, *Church Dogmatics*, III/3:3, 155. Barth writes at length on the rule of God. As Geoffrey W. Bromiley has explained, Barth breaks the divine ruling into four components: "God actively orders creaturely occurrence. He comprehensively controls it, both in its execution and its results. He directs it to a common goal, without invalidating its individual features and aims. He coordinates it, mutually conditioning the individual moments and actions to the individual and corporate praise of God." Bromiley continues by noting that the God of providence is not just a supramundane being "but the God of the covenant, the King of Israel" and finally "the incarnate Word." See Geoffrey W. Bromiley, *An Introduction to the Theology of Karl Barth* (Grand Rapids: Wm. B. Eerdmans Publishing Co., 1979), 146. See also Barth, *Church Dogmatics* III/3:164–82.

67. Kathleen Norris, *The Cloister Walk* (New York: Riverhead Books, 1996), 275.

68. See John Winthrop's 1630 sermon, "A Modell of Christian Charity," in which with great assurance he stated that "the God of Israel is among us" and that "the Lord our God may bless us in the land whither we go to possesse it" (H. Shelton Smith, Robert T. Handy and Lefferts A. Loetscher, eds., *American Christianity*, vol. 1 [New York: Charles Scribner's Sons, 1960], 98–102); Samuel Danforth's sermon, *A Brief Recognition of New England's Errand into the Wilderness* (Cambridge, Mass., 1671); and Perry Miller, *Errand into the Wilderness* (Cambridge, Mass.: Harvard University Press, 1956), 1–15. For a survey of American millennial thought in the eighteenth century, see Ruth Bloch, *Visionary Republic: Millennial Themes in American Thought, 1756–1800* (New York: Cambridge University Press, 1985, 1994) and James H. Smylie, "American Millennium Visions, 1776–1800," *Journal of Presbyterian History* 77, no. 2 (1999): 119–28.

69. Baldwin's 1776 sermon was titled "The Duty of Rejoycing under Calamities and Afflictions," and Sherwood's, based on Revelation 12:14–17, bore the title, "The Church's Flight into the Wilderness." Both sermons are discussed in Harry S. Stout, *The New England Soul: Preaching and Religious Culture in Colonial New England* (New York: Oxford University Press, 1986), 308–11. The full text of Sherwood's sermon can be found in Ellis Sandoz, ed., *Political Sermons of the American Founding Era, 1730–1805* (Indianapolis: Liberty Fund, 1991), 495–527. Part of Sherwood's vision was to be found in the way providence had planted the church as a choice vine in the "howling wilderness" of early Amer-

ica (503, 522). Witherspoon, too, once spoke of America as "a howling wilderness" but without any millennial overtones. See "Lectures on Divinity," *Works*, 4:87.

70. See my discussion of Witherspoon's ideas on a just war, based on his "Druid Essay Number II," *Works*, 4:153–60, in *New Jersey History* 100 (fall/winter 1982): 31–46.

71. Specifying inhumane methods of warfare was common enough in some of the political writings of the seventeenth and eighteenth centuries. Witherspoon was dependent upon three earlier thinkers: Francis Hutcheson (1694–1746), Hugo Grotius (1583–1645), and Samuel von Pufendorf (1632–1694).

72. "Lectures on Divinity," *Works*, 4:22.

73. "Address to the Senior Class," *Works*, 2:630–31. Sloan has also remarked how much Witherspoon had "imbibed the modern spirit" over the years as evidenced in his "Lectures on Eloquence." See Sloan, *Scottish Enlightenment*, 133–35. Albert Outler concludes that none other than John Wesley had also imbibed the modern spirit, so much so that he can be described as representing "enlightened pietism." See Albert Outler, "Pietism and Enlightenment: Alternatives to Tradition," in *Christian Spirituality: Post-Reformation and Modern*, ed. Louis Dupré and Don E. Saliers (New York: Crossroad, 1989), 252–55.

74. Scott, ed., *Lectures on Moral Philosophy*, 64. On special revelation, see pp. 64, 102–7, 126, 187.

75. "Happiness of the Saints," *Works*, 2:235; "Justification," 1:67.

76. Scott, ed., *Lectures on Moral Philosophy*, 87.

77. Two complete lectures (4, 5) are devoted to the nature, foundation, and obligation of virtue (Ibid., 83–94, also 187).

78. "Christian Magnanimity," *Works*, 2:599–632. Ashbel Green was so taken with the sermon that he judged it difficult to find elsewhere "so much wise, useful and appropriate advice to liberally educated youth, as is contained in this address. It has been of more practical utility to the [present] writer than every thing else of the kind, that he has either read or heard." See Ashbel Green, *The Life of the Revd John Witherspoon, D.D., LL.D.*, ed. Henry Lyttleton Savage (Princeton, N.J.: Princeton University Press, 1973), 149.

79. "Christian Magnanimity," *Works*, 2:601.

80. Ibid., 602.

81. There is a possible suggestion of resistance to the king when, toward the end of the sermon, he declares that the gospel is strong enough to make believers "withstand a king upon his throne." (Ibid., 610).

82. Ibid., 606–9.

83. Ibid., 609.

Chapter 6—Practical Improvement

1. John H. Leith, *Basic Christian Doctrine* (Louisville, Ky.: Westminster/John Knox Press, 1993), 5–9.

2. Douglas F. Ottati, *Reforming Protestantism: Christian Commitment in Today's World* (Louisville, Ky.: Westminster John Knox Press, 1995), 41–45.

3. Ibid., 44.

4. John H. Leith, *Crisis in the Church: The Plight of Theological Education* (Louisville,

Ky.: WestminsterJohn Knox Press, 1997), 46–47, 29–30. Kuklick's judgment is found in *Church History* 67 (June 1998): 402.

5. Shirley C. Guthrie, *Christian Doctrine*, rev. ed. (Louisville, Ky.: Westminster John Knox Press, 1994), 398–99.

6. David Willis and Michael Welker, eds., *Toward the Future of Reformed Theology: Tasks, Topics, Traditions* (Grand Rapids: Wm. B. Eerdmans Publishing Co., 1999), 191.

7. John McIntyre, *The Shape of Christology* (Edinburgh: T. & T. Clark, 1992), 120. Other theologians urging a return to a theology of the atonement include Gerhard Forde of Luther Seminary in St. Paul, Minnesota, who proposes a theology of the cross. This theology, based on the thought of Martin Luther, addresses us as real sinners, Forde argues, not as lost souls languishing as pitiable victims in a meaningless universe. Consequently, we need evangelical help, not the therapeutic kind. See Gerhard Forde, "On Being a Theologian of the Cross," *Christian Century* 114 (October 22, 1997): 947–49. Forde's thesis is fully developed in his 1997 book of the same title (Grand Rapids: Wm. B. Eerdmans Publishing Co.). Theologian Miroslav Wolf of Yale University Divinity School has written that at the core of the Christian faith lies a vision of reconciliation through Christ, between the individual and God and among men and women as well. He clinches his argument by quoting Colossians 1:19–20: "For in [Christ] all the fullness of God was pleased to dwell, and through him God was pleased to reconcile to himself all things." Wolf seems unconsciously to echo the theme of reconciliation so prominent in the Presbyterian Confession of 1967. Miroslav Wolf, "The Core of the Faith," *Christian Century* 115 (March 4, 1998): 239.

8. Richard Lischer, *A Theology of Preaching: The Dynamics of the Gospel*, rev. ed. (Durham, N.C.: Labyrinth Press, 1992), 3–4.

9. Published in Robert Farrar Capon, *The Foolishness of Preaching: Proclaiming the Gospel against the Wisdom of the World* (Grand Rapids: Wm. B. Eerdmans Publishing Co., 1998), 13, 9.

10. See Karl Barth, foreword to *Reformed Dogmatics*, rev. ed., by Heinrich Heppe (London: George Allen & Unwin, 1950), v–vi; Paul Tillich, *A History of Christian Thought* (New York: Harper & Row, 1968), 276–83; William Stacy Johnson and John H. Leith, eds., *Reformed Reader: A Sourcebook in Christian Theology*, vol. 1 (Louisville, Ky.: Westminster/John Knox Press, 1993), xxvi.

11. "Address to the Senior Class," *Works*, 2:632.

12. "Preface," *Works*, 1:3.

13. "Fervency in Prayer," *Works*, 2:11.

14. "Regeneration," *Works*, 1:95; "Object of a Christian's Desire," 2:79.

15. Alexis de Tocqueville, *Democracy in America* (New York: Alfred A. Knopf, 1945), 2:126–27. Tocqueville's tour of America occurred 1831–32.

16. Robert C. Kimball, ed., *Theology of Culture* (New York: Oxford University Press, 1959), 164–76.

17. "The Druid, Number IV," *Works*, 4:168–79; "Lectures on Eloquence," 3:384. See also "Trial of Religious Truth," 1:296: "There often is great virtue and goodness in mean capacity, and great depravity in persons of eminent ability."

18. Scott, ed., *Lectures on Moral Philosophy*, 73–74, 97; Douglas Sloan, *The Scottish*

Enlightenment and the American College Ideal (New York: Teachers College Press, 1971), 129. Other sources that recount the common sense tradition in America, and Witherspoon's part in it, include: Sydney Ahlstrom, "The Scottish Philosophy and American Theology," *Church History* 24 (September 1955): 257–72; James L. McAllister, "John Witherspoon: Academic Advocate for American Freedom," in *A Miscellany of American Christianity,* ed. Stuart C. Henry (Durham, N.C.: Duke University Press, 1963), 183–224; Mark A. Noll, "Common Sense Traditions and American Evangelical Thought," *American Quarterly* 37 (summer 1985), 216–38; J. David Hoeveler, *James McCosh and the Scottish Intellectual Tradition: From Glasgow to Princeton* (Princeton, N.J.: Princeton University Press, 1981). The "late writers" Witherspoon had in mind would surely include Thomas Reid and quite probably James Beattie (1735–1803), professor of moral philosophy at Aberdeen. In the 1753 *Scots Magazine* article, Witherspoon had set forth certain ideas that he later claimed predated Reid's more comprehensive work. See chapter 3, note 30 of the present study, and Green, *Life of the Revd John Witherspoon,* 132. The account of how common sense philosophy entered Princeton Theological Seminary is found in Lefferts A. Loetscher, *Facing the Enlightenment: Archibald Alexander and the Founding of Princeton Theological Seminary* (Westport, Conn.: Greenwood Press, 1983), 33–35.

19. "An Address to the Senior Class," *Works,* 2:615.
20. Saxe Commins, ed., *Basic Writings of George Washington* (New York: Random House, 1948), 637.
21. Clinton Rossiter, *Seedtime of the Republic: The Origin of the American Tradition of Political Liberty* (New York: Harcourt, Brace & Co., 1953), 59, 138, 295. See also Gordon S. Wood, "Religion and the American Revolution," in *New Directions in American Religious History,* ed. Harry S. Stout and D. G. Hart (New York: Oxford University Press, 1997), 175.
22. See Stone's essay, "Introduction to Reformed Faith and Politics," in Ronald Stone, ed., *Reformed Faith and Politics* (Washington, D.C.: University Press of America, 1983), 1–4.
23. "Christian Magnanimity," *Works,* 2:607; see also "Letters on Education," 3:531.
24. "Public Thanksgiving," *Works,* 2:474.
25. "Dominion of Providence," *Works,* 2:431, 435–36. See also Witherspoon's statement in Scott, ed., *Lectures on Moral Philosophy,* 159: "Love to God, and love to man, as the substance of religion; when those prevail, civil laws will have little to do." See also Mark A. Noll, *Princeton and the Republic, 1768–1822: The Search for a Christian Enlightenment in the Era of Samuel Stanhope Smith* (Princeton, N.J.: Princeton University Press, 1989), 51–52, 81.
26. Tocqueville, *Democracy in America,* 1:305–6; 2:20–32, 143.
27. David Little, "Reformed Faith and Religious Liberty," *Church and Society* (May/June 1986): 5–28. Little's essay has been reprinted in Donald K. McKim, ed., *Major Themes in the Reformed Tradition* (Grand Rapids: Wm. B. Eerdmans Publishing Co., 1992), 196–213. In his *Habits of the Heart,* Robert Bellah and his colleagues have repeated Witherspoon's conviction of the necessity of piety by stating that "a good society thus depends in the last analysis on the goodness of individuals, not on the soundness of institutions or the fairness of laws." They

also cite Martin Luther King Jr. as one whose goal was building a just national community, employing biblical and republican themes in a way that transformed the negative features of the culture of individualism. See Robert N. Bellah et al., *Habits of the Heart: Individualism and Commitment in American Life* (Berkeley, Calif.: University of California Press, 1985), 183, 249.

28. *A Nation of Spectators: How Civic Dis-engagement Weakens America and What We Can Do about It*, final report of the National Commission on Civic Renewal (College Park, Maryland, 1998), 12.

29. G. C. Berkouwer, *The Providence of God*, trans. Lewis Smedes (Grand Rapids: Wm. B. Eerdmans Publishing Co., 1952), 12–16, quoted in George W. Stroup, ed., *Reformed Reader: A Sourcebook in Christian Theology* (Louisville, Ky.: Westminster/John Knox Press, 1993), 2:135. Stroup himself admits that theologians today have a problem in what to say about God's activity in history, given the horrors of the twentieth century (xxvii). In a formal way, Benjamin Farley has offered suggestions for how providence may become a vital part of contemporary Christian experience. For a more formal understanding of the doctrine, see Farley, *The Providence of God* (Grand Rapids: Baker Book House, 1988), 232–37.

30. Guthrie, *Christian Doctrine*, 166; see also his *Always Being Reformed: Faith for a Fragmented World* (Louisville, Ky.: Westminster John Knox Press, 1996), 86–87.

31. "Visible Religion," *Works*, 1:389, 400; Kathleen Norris, *Amazing Grace: A Vocabulary of Faith* (New York: Riverhead Books, 1998), 7, 9, 186, 211–14; Barbara Brown Taylor, *When God Is Silent* (Cambridge, Mass.: Cowley Publications, 1998), 9, 29.

32. Susanne K. Langer, "Language and Thought," in *Exploring Language*, 6th ed., ed. Gary Goshgarian (New York: HarperCollins, 1992), 25.

33. "Lectures on Eloquence," *Works*, 3:396–97; "The Druid, Number V," 4:184.

34. John Simon, "Why Good English Is Good for You," in Goshgarian, ed., *Exploring Language*, 339. Others who have deplored a decline in proper English are George Orwell, whose essay, "Politics and the English Language," appears in Goshgarian, ed., *Exploring Language*, 141–51; and TV news commentator Edwin H. Newman. Newman explains that a civil tongue means "a language that is not bogged down in jargon, not puffed up with false dignity, not studded with trick phrases. . . . It doesn't consider 'We're there because that's where it's at' the height of cleverness. . . . It is direct, specific, concrete, vigorous, colorful, subtle, and imaginative when it should be, and as lucid and eloquent as we are able to make it." See Edwin H. Newman, *A Civil Tongue* (Indianapolis: Bobbs-Merrill Co., 1975), 6.

35. "The Druid, Number V," *Works*, 4:180. At the time, Witherspoon was only one of several voices arguing for proper English. In both Scotland and America in the eighteenth century, a number of writers were urging a proper English that would be satisfactory to the English themselves, eliminating "Scotticisms" and what Witherspoon came to call "Americanisms." This effort was part of the growing interest in rhetoric and belles lettres in Scottish and American institutions of higher learning. See "The Scottish Invention of English Literature" in Robert Crawford, *Devolving English Literature* (Oxford: Clarendon Press, 1992),

16–44, and Robert Crawford, ed., *The Scottish Invention of English Literature* (New York: Cambridge University Press, 1998), 147–48.

36. "Ecclesiastical Characteristics," *Works*, 3:132.
37. "Visible Religion," *Works*, 1:396. See also "Christian Magnanimity," 2:610–11.
38. Green, *Life of the Revd John Witherspoon*, 263–64; Rodgers reports the same information in his funeral sermon for Witherspoon in *Works*, 1:35.
39. Alan Geyer, "Reformed Faith and World Politics," in Stone, *Reformed Faith and Politics*, 159.
40. "World Crucified," *Works*, 1:549.
41. "Nature and Effects of the Stage," *Works*, 3:71.
42. "Dominion of Providence," *Works*, 2:436.

Selected Bibliography

Ahlstrom, Sydney E. "The Scottish Philosophy and American Theology." *Church History* 24 (September 1955): 257–72.

Atwater, Lyman H. "Witherspoon's Theology." *Biblical Repertory and Princeton Review*, 35, no. 4 (October 1863): 596–610.

Bartley, David D. "John Witherspoon and the Right of Resistance." Ph.D. dissertation, Ball State University, 1989.

The Book of Confessions. Louisville, Ky.: The Presbyterian Church (U.S.A.), 1996.

Bouwsma, William J. *John Calvin: A Sixteenth Century Portrait*. New York: Oxford University Press, 1988.

Bower, Alexander. *The History of the University of Edinburgh: Chiefly Compiled from Original Papers and Records Never Before Published*. 3 vols. Edinburgh: Printed by Alex. Smellie, Printer to the University, 1817–30.

Brackett, William Oliver. "John Witherspoon: His Scottish Ministry." Ph.D. dissertation, University of Edinburgh, 1935.

Burleigh, J. H. S. *A Church History of Scotland*. London: Oxford University Press, 1960.

Butterfield, L. H., ed. *John Witherspoon Comes to America: A Documentary Account Based Largely on New Materials*. Princeton, N.J.: Princeton University Library, 1953.

Collins, Varnum Lansing. *President Witherspoon: A Biography*. 2 vols. Princeton, N.J.: Princeton University Press, 1925. Reprint (New York: Arno Press and the New York Times, 1969).

Crichton, Thomas. "Memoir of the Life and Writings of John Witherspoon." *Edinburgh Christian Instructor* 28 (October 1829): 673–94.

Drummond, Andrew L. and James Bulloch. *The Scottish Church, 1688–1843: The Age of the Moderates*. Edinburgh: Saint Andrew Press, 1973.

Farley, Benjamin Wirt. *The Providence of God*. Grand Rapids: Baker Book House, 1988.

Fechner, Roger J. "The Moral Philosophy of John Witherspoon and the Scottish-American Enlightenment." Ph.D. dissertation, University of Iowa, 1974.

Graham, Henry Grey. *The Social Life in Scotland in the Eighteenth Century*. London: Adam & Charles Black, 1950 (first published in 2 vols., 1899).

Green, Ashbel. *The Life of the Revd John Witherspoon, D.D., LL.D.: With a brief review of his writings: and a summary estimate of his character and talents*. Edited by Henry Lyttleton Savage. Princeton, N.J.: Princeton University Press, 1973.

_____, ed. *The Works of the Rev. John Witherspoon.* 4 vols. Philadelphia: William Woodward, 1801–1802.

Heron, Alasdair I. C., ed. *The Westminster Confession in the Church Today.* Edinburgh: Saint Andrew Press, 1982.

Hunt, George L., ed. *Calvinism and the Political Order.* Philadelphia: Westminster Press, 1965.

Johnson, William Stacy and John H. Leith, eds. *Reformed Reader: A Sourcebook in Christian Theology.* Vol. 1. Louisville, Ky.: Westminster/John Knox Press, 1993.

Klauber, Martin I. "Reformed Orthodoxy in Transition: Bénédict Pictet (1655–1724) and Enlightened Orthodoxy in Post-Reformation Geneva." In *Later Calvinism: International Perspectives,* edited by W. Fred Graham. Kirksville, Mo.: Sixteenth Century Journal Publishers, 1994.

Leith, John H. *Assembly at Westminster: Reformed Theology in the Making.* Atlanta: John Knox Press, 1973.

Marty, Martin E. *Pilgrims in Their Own Land: 500 Years of Religion in America.* Boston: Little, Brown & Co., 1984.

Maxwell, William D. *A History of Worship in the Church of Scotland.* London: Oxford University Press, 1955.

May, Henry F. *The Enlightenment in America.* New York: Oxford University Press, 1976.

McAllister, James L. "John Witherspoon: Academic Advocate for American Freedom." In *A Miscellany of American Christianity: Essays in Honor of H. Shelton Smith,* edited by Stuart C. Henry. Durham, N.C.: Duke University Press, 1963.

McIntosh, John R. *Church and Theology in Enlightenment Scotland: The Popular Party, 1740–1800.* East Linton, East Lothian, Scotland: Tuckwell Press, 1998.

McKim, Donald K., ed. *Encyclopedia of the Reformed Faith.* Louisville, Ky.: Westminster/John Knox Press, 1992.

Noll, Mark A. *Christians in the American Revolution.* Washington, D.C.: Christian University Press, 1977.

_____. *Princeton and the Republic, 1768–1822: The Search for a Christian Enlightenment in the Era of Samuel Stanhope Smith.* Princeton, N.J.: Princeton University Press, 1989.

Rich, George E. "John Witherspoon: His Scottish Intellectual Background." D.S.S. dissertation, Syracuse University, 1964.

Scott, Jack, ed. *An Annotated Edition of Lectures on Moral Philosophy by John Witherspoon.* Newark, Del.: University of Delaware Press, 1982.

Sher, Richard B. *Church and University in the Scottish Enlightenment: The Moderate Literati of Edinburgh.* Princeton, N.J.: Princeton University Press, 1985.

Sher, Richard B. and Jeffrey R. Smitten, eds. *Scotland and America in the Age of the Enlightenment.* Princeton, N.J.: Princeton University Press, 1990.

Sloan, Douglas. *The Scottish Enlightenment and the American College Ideal.* New York: Teachers College Press, 1971.

Smylie, James H. *A Brief History of the Presbyterians.* Louisville, Ky.: Geneva Press, 1996.

Stohlman, Martha Lou Lemmon. *John Witherspoon: Parson, Politician, Patriot.* Philadelphia: Westminster Press, 1976.

Stone, Ronald, ed. *Reformed Faith and Politics*. Washington, D.C.: University Press of America, 1983.

Stroup, George W., ed. *Reformed Reader: A Sourcebook in Christian Theology*. Vol. 2. Louisville, Ky.: Westminster/John Knox Press, 1993.

Tocqueville, Alexis de. *Democracy in America*. 2 vols. New York: Alfred A. Knopf, 1945.

Torrance, Thomas F. *Scottish Theology: From John Knox to John McLeod Campbell*. Edinburgh: T. & T. Clark, 1996.

Trinterud, Leonard J. *The Forming of an American Tradition: A Re-examination of Colonial Presbyterianism*. Philadelphia: Westminster Press, 1949.

Witte, Wayne W. "John Witherspoon: An Exposition and Interpretation of His Theological Views as the Motivation of His Ecclesiastical, Educational, and Political Career in Scotland and America." Th.D. dissertation, Princeton Theological Seminary, 1953.

Index